EZRA-NEHEMIAH

In this provocative study Lester L. Grabbe dispenses with the trend in Biblical scholarship towards new literary study and postmodernist criticism to advocate a 'close reading' of the text itself. The main focus of this book, discussed in Part I, gives a close reading of the final form of the text; the Hebrew Ezra, the Hebrew Nehemiah, 1 Esdras and other Ezra and Nehemiah traditions. Lester L. Grabbe also discusses intertextuality and questions of historicity raised by a close reading of the texts.

This book presents a unique approach to Ezra-Nehemiah in the combination of literary and historical approaches. Lester L. Grabbe challenges commonly held assumptions about Joshua and Zerubbabel, the initial resettlement of land after the exile, the figure of Ezra and the activities of Nehemiah. Controversially, the challenge comes, not from radical theory, but from paying careful attention to the text of the Bible itself.

Lester L. Grabbe is Professor of Hebrew Bible and Early Judaism at the University of Hull.

EZRA-NEHEMIAH

Lester L. Grabbe

London and New York

First published 1998
by Routledge
11 New Fetter Lane, London EC4P 4EE

Simultaneously published in the USA and Canada
by Routledge
29 West 35th Street, New York, NY 10001

Typeset in Garamond by
BC Typesetting, Bristol
Printed and bound in Great Britain by
Creative Print & Design (Wales), Ebbw Vale

British Library Cataloguing in Publication Data
A catalogue record for this book is available from the British Library

Library of Congress Cataloguing in Publication Data
Grabbe, Lester L.
Ezra-Nehemiah/Lester L. Grabbe.
p.   cm. – (Old Testament readings)
Includes bibliographical references and index.
ISBN 0–415–14153–2 (hardcover). – ISBN 0–415–14154–0 (pbk.)
1. Bible.   O.T.   Ezra–Commentaries.   2. Bible.   O.T.   Nehemiah-
-Commentaries.   I. Title.   II. Series.
BS1355.3.G73   1998
222′.707–dc21   98.9271
                                                                 CIP

ISBN 0–415–14153–6 (hbk)
ISBN 0–415–14154–0 (pbk)

1001381784

CONTENTS

CONTENTS

ABBREVIATIONS

AB	Anchor Bible
AGAJU	Arbeiten zur Geschichte des antiken Judentums und des Urchristentums
ALGHJ	Arbeiten zur Literatur und Geschichte des hellenistischen Judentums
ANET	James B. Pritchard, *Ancient Near Eastern Texts Relating to the Old Testament*, 3rd edn with Supplement; Princeton: Princeton University Press, 1969
AOS	American Oriental Series
b.	Hebrew *ben*/Aramaic *bar* = 'son of'
BZAW	Beihefte zur *Zeitschrift für die alttestamentliche Wissenschaft*
CBC	Century Bible Commentary
CBQ	*Catholic Biblical Quarterly*
EI	*Eretz-Israel*
FRLANT	Forschungen zur Religion und Literatur des Alten und Neuen Testaments
HAT	Handbuch zum Alten Testament
ICC	International Critical Commentary
IEJ	*Israel Exploration Journal*
JBL	*Journal of Biblical Literature*
JNES	*Journal of Near Eastern Studies*
JSOT	*Journal for the Study of the Old Testament*
JSOTSup	Supplements to *Journal for the Study of the Old Testament*
JTS	*Journal of Theological Studies*
KAT	Kommentar zum Alten Testament
LXX	Septuagint version of the Old Testament
MT	Masoretic text
NJPS	New Jewish Publication Society translation of the Hebrew Bible

NM	Nehemiah memorial/memoir
OT	Old Testament/Hebrew Bible
RB	*Revue Biblique*
SBLMS	Society of Biblical Literature Monograph Series
SUNT	Studien zur Umwelt des Neuen Testaments
VT	*Vetus Testamentum*
VTSup	Supplements to *Vetus Testamentum*
WBC	Word Bible Commentary
WMANT	Wissenschaftliche Monographien zum Alten und Neuen Testament
ZAW	*Zeitschrift für die alttestamentliche Wissenschaft*

1

INTRODUCTION

The books of Ezra and Nehemiah have not been the most popular of the books in the Hebrew Bible. Yet they have had great influence on how the Jewish religion is assumed to have developed. They describe the reconstruction of the Jewish temple and state after their destruction by the Babylonians in 587/586 BCE and set the theme for the concerns and even the basis of Early Judaism which is usually seen as the Torah. The figure of Ezra has been profoundly associated with the origin or promulgation or interpretation of that Torah. The consequence is that the books of Ezra and Nehemiah are in many ways the foundation of much scholarship, not only about the development of the Jewish religion but even of how the Old Testament (OT) literature emerged.

The aim of this book is to make a contribution to a better understanding of these two books which, in my opinion, are crucial writings in the Hebrew Bible. My study has implications for the history of Israel and Judah, the religion of Israelites and Judaeans, the literary development of the OT, and OT theology. This is inevitable because of the importance of Ezra and Nehemiah for all these areas. All the various implications are not drawn here because of my focus purely on Ezra and Nehemiah. Some of the consequences were drawn in chapter 2 of my *Judaism from Cyrus to Hadrian* (1992a) and will be dealt with in more detail in my forthcoming *Yehud: The Persian Province of Judah* (in preparation).

As a part of the series 'Readings' the heart of this study is a close reading of the books of Ezra and Nehemiah. Part I focuses purely on the literary aspects of the two books; it is primarily a close reading of the Hebrew books of Ezra and Nehemiah plus 1 Esdras and other Ezra and Nehemiah traditions. The aim is to read the texts as they exist in their final form. This does not reject the concept of authorial intent – indeed, authorial intent will be frequently discussed in

1

Part II – but the emphasis in Part I is asking what the text actually says and what its structure implies. Questions of literary growth and source criticism come only as secondary questions: they are not the concern of chapters 2 to 4; however, occasional references may be given in anticipation of the later discussion, for questions of literary growth and sources and, especially, the historical questions will eventually be addressed. Chapter 5 asks about the relationship between the various traditions and goes on to discuss not only how the Hebrew books of Ezra and Nehemiah are put together but also what their structure and content imply about the growth of the traditions. It is necessary for these matters of sources and literary growth to be dealt with before historical questions can be asked in Part II. Therefore, the analysis in chapters 2 to 4 goes beyond a conventional literary analysis; it also looks at the implications of content as well as structure to consider what these imply about the development and redaction of the traditions.

In my view, it is a mistake to assume that a close reading or a stucturalist analysis will clarify all aspects of the text. In some cases they will but often, especially with traditional literature, they show the imperfections and the disjunctures in the text as well as the literary skill of the compiler/author/redactor. Part of a holistic reading is not just to see how the text is structured and the parts fit the whole but also to recognize that sometimes a purely literary reading of the final form of the text does not do justice to what lies before us. A full analysis of the text may require one to ask how it came about – about its history, evolution, redaction, compilation. The emphasis in some of the literary approaches has been on how the work is structured and how the various elements within the narrative contribute to the message of the book; that is, they emphasize unity and integrity of the narrative. Such analyses have often been very helpful in appreciating the literature, have brought previously unrecognized meanings to the surface, and have corrected an earlier over-emphasis on traditio-historical criticism. However, a close reading does not always show literary skill; on the contrary, it may well disclose textual disharmony, bad writing, and clumsy editing. It may raise questions about the use of earlier traditions (which is, of course, a form of intertextuality), and it may well call into question the matter of authorial competence. Such points are noted in chapters 2 and 3 wherever they arise. Discussion of sources is also essential to chapter 4 because the other Ezra and Nehemiah traditions cannot be discussed without reference to the Hebrew books of Ezra and Nehemiah.

The analysis in Part I was done as independently as possible. Although the standard commentaries were consulted at various points when the need was felt, the aim was to try to put previous interpretations out of mind – as far as that was possible to do – and to approach the texts afresh, trying to eliminate preconceived ideas. Most of the secondary literature was read or reviewed only after the texts had been analysed. This is why few references to secondary literature are found in Part I, especially in chapters 2-4.

The various Ezra and Nehemiah traditions occur in a variety of text types and languages, each of which can be analysed in its own right. However, the core of the study is the Hebrew texts of Ezra and Nehemiah (using the text in the *Biblia Hebraica Stuttgartensia*). We know these mainly from the Masoretic tradition (MT) which is the basis of the analysis. The Greek versions of Ezra and Nehemiah (often called Esdras β or Esdras B or occasionally even 2 Esdras – but not to be confused with 4 Ezra which is also often called 2 Esdras) are fairly literal translations of a Hebrew text which was very close to our present Masoretic text. Therefore, these Greek translations were not investigated further (except as they might be used for purposes of textual criticism). 1 Esdras was different, however. Although for much of its length it is parallel to sections of 2 Chronicles, Ezra, and Nehemiah, it represents a different textual tradition. The contents are in a different order from anything in the Hebrew Bible and, as far as one can tell from a translation, often represent a slightly divergent Hebrew original. The Göttingen edition (Hanhart 1974) was used for this text.

Part II relies heavily on the close reading of Part I, but it asks about history: What is the relationship between the Hebrew Ezra and Nehemiah and the other Ezra and Nehemiah traditions and the historical events of the time? Granted that the Hebrew books are a part of our historical sources, how trustworthy are they and can we ultimately accept them as historical – or, to put it another way, to what extent are they historical? What quality of sources are they? To answer these questions we need to look at other sources and also to bring in our knowledge of history in the Persian period generally.

These sources for Persian history and especially for the Persian province of Yehud are surveyed in my *Judaism from Cyrus to Hadrian* (1992a: ch. 2). Although some of the points made in the earlier work are also included here, this is because they still seem to be valid in the light of subsequent study. I have attempted to rethink the books of Ezra and Nehemiah and also to go beyond what was included in my study of 1992. My thinking on the two books continues to develop, and a number of further studies relating to this investigation here have been done since then as well (see Bibliography).

One might think that we can all take for granted what is meant by historical study. I find that this is not the case: some biblical scholars seem to mistake the aims and methods of historical study and do not understand the difference between it and study of the Bible for theological, literary, hermeneutical, or other 'applied' reasons. There are, sadly, those who think that the theological or ideological needs in modern society can allow one to override critical debate. An example of this which has come forcibly to my attention is found in a review of my book *Priests, Prophets, Diviners, Sages* (1995) by Walter Brueggemann (1996). The general tenor of the review is actually complimentary, with such statements as the following: 'There is no doubt that Grabbe's study is well informed, and his critical judgments are well measured and balanced. The book will be an important and useful reference' (Brueggemann 1996: 729). However, in one particular area Brueggemann is unhappy with my approach, which may be summed up by the following quotations (p. 729):

> Grabbe here voices what has become almost a criticial *de rigueur* concerning older 'theological interpretations' of the prophets. . . . The methodological rigor of Grabbe's study, however, leads to the odd conclusion that there is no reliable distinction, in terms of the methods here championed, between the false prophets of Israel and the true ones. . . . The methods of Grabbe rule out any theological, Yahwistic, or canonical claims, so that all criteria then perforce disappear. I suppose this is a legitimate perspective. But it is striking that the method is willing to host the evidence of seemingly everyone except the voices of the text themselves who thought they could make distinctions, which Grabbe dismisses as 'the subjective judgment of the editors and tradents.' The editors or ideologues are accused of wanting to present a certain 'view of religion and society.' But of course! Thus the attempt to drive a wedge between 'scientific' data and 'theological interpretation' is here a complete one.

Brueggemann has a considerable reputation for his work on theology and literary study, but he is not known as a historian. If he wishes to do a theological study of true and false prophecy as presented by the biblical text, he is welcome to do that; he is also welcome to give the perspective of the text pre-eminence in such a treatment. But it would not be a historical study. Brueggemann does not, however, seem to understand the difference – and he is not the only biblical scholar to make this mistake. The viewpoint of the text is a sociological and historical datum. The fact that the text thinks, for example, that it can distinguish between true prophets and false prophets is a piece of information which the historian should take into account. But this view is not determinative of the historian's conclusions; it is only a part of the raw data to be weighed and critically evaluated. After all, the text makes all sorts of claims which few of us (including Brueggemann) would accept, such as that the Canaanites deserved to be exterminated, or that in the sixth century BCE Daniel prophesied the coming of Antiochus Epiphanes, or that the one who seizes Babylonian babies and smashes their brains out against the stones is blessed. The text makes all sorts of statements that we would reject for theological and moral reasons, but in particular it makes historical statements that cannot be taken at face value.

When carrying on debates about history in relation to the Bible, one occasionally hears voices raised that such and such an interpretation unfairly slights or promotes the cause of the Jewish people or the Palestinian peoples or the state of Israel or the poor and disadvantaged or a particular gender, or whatever. Such arguments should be irrelevant to scholarship. It is the equivalent of judging a book by its cover. History has, of course, always been used in aid of propaganda and distorted by propaganda. But if propaganda is what you have in mind, why wrap it up in the package of critical history? If critical historical study conducted carefully and fairly comes to uncomfortable conclusions, then so be it. The question of whether someone might use such conclusions for purposes which we would find objectionable is not an issue which should influence the conclusions.

Above all, our historical judgements should be made on the basis of historical principles and methodology. Once we let ideology be the basis, we are already going down a dangerous road. One only has to consider a court case in Japan that concluded in 1997. It was actually illegal in Japan to tell the true story of Japanese atrocities in the Second World War because this was considered a negative portrait of the country and people. Thus, textbooks had such matter censured from them, and it is only now – half a century after the end of the war – that Japanese students can be told the truth in school texts. To decide one's history on the basis of theology is just as mistaken and just as dangerous – whether to scholarship or to our status as free moral agents.

Naturally, no one can doubt that every historian is limited by personal experiences, prejudices, intellectual failings, and many other lacks which prevent a completely neutral and dispassionate evaluation of the data. There is, however, a difference between these human weaknesses which historians try to allow for and overcome, and the deliberate overriding of proper historical judgement by promoting a particular point of view because it suits certain needs beyond academic interpretation and reconstruction of history. Any historical reconstruction will, of course, be subjective to some extent. But just because this is true and inevitable does not mean that, therefore, one reconstruction is as valid as another. There is such a thing as bad historical study and bad scholarship.

On the other hand, sincere individual historians striving to be as fair to the data as possible may still come up with quite different scenarios from others equally conscientious; indeed, the same historian may come up with a very different interpretation at one particular time than at another. The discussion in chapters 6–7 is without question my own particular interpretation at this point in my scholarly odyssey. It may be that at some point in the future, I shall be giving a completely different interpretation, though the likelihood is that future discussion will be a development of present views, not a complete disowning of them. This is not because I am not capable of changing my mind, for my views have actually changed radically on Ezra-Nehemiah. About a decade ago they changed from a perspective fairly close to that found, for example, in Hugh Williamson's commentary (1985) to the one found in chapter 2 of *Judaism from Cyrus to Hadrian* (1992a). There were a number of causes but an important one was reading Gunneweg's commentary on Ezra (Gunneweg 1985; cf. my remarks in Grabbe 1991).

Lest Professor Brueggemann or other non-historians should be reviewing this book, let me say that I do not doubt the value of Ezra-Nehemiah for theological or hermeneutical purposes or for its place in literary appreciation and aesthetics. The literary and theological sides are discussed at some length, though there is a great deal more that could be said. But when I come to chapters 6 and 7, I am asking historical questions and dealing in critical history. I hope readers will understand that and not assume that I am doing like so many biblical scholars who talk about 'history' when they really mean theology or ideology.

6

Some practical points about use of this book need to be made at this juncture. Citation of the biblical text is to the chapter and verse numbering found in the Hebrew Bible. This usually corresponds to the English, but there are occasional differences (e.g. 10:1 in Hebrew is 9:38 in English). The Greek text of Esdras B is seldom cited since it usually only confirms the Hebrew; however, the text of Esdras B is not divided into two books, which means that the chapters are numbered consecutively. Thus, Nehemiah 1–13 corresponds to Esdras B 11–23. The verse numbering of 1 Esdras in various English translations sometimes differs by a number or two from that in most Greek editions.

The transliteration of Hebrew should be clear to those who know the language. I have used *v* and *f* for the non-*dagesh*ed forms of *bet* and *pe*, while *w* is always used for *waw* (even though now pronounced *v* by most modern users of Hebrew). English translations are generally my own, though I have consulted various English translations at different times, especially the New Jewish Publication Society version.

I use a number of words purely as descriptive terms without any political or sectarian motivation: Old Testament (OT) and Hebrew Bible are normally used interchangeably to mean the collection of writings found in the present Hebrew canon. However, if I am referring to the Septuagint version or any other which includes the deutero-canonical books, I shall use 'OT' (or 'Septuagint'); it has no sectarian or theological significance. 'Palestine' is purely a geographical term, used because it has been widely accepted for many years and because it is difficult to find a suitable substitute. Whenever the term 'the exile' is mentioned, it is both a convenient chronological benchmark to refer to the watershed between the monarchy/First Temple period and the Second Temple period and also a means of referring to the deportations from Judah that took place in the early sixth century BCE (cf. the discussion and essays in the edited volume of Grabbe 1998b).

The divine name for the God of Israel is written as 'Yhwh'; although often vocalized as 'Yahweh', the precise pronunciation is in fact unknown. The term *golah* is used to refer to the community of those who are alleged to have returned from exile. The name of the large Persian satrapy to the west of the Euphrates occurs in a variety of forms in our sources, depending on the particular administrative language in question. I give it in the form of 'Ebir-nari' which means 'Beyond (to the West of) the River (Euphrates)'.

Part I

LITERARY ANALYSIS

Chapters 2, 3, and 4 of this section give a close reading of the Hebrew books of Ezra and Nehemiah, of the Greek book of 1 Esdras, and of the other Ezra and Nehemiah traditions. The aim in these is to look at the text in its final form in all its detail and diversity. The emphasis is on an independent detailed study, asking the simple question: What do these texts actually say? Chapter 5 brings together and summarizes some of the main conclusions arising from the literary study.

2

EZRA IN THE HEBREW BIBLE

Analysis of the text

Ezra 1

Ezra 1:1–3a is the same as 2 Chron. 36:22–23. This has the clear aim of making Ezra a continuation of Chronicles. Just as 2 Chronicles ends on an optimistic note, so Ezra begins on the same optimistic note: as soon as Cyrus took the throne – in his very first year – the exile came to an end. His actions were not just those of a self-interested king (or, indeed, a benevolent king); they had actually been instigated by Yhwh to fulfil his own word as given through Jeremiah. The specific prophecy of Jeremiah is not indicated, but it seems to be the 'seventy years prophecy' of Jer. 25:11–14; 29:10–14 (though one might also think of the prophecy about Cyrus in Deutero-Isaiah [Isa. 45:13]). Cyrus issued a decree throughout his kingdom both orally (*qôl*) and in writing.

This decree (1:2–4) shows that Cyrus was not ignorant of the hand of Yhwh in his activities because he acknowledges that 'the God of the heavens' had given all the kingdoms of the earth into his control. Therefore (the decree continues), God has visited upon Cyrus the task of rebuilding God's house in Jerusalem, and he orders that whoever among all God's people so wishes can go to Jerusalem and build the house of Yhwh (with the help of his local community). This decree (which is in Hebrew even though the standard language of communication in the Persian empire was Aramaic) combines a rather specific reference to Yhwh the unique God of Israel with language of the outsider: 'the God of the heavens', 'Jerusalem which is in Judah' (twice), 'his people, his God', 'Yhwh the God of Israel'. The writer of the decree also knows about 'free-will offerings' (1:4: *nĕdāvāh*), and he also calls on the people as a whole (the 'men of his place') to provide support. This seems to contradict Ezra 6:3–4 in which Cyrus orders the costs to be paid from the royal treasury.

The rest of the chapter (1:5–11) emphasizes the enthusiastic response of both the Jews and Cyrus himself to this decree. The heads of families (1:5: *rāʾšê hāʾāvôt*) from Benjamin and Judah, and the priests and Levites, were all involved, though their precise activity is not made very clear. But the neighbours (Jews only or Gentiles as well?) of those going to Jerusalem helped them out with vessels of precious metal, animals, and other sorts of gifts, not to mention free-will offerings (whatever that means). Cyrus does his part by returning the vessels looted from the Jerusalem temple by Nebuchadnezzar, which had been placed in a pagan temple. Cyrus gives the task to Mithradat the treasurer who inventories them to Sheshbazzar, a prince or official (*nāśîʾ*) of Judah.

The inventory itself follows, showing the emphasis placed on the exact number of vessels: thirty bowls (?: *ʾăgarṭĕlîm*) of gold and 1,000 silver; twenty-nine vessels of another sort (*maḥălāfîm*); thirty bowls of some sort (*kĕfôrîm*) of gold and 410 things (*miśĕnîm*) made of silver; plus another thousand vessels, all adding up to a total of 5,400 vessels of gold and silver. This is all very puzzling. The actual number listed do not add up to anywhere near the total sum, and a number of the vessel names have not been figured out by modern scholars. Since the names of vessels and instruments in the temple are listed elsewhere (e.g. 1 Chron. 28:14–17), we would expect conventional names. The meanings of a couple of other Hebrew words are also unexplained in this context. Either we have a list whose text has been damaged in transmission or we have someone's (the author's?) attempt to create a list to make a point. Since the temple vessels were all supposed to have been destroyed by Nebuchadnezzar (2 Kings 24:13; 25:13–17), the latter seems to be the more likely.

The chapter ends by asserting that these vessels were brought to Jerusalem by Sheshbazzar with the 'great migration' from Babylonia to Jerusalem. Curiously, no list of the immigrants is given (cf. Ezra 8:1–14). In the context, Ezra 2 immediately follows; it is a settlement list rather than one of immigrants, but it serves. However, it looks as if the writer had no list of immigrants or he would have included it here. So both the exiled people and the exiled holy contents of the destroyed temple return together to restore that which had been taken away almost half a century earlier.

Ezra 2

This chapter describes the settlement of the captives who returned from Babylonia to Jerusalem and Judah. They are called the 'sons of the province' (2:1: *běnê hammědînāh*), presumably referring to the province of Judah. It seems a strange designation for people who have just come back, which suggests that the list was of those who had already become established in the province. If so, this might imply a list made up rather later than just after the return described in Ezra 1. What this list does above all is inventory the population solely in terms of returnees; there is no hint that others were already living in the land or that they might also have rights. This chapter is firmly in the tradition of 'the myth of the empty land' (Carroll 1992; Barstad 1996).

A list is given of apparent leaders (2:2): Zerubbabel, Joshua, Nehemiah, Seraiah, Reeliah, Mordecai, Bilshan, Mispar, Bigvai, Rehum, Baanah. These are names known from the period and might be taken as simply the names of those who led the entourage of returnees. Yet there is a remarkable coincidence between a number of the names and individuals important elsewhere in literature of this period. Joshua and Zerubbabel are the leaders of the *golah* (returnee) community according to Ezra 3–5. Yet they were not mentioned in Ezra 1; instead, the leader of the return is Sheshbazzar (1:8, 11). This Sheshbazzar disappears from the narrative, though, except for a brief mention in a document later on (5:14).

Of the other names in 2:2 the name of Nehemiah is particularly striking. Apart from Neh. 3:16, no other individual by this name is known other than the figure in the book of Nehemiah who was made governor of the province of Yehud. Seraiah is the father of Ezra (7:1); indeed, in the parallel form of the list found in Nehemiah 7, the name appears as Azariah (*'ăzaryāh*) which is often seen as a variant of Ezra (*'ezrā'*). Mordecai is the name of Esther's uncle and an important figure in the book of Esther. Bigvai is mentioned a few verses later (2:14) as the name of a clan; it is also apparently a variant of the name Bagohi, known from the Elephantine as a governor of Yehud (but not mentioned in the Bible). Bilshan is the name of an individual, possibly an official, who wrote to Artaxerxes about Jerusalem (Ezra 4:7); it is also a form of *Bēlšunu* who is now known to have been a satrap of Ebir-nari in the late fifth century (Stolper 1987). The name Rehum occurs in several contexts. A person by this name is a Persian official in the time of Artaxerxes (Ezra 4:8–9, 17, 23). Also, one of the Jewish 'heads of the people' in Neh. 10:26 has the name Rehum, and a Levite with this name is mentioned among those repairing the walls of Jerusalem (Neh. 3:17). The name Baanah is among the Jewish 'heads of the people' in Neh. 10:28, and may be a variant of the father's name of one of those repairing the city wall (Neh. 3:4). Reeliah and Mispar are otherwise unknown.

What are we to make of this list of names in 2:2? It is ostensibly a list of leaders of the return at the beginning of Cyrus' reign. Several factors call that into question: the name of Sheshbazzar is missing; several of the names on it are of prominent individuals but whose activities seem to lie in a different context (Nehemiah, Ezra?, Mordecai, Bilshan, Bigvai?); a couple of the names are otherwise attested in the time of Nehemiah (Baanah, Rehum?). Any conclusions must be far from certain, but the most likely at this point is that either the list has been cobbled together from a collection of general names for this period, or it represents genuine leaders but over a period of time; indeed, a combination of these two factors cannot be ruled out.

The next section of the list (2:2–35) is of the 'men of the people of Israel' (2:2: *'anĕšê 'am Yiśrā'ēl*) and is divided into two parts: the first part (2:3–19) lists according to 'phratries' (families); the second part is mostly a geographical listing (2:20–35). A majority of the family names occur elsewhere in Ezra-Nehemiah (e.g. Ezra 8; 10; Neh. 10). The listing by place of settlement falls into the old territory of Benjamin. Much of the province of Yehud was taken up by what had been Benjamin, and the southern portion of the old kingdom of Judah seems to have come under Edomite jurisdiction.

The next portion of the list (2:36–58) is made up of temple personnel of various sorts: priests (2:36–39); Levites (2:40); singers (2:41); gatekeepers (2:42); Netinim servants (2:43); Solomon's servants (2:55–58). There are several peculiarities about this list. First, there are several different groups here which are not found elsewhere in Ezra-Nehemiah or Chronicles, suggesting that some may have merged together or become assimilated to the Levites. Secondly, the priests are quite numerous (well over 3,000) whereas the Levites are fewer than seventy-five, and the temple servants of various sorts do not reach 400.

Some who expected to claim their part in Israel were excluded because their genealogy could not be proved (2:59–63). This is understandable with regard to the priests since the priesthood was purely a matter of proper descent, but the idea that people could be excluded from 'Israel' because of ethnic descent goes against

14

everything else in the OT. Gentiles were allowed to convert, and the three families of lay Israelites excluded seem to have been observing the Jewish law, including circumcision, since non-observance is likely to have been mentioned (2:59–60). Curiously, the name Delaiah is known from the Elephantine papyri to be a son of Sanballat who opposed Nehemiah, while Tobiah is the name of one of Sanballat's colleagues (Neh. 2:10). Nothing further is known of Nikoda, though a person of that name is found in the list of Netinim (2:48). The implications of not being able to prove their ancestry are not further spelled out.

Three families of priests were also excluded. Barzillai may be debarred because of descent through the female line since the priesthood was inherited primarily through the male line. It is interesting to note that one of the excluded families of priests apparently occurs as a fully accepted sacerdotal family in other texts (cf. Ezra 8:33; Neh. 3:4, 21; 1 Macc. 8:17). The three families claiming to be priestly were prevented from eating of the food reserved for the priests until their ancestry could be established. No suggestion is made that one might look to prophets for a judgement. This suggests (contrary to several passages in Nehemiah) that prophets were not ‑envisaged or that their word would not be sufficient. Reference is made instead to the traditional priestly method of divination of Urim and Thummim which seem to have been a form of lot (cf. Grabbe 1995: 120–21). The implication is that they were not currently available, though their future use is certainly allowed for; however, no other Second Temple text suggests that the use of the Urim and Thummim was revived.

The matter was handled by 'his excellency' (*hattiršātā'*). The Tirshata was an Aramaic title apparently used for the provincial governor elsewhere (Neh. 8:9; 10:2). The list ends with totals not only of the community members but also of their servants, singers (apparently for their entertainment, since the temple singers occur earlier in 2:41), and even their pack animals (2:64–69). Donations for the temple are also mentioned. The first total of more than 42,000 for the members of the community is about 12,500 more than the sum of the numbers given through the list. This indicates that the text is more interested in giving an impression of sizeable numbers than simply preserving an accurate record of numbers. That well over forty thousand Israelites, with a large number of servants and a sizeable number of animals for transport, returned as soon as Cyrus gave his command would be impressive to most readers. This large group who returned to settle an empty land in their old places of habitation would confirm the divine will behind the decree of the pagan kings. These people were also not destitute or refugees, for they had not only servants and property but also a sizeable amount of gold and silver for the temple, along with the necessary priestly garments. The wealth and generosity of the community is shown in the donation of 61,000 drachmas of gold (roughly 500 kilograms or half a tonne) and 5,000 minas of silver (roughly 2,500 kilos or 2.5 metric tonnes).

The chapter ends with the priests and Levites and all the other people settled in their respective cities (2:70). The stage is now set for taking up the task for which they had come – the rebuilding of the temple.

Ezra 3

This chapter describes how the people, having arrived and settled into their cities, begin the most important task before them: rebuilding the temple which had been desolate for almost fifty years. We immediately run into an anomaly in the narrative. First, two new leaders, not mentioned in Ezra 1 and only as two among eleven in 2:2, suddenly emerge; these are Joshua (or Jeshua) and Zerubbabel. But the second curious point is the author's reticence to tell us who these two men are, identifying them only by their fathers' names. It is clear in context that Joshua is a priest because v. 2 mentions 'his fellow priests', but we are not told that he is high priest nor are we told who Zerubbabel is. We know from other passages that Joshua holds the office of high priest (Hag. 1:1, 12, 14; 2:2; Zech. 3:1) and that Zerubbabel is actually the provincial governor appointed by the Persians (Hag. 1:1, 14; 2:2). Why are we not told this straightforwardly? It does not seem to be because the author wishes to deny these offices – indeed, the office of Joshua is not too difficult to infer. The answer seems to be that he wishes to emphasize the place of the entire people in the process of building, as an analysis of the following verses indicates (Japhet 1982, 1983).

Ezra 3:1 gives the setting of rebuilding. It is the 7th month (Tishri or September/October) which contained a number of important holy days and festivals, including the Day of Trumpets (1 Tishri), the Day of Atonement (10 Tishri), and the Festival of Tabernacles (15–22 Tishri). The people would need to gather in Jerusalem to celebrate this period; their doing so 'as one man' (v. 1) is evidence of their piety and intent. Although the two leaders are unavoidably given prominence, the emphasis is on the people as a whole: the fellow priests of Joshua and the fellow countrymen ('brothers') of Zerubbabel. It is what 'they' do that is important. They build the altar to Israel's God to offer offerings as instructed in the written law (*tôrāh*) of Moses the man of God, and begin offering the daily morning and evening sacrifice (*tāmîd*). Ezra 3:3 already anticipates Ezra 4–6 by hinting at opposition from 'the peoples of the land', though nothing further is said in this chapter.

Verses 4–5 make the point not only that they observed Sukkot (the Feast of Tabernacles) but that they did it 'as it was written', including the various sacrifices required for 'day by day'. This is an allusion to Num. 29:12–39 which specifies the particular sacrifices to be offered each day of Sukkot, as well as those to be offered daily, weekly, monthly, and at the other festivals (Num. 28–29). The altar was set up in time to begin offerings from 1 Tishri (3:6) even though work on the temple itself had not begun.

The work begins in earnest with 3:7 when silver is paid to hire workmen, obtain provisions, and import cedar wood from Lebanon. This began in the 2nd month (Iyyar or April/May) of the 2nd year of their return, which is somewhat curious since this is about seven months after the altar was first set up. Why the gap of more than half a year? Again, the work is done by Zerubbabel and Joshua and 'the rest of their fellows, the priests and the Levites and all those who returned from captivity', with the Levites aged twenty and above acting as supervisors. Joshua and his sons and his brother Kadmiel were apparently in overall charge (though 3:9 is somewhat puzzling and often thought to be partially corrupted). As soon as the foundations were laid, the priests and Levitical descendants of Asaph stood by with musical instruments to praise God, and the people shouted with a great shout, praising God at the laying of the foundations. Many of the older priests, Levites, and family heads had remembered the First Temple and wept loudly, blending their cries with the glad shouting of the rest of the people. Why they wept is not stated, though it would be an expected emotion at this time.

Ezra 4

One of the elements of a good story is that things cannot go forward with uninterrupted progress. Life is not like that, and without tension stories soon become boring. Whatever the historical reality behind Ezra, the account of rebuilding the temple in 1–6 is a ripping yarn. The foundation laid with such hope and expectations in Ezra 3 suddenly meets determined opposition in Ezra 4. The opponents' efforts eventually lead to the suspension of the work for a number of years.

In 4:1–2 the unspecified 'enemies of Judah and Benjamin' hear that the returnees are building a temple to Yhwh and approach Zerubbabel and the 'heads of the families' (note that the narrator takes some of the limelight off Zerubbabel by sharing the leadership with the heads of families) with a proposition. They claim to worship the same God, though this has been since the days of Esarhaddon king of Assyria (681–669 BCE) who brought them there. This makes the point that they are foreigners, even though they have been in the land for at least 150 years. Therefore, Zerubbabel and Joshua (mentioned now though not in 4:2) and the heads of families reject their offer. No real reason for this refusal is given, though a brief appeal is made to the command of Cyrus (4:3). However, having been rejected as allies these people now become opponents, weakening the hands of the builders by trying to frighten them.

The two opposing groups are named as the 'people of the land' ('am-hā'āreṣ) and the 'people of Judah' ('am-Yĕhûdāh). The 'people of Judah' seems to be identified with the returnees. The 'people of the land' has been much debated. We know that in rabbinic literature, it comes to mean the ordinary Jews who were not very observant about the finer points of rabbinic law in matters of ritual purity, tithing, and the like. The term is not usually used of non-Jews. In the books of Kings, the 'people of the land' seem to be a sort of rural aristocracy made up of people with money and influence who could be called on for support by the king but who also occasionally intervened to remove an unacceptable ruler (e.g. 2 Kings 11:14, 18, 20; 21:24; 25:19; Hag. 2:4; Zech. 7:5). In Ezra and Nehemiah, however, the term appears to be used to label individuals as foreigners and non-Jews with pagan practices and thus a potential corrupting influence on the community. Whether this picture is a fair one will be discussed in chapter 6 below.

The opposition continued to harass the community for many years, all during the rest of Cyrus' reign, and into the reign of Darius I (4:5) – the reign of Cambyses seems to be overlooked. The nature of this harassment is a bit vague but seems to be diplomatic rather than the use of violence or force. They hired 'counsellors' against them, probably a reference to bribing Persian officials. The rest of the chapter is a detailed description of how the opponents eventually managed to get the work of rebuilding stopped until the 'second year' of Darius I's rule (4:24). This account fits the situation well and is consistent with the story overall. However, it is a very strange episode once we step outside the story and attempt to match up the named kings with the actual Persian rulers.

'At the beginning of the reign of Ahašweroš [usually identified with Xerxes] they wrote in opposition [?: śiṭnāh] to/about ['al] the inhabitants of Judah and Jerusalem' (4:6). This is perhaps one of the most puzzling verses in the Bible. It looks like the start of a narrative, but 4:7 immediately leaps ahead to the reign of another king and thus begins a new narrative. Therefore, 4:6 may be only a fragment of another narrative which has otherwise been lost. If so, there is no context to explain the unusual wording. The word śiṭnāh is a *hapax legomenon*, and commentators and lexicographers translated it more or less by guesswork. It might be related to the root śṭn which means 'oppose, be hostile', and most commentators take it to have some sense like this, though the exact nuance is uncertain. The preposition 'al in conjunction with the word 'write' (kātav) can mean either 'to' or 'concerning, about'. In other words, 'they' (apparently the opponents previously mentioned in the chapter) could have written *about* the people of Judah to someone else, perhaps the Persian officials, or they could have written *to* the inhabitants, in which case the subject 'they' would probably refer to Persian officials.

As just noted, 4:7–24 forms a new narrative. During the reign of Artaxerxes, 'Bishlam, Mithredat, Tabeel, and the rest of their companions' wrote to the king (v. 7). The quoted phrase is only one way of translating this somewhat difficult text. Some have seen the word *bišlām* not as a proper name but as a phrase meaning 'in peace' or 'in agreement (with)' or even have emended it to read 'in Jerusalem' or 'in matters concerning Jerusalem'. In any case, we are not told who these two or three individuals are. The verse goes on to state that the writing was in Aramaic and translated into Aramaic. From 4:8 to 7:18 the text is now in Aramaic rather than Hebrew. The reason for this is unclear. The Persian documents embedded in the text would be expected to be in Aramaic since this was the common medium of communication in the Persian empire (a situation which had already begun in the days of the Neo-Assyrian empire); however, the narrative itself could have continued in Hebrew (as in fact it does in Ezra 7 where the narrative is in Hebrew but the document is in Aramaic). The fact that both the documents and the narrative are in Aramaic is an issue which will be discussed further when the question of the authenticity of the documents is looked at (ch. 6 below).

The new narrative beginning in 4:7 is immediately interrupted in v. 8, not by the formal aspects of the text but by the content. Verse 7 says that Mithredat, Tabeel, and others wrote to the king, and then v. 8 begins the supposed letter which is indeed addressed to king Artaxerxes. Yet the senders of the letter are said to be Rehum the commissioner (*bĕ'ēl-ţĕ'ēm*) and Shimshai the scribe. One can only conclude that a wrong letter has somehow got inserted in the narrative in place of the one referred to in v. 7. The writers and 'the rest of their companions' speak in the name of various officials and various ethnic groups. The senders of the letter can be divided into two groups: first are the 'officials', though the precise meaning of the terms is not always clear. The ethnic groups are those from the Mesopotamian cities of Erech and Babylon and from the Elamite city of Susa. These had been settled in the city of Samaria and other cities in the province of Ebir-nari (i.e. the province of Across-the-River-Euphrates which included Syria and Palestine).

This list of ethnic groups reminds one immediately of 2 Kings 17 which describes a group of eastern peoples brought into Samaria when some of the Northern Kingdom were sent into exile about 722 BCE. However, the only name they have in common is men from 'Babylon'. Also, the men of this letter in Ezra are said to have been deported by the 'great and noble king Asnappar'. The king who deported some of the population of Samaria was Shalmaneser V (2 Kings 17:3 and *Babylonian Chronicle 1* i 27–28 [Grayson 1975: 73], though Sargon II takes credit for the deed in some of his inscriptions). Asnappar may be a reflex or corruption of Ashurbanipal (668–627 BCE); if so, he could hardly be associated with the fall of Samaria some half a century earlier in 722 BCE. Either the writer has confused the data about the fall of Samaria, or he has a different tradition from the one in 2 Kings 17, or he knows of an entirely different deportation under Ashurbanipal. Choosing one of these three over the others is not easy.

The text of the letter (4:12–16) asserts that the Jews are rebuilding the city of Jerusalem and the walls. Then follows a long list of the losses to the Persian empire if this is allowed to continue. Jerusalem has a long history of being rebellious and wicked (4:12). The main loss would be of tax revenue, which is listed in detail (though the precise taxes in question are difficult to determine at this distance from the Persian administration). The king should search the records, and he will find that Jerusalem has always been rebellious and destructive to kings and provinces, which is why it was destroyed in the first place. Therefore, if this building continues, the king will no longer have control of the region of Ebir-nari. The letter emphasizes the rebuilding of the city walls, which would be the first thing done if the intent was to rebel. Nothing seems to be said about rebuilding the temple (unless this is implied at the end of 4:12). Are the writers of the letter making up this accusation in order to frighten the authorities, or does it in fact refer to a completely different building project from that focusing on the temple?

The king's reply comes in 4:17–22. Their letter had been read to him and a search was made, confirming the rebellious nature of Jerusalem. Great kings had ruled in the city and even over the whole province of Ebir-nari, collecting taxes of various sorts. Therefore, he commands the original communicators to stop the work of building immediately, until further orders might come from the king. Rehum the commissioner and Shimshai the scribe do as they are told, and work on the house ceases (v. 23). This cessation of work continues until the second year of king Darius of Persia (Darius I [522–486 BCE]).

As noted above, from the point of view of literary form and internal coherence the narrative is straightforward. A group of locals ask to participate in building. They are refused and so begin a campaign directed at the Persian authorities against the builders. Eventually, letters are written to the king, making accusations. The king examines the matter, accepts that the accusations are true, and stops the building of the temple. When the *contents* of the chapter are compared with *external history*, however, the message becomes nonsense. The building begins in the reign of Cyrus (who died in 530 BCE). The harassment continues during the reign of Cyrus until that of Darius. Cambyses (530–522 BCE) is not mentioned. He does not have to be, but it is a bit surprising that he is ignored. However, the narrative suddenly leaps ahead to a writing in the reign of Xerxes (486–465 BCE), which is not quoted, and then another writing in the reign of Artaxerxes (I? [465–424 BCE]). This writing in the reign of Artaxerxes, when actually quoted, turns out to be written by a different set of individuals from those said to have written it. King Artaxerxes writes back to order the building stopped. This writing – of Artaxerxes – is then used to stop building work in the time of Cyrus, almost a century earlier! The work then ceases until the reign of Darius who died several decades before the reign of Artaxerxes. Something is clearly amiss here!

Ezra 5

After a considerable period of inactivity – from the early years of Cyrus to the second year of Darius, or almost two decades, according to 4:23 – two prophets stood up and prophesied. Their names are given as Haggai and Zechariah, the same as the two prophetic books by these names. This raises the question of identity, but it soon becomes clear that the prophets in Ezra are meant to be identical with those in the books of Haggai and Zechariah; however, the contents of Haggai and Zechariah 1–8 are not fully compatible with the situation described in Ezra 5. For example, both Haggai (1:9; 2:1–4) and Zechariah (4:9–10) seem to envisage a single beginning and give no hint of a project started and then stopped by enemies. The context is that the temple is not being built because people have their mind on their own prosperity, not that enemies have caused the project to be held in abeyance. Strangely, here in Ezra their specific prophecies are also not given. One infers from the context that they prophesied to begin the temple building again (5:1–2), yet the expected content of the prophecies is not narrated here. The community leadership is roused by the prophecies. Zerubbabel, Joshua, and their fellow officers resume the work, though this time they are supported by the two prophets of God.

Not surprisingly this renewed activity quickly comes to the attention of the Persian authorities. Tattenai the satrap of the entire province of Ebir-nari, along with Shetar-boznai and their companions, came personally to investigate. The residence of the satrap was likely to have been a long way from Jerusalem; therefore, his coming in person attests to the seriousness of the matter and also the importance of Jerusalem. He asks who authorized the building and is given a list of those doing the work. However, they did not cease work while an official inquiry went to king Darius and his reply was awaited, because the eye of God was on the 'Jewish elders' (*śāvê Yĕhûdāyē*'). The contents of the letter then follow in 5:6–10.

The letter begins with a greeting to Darius the king. This is surprisingly short and not the elaborate flattery one might have expected, but this seems to conform to actual correspondence at the time. They then say that they went to 'Yehud the province' (*lîhûd mĕdîntā*'), one of the few specific designations of the area as a province in Ezra-Nehemiah. They saw the building of the house of 'the great God' – a title which shows no particular deference to Israel's God as opposed to any other. The progress of the building is described in some detail. Their question of who authorized the building and the request for the names of those involved, or at least their leaders, is recounted. The language used here is almost exactly the same as in 5:3–4, which suggests that one has borrowed from the other. If the document is original, it is likely that it is the source of the information in 5:3–4; if it is not, 5:9–10 is likely just a repetition of the description in 5:3–4 (see further in ch. 6 below).

The reply of the builders, as described in the continuing text of the letter, is very instructive. They say they are servants of the 'God of heaven and earth' who was angered by their ancestors and gave them into the hand of Nebuchadnezzar the Chaldean, king of Babylon, who destroyed the temple and exiled the people to Babylon. However, in his first year Cyrus the king of Babylon gave an order that the house of God should be rebuilt. Further, Cyrus took the vessels which Nebuchadnezzar had removed from the Jerusalem temple and placed in a temple in Babylon and turned them over to a man named Sheshbazzar. This Sheshbazzar Cyrus made governor, presumably over Judah. This Sheshbazzar not only brought back the vessels but he also laid the foundations of the temple in Jerusalem whose building has continued since then but is still not complete.

The writers of the letter then request king Darius to give the order to have the archives searched to see whether Cyrus gave such a decree to rebuild the Jerusalem temple as claimed. This might seem a bit presumptuous, since it was up to Darius to decide whether the rebuilding should continue. Yet it is also believable that a powerful satrap should suggest even to the king that it might be good to see what his predecessor had actually ordered. The king, receiving regular communication from all parts of the empire, was not likely to resent a suggestion from the regional governor if given sincerely and respectfully. Therefore, most of this is quite credible; whether it is historical or not is, of course, another question.

Ezra 6

The chapter break does not form a break in the story, since the question of whether the new phase of rebuilding can continue moves seamlessly from Ezra 5 to 6. Darius complies with the request from the satrap Tattenai and has a search made in the archives of Babylon. However, the document was found not in Babylon itself but in Ecbatana, a city which was used as the summer residence of the later Persian kings (cf. Xenophon, *Anabasis* 3.5.15; *Cyropaedia*

8.6.22). The document gives all that the builders could hope for (6:3–5). It says that in his first year Cyrus issued an order to let the house of God in Jerusalem be rebuilt, with sacrifices being offered. Not only that, the height and breadth are both specified as 60 cubits though, strangely, the length is not given. It is to be built of layers of stone and wood, with three layers of stone to one of wood, with the cost being met from the palace. The temple vessels taken away by Nebuchadnezzar are to be returned.

Although it is not said explicitly, the decree from Cyrus apparently forms part of a reply from Darius to Tattenai because 6:6–12 continues on as such a letter from the king to the satrap. The letter which follows could only be an answer to prayer because it orders all that the builders could possibly want. Therefore, continues the letter, Tattenai the governor of Ebir-nari, Shetar-boznai, and the others are to keep away from the work at Jerusalem. It is to be left to the 'governor of the Jews' (*paḥat Yĕhûdāyē'*) and the elders. Furthermore, Darius commands that in order to assist the building, the expenses are to be paid from the tax revenues gathered in Ebir-nari. Also, whatever the priests say is needed for the sacrifice to the God of heaven – bullocks, rams, lambs, wheat, salt, wine, oil – is to be given to them on a daily basis. The priests are to be offering up a sweet smell to the God of heaven and praying for the life of the king and his sons. And if anyone attempts to change this message, a beam is to be pulled out of his house and he is to be impaled upon it and his house turned into a dungheap. Let the God who makes his name dwell there overthrow any king or people who attempts to alter the decree or destroy this temple. Darius has issued a decree; let it be done.

What a powerful affirmation of the work of the rebuilders! It could not have been more opportune than if they had written the decree themselves. Indeed, this very fact immediately makes one suspicious of the origins of this edict from Darius. That Darius might have written an order on behalf of the temple is quite possible, but he is unlikely to have written this order. He rebukes the Persian officials who are only doing their duty, he provides for the work from the central treasury, and he uses Deuteronomistic language in 6:12 on God's name dwelling in Jerusalem. This does not look like the work of chancellery scribes but of a Jewish theologian.

As a theological document, though, the Darius decree fits the story very well. The builders went ahead in faith, trusting in the word of Yhwh through the prophets, and God has used the Persian king as his instrument to see that the work is placed on an even more secure basis. The rest of the chapter (6:13–22) describes how the work is brought to completion according to the divine plan. Tattenai and his fellow officials immediately implement the terms of Darius' decree. The elders continued to build at the prophecy of Haggai and Zechariah, and at the order of the God of Israel and the decrees of Cyrus, Darius, and Artaxerxes. Artaxerxes? Artaxerxes had probably not been born when the temple is supposed to have been finished. Thus, the confusion of kings and their relationship to the temple rebuilding seen in Ezra 4 surfaces here once again.

The building is finally completed on 3 Adar (February/March) in Darius' 6th year (6:15). The sons of Israel, the priests, the Levites, and the rest of the returnees dedicated the temple in joy. Note that the narrative speaks of the various groups of people, but no leader. This corresponds to previous passages which placed the emphasis on the people rather than the leaders; however, it is rather surprising that Zerubbabel and Joshua are not even mentioned. Notice that it is not 'sons of Judah' but 'sons of Israel'. Who the 'rest of the returnees' might be after one takes out the Israelites, the priests, and the Levites is a question; 'the rest of the returnees' seems redundant. In conformity with the usual description of temple dedications, a great deal of stress is placed on the quantity of animals killed. In this case, they offered up 100 bulls, 200 rams, 400 lambs, and twelve goats for a sin offering (purification offering) for all Israel, one goat for each of the twelve tribes of Israel. The priests and Levites, organized according to their divisions, performed the work as written in the law of Moses.

The narrative now switches back to Hebrew (6:19–22), but the thought seems to continue without interruption. On the 14th of the 1st month (Nisan or March/April) they celebrated the Passover, all the priests and Levites being ritually pure as one. The sons of Israel and the elders were separated from the impurity of the nations or peoples of the land (*gôyê-hā'āreṣ*). They then celebrated the seven days of the Festival of Unleavened Bread following the Passover with rejoicing because Yhwh had made them rejoice and had changed the heart of the king of Assyria to strengthen their hand in the work of rebuilding the house of the God of Israel. Why the Persian king should be called 'king of Assyria' is somewhat puzzling (cf. Neh. 9:32 which sees the kings of Assyria as all in the past).

This chapter is redolent with theologically significant motifs. These include:

- The king of Persia as only an instrument in God's hand to aid the Jews in rebuilding the temple. He not only gives permission and protection (6:7); he also provides imperial funds (6:8–9).
- Stress placed on Israel, even though terms such as 'Jews' are also used.
- Emphasis placed on the community and its various groups; the leadership is mentioned only once and then anonymously (6:7: 'the governor and the elders of the Jews').
- The full operation of the cult, with the priests and other personnel appropriately organized (6:18), and proper celebration of God's festivals (specifically the Passover and Unleavened Bread).

Ezra 7

Ezra 7–10 forms the story of Ezra. If we look at a historical list of the Persian kings, Ezra does not come on the scene any earlier than 458 BCE, which is the 7th year of Artaxerxes I; it could be 398 BCE if the king in question is Artaxerxes II. Yet there is no apparent awareness in the narrative that Ezra comes anything other than shortly after the completion of the temple. In fact, we have the curious move from the *6th* year (of Darius) to the *7th* year (of Artaxerxes). This looks more than just accidental, especially if all the dates in Ezra-Nehemiah are taken into account. Ezra's mission is not separate from the rebuilding of the temple but is, rather, complementary to it. The continuation from Ezra 1–6 is made clear in the opening words: 'after these things'. By this phrase, the author signals that the story still continues – there is no real break, even though a simple check of the dates would show that at least half a century had intervened, if any of this is historical.

In 7:1–5 Ezra is identified. The means of this identification is quite interesting because it tells us some of the things thought to be important about Ezra. He is identified by means of his genealogy which goes back to Aaron the high priest. Ezra is a priest; furthermore, he is of the line of the pre-exilic high priests. This is significant because he nowhere claims the office of high priest, but the text seems to be implying that he deserves this office even if he does not have it formally. His immediate predecessor was Sariah (7:1), the last of the pre-exilic high priests, who was executed when Nebuchadnezzar took Jerusalem (2 Kings 25:21). It cannot be literally true that Ezra was son of Sariah, for he would have been at least 120 years old. Yet it seems that this is what the text wants us to believe. It is not common for a more distant ancestor to be used as a patronymic, and there is nothing linguistic to make us think Sariah is anything but Ezra's father. It is only when we calculate the chronology from data outside Ezra that the absurdity of the situation becomes clear.

The text then gives us a second means of identifying Ezra. He is 'the swift [or "ready"] scribe in the *tôrāh* of Moses which Yhwh the God of Israel gave' (7:6). The term 'scribe' (*sōfēr*) implied reading, writing, and books. In a time and place where very few could read, much less write, the scribe's job was to take care of all those duties which involved reading and writing. As well as letters, documents, and books this might include keeping records, inventories, and accounts. Yet what is emphasized about Ezra is not the normal duties of a scribe but the particular concern with the 'teaching' of Yhwh (which is the basic meaning of *tôrāh*). Thus, Ezra 'had set his heart to research the *torah* of Yhwh and to do and to teach the statute and judgement in Israel' (7:10). He is 'the scribe of the words of Yhwh's commandment and his statutes over Israel' (7:11), the 'scribe of the law (*dat*) of the God of heaven' (7:12).

This in some ways gives a new meaning to the word 'scribe' in Israel since there is no suggestion up until now that the scribe had any special connection with the law or teaching of Yhwh. Yet this is not incompatible with the concept of scribe in the ancient Near East in general. In Mesopotamia and Egypt scribes were responsible for all intellectual activity, from measuring fields to the production of cultic texts. There were scribes associated with temples and with jurisprudence. In Ezra's case there does not seem to be a clear distinction made between his being a priest and his being a scribe. He is both – and he is particularly concerned with the teaching of Yhwh the God of Israel in its broadest sense. He is a scribe but not a normal scribe; he is more than a scribe (on scribes, see Grabbe 1995: 152–80).

This Ezra went up from Babylon, and the king gave him all that he desired, because the hand of Yhwh was upon him (Ezra? the king? – 7:6). A group went to Jerusalem with Ezra in the 7th year of Artaxerxes: Israelites, priests, Levites, singers, gatekeepers, Netinim (temple servants of some sort). They set out on new year – the 1st day of the 1st month (March/April) – and arrived on the 1st day of the 5th month (July/August), for God's good hand was on Ezra because of his commitment to study and teach the law (7:9–10). Now comes a transitional verse (7:11), in Hebrew but introducing the Aramaic royal decree which follows. Again, it is emphasized that Ezra is priest and scribe, scribe of the words of Yhwh's commandment and his statutes over Israel.

The decree (7:12–26) is in Aramaic as one would expect of a decree from the Persian king. It makes available power and resources to Ezra beyond his wildest dreams. Anyone who wishes may go to Jerusalem with Ezra, whether from the people of Israel or the priests or the Levites. Ezra is sent by the king and his seven counsellors to make investigation in Judah and Jerusalem on the basis of the 'law which is in your hand' (7:14) and also to convey the silver and gold which the king and his counsellors have donated to the God of Israel (7:15). Furthermore, all the silver and gold found in the province of Babylon, along with that donated by the people and priests, is given for the temple in Jerusalem (7:16). They are to use the money to buy bullocks, rams, and lambs, with their cereal and drink offerings, and to offer them up on the altar in Jerusalem (7:17). The rest of the silver and gold can be used for whatever seems good to Ezra and his brethren, according to God's will (7:18), and vessels given for service of the temple are to be delivered to the God of Jerusalem (7:19). What is more, any other needs for the temple are to be paid from the king's treasury, with Artaxerxes himself issuing an order to all the treasurers of Ebir-nari that anything which Ezra (the priest and scribe of the law of the God of heaven) asks is to be done precisely, up to a hundred talents of silver, a hundred *cor*s of wheat, a hundred *bath*s of wine and a hundred of oil, and salt without any limit (7:20–22). All required of the God of heaven let be done diligently for his temple, for why should he be wrathful over the rule of the Persian king and his sons (7:23)? Let it be announced that none of the temple personnel – priest, Levite, temple singer, gatekeeper, Netin, temple servant – are to pay tax, tribute, or revenue (7:24).

The decree goes on to give Ezra the task of appointing judges and magistrates to be judging the people who are in Ebir-nari, all those who know the law (*dat*) of his God. All those who do not know the law of the God are to be taught it. Ezra is to do this by 'the wisdom of God which is in your hand' (7:25). Anyone who is not observing the law of Ezra's God and the law of the king is subject to strict judgement, whether banishment, fine, or imprisonment (7:26). The Aramaic text, and presumably the decree itself, comes to an end at this point; however, it is only the change of language which signals the end of the decree since what follows in v. 27 otherwise seems to be a continuation of v. 26. Apparently Ezra now speaks (the narrative is in the first person), blessing the God of the fathers who has put in the king's heart to glorify the Jerusalem temple, who extended mercy on Ezra from the king, his counsellors, and all his mighty officers. Thus strengthened by the hand of God Ezra gathers the leaders (*rā'šîm*) from Israel to go up with him. In this manner, 7:28 serves to finish off the decree of Ezra 7 and to preface the journey to Jerusalem which follows in Ezra 8.

Ezra 8

This chapter describes the journey to Jerusalem, including a list of those who went and the amount of donated precious metals they took with them. The details of the journey are not given because the focus is on other, more theological matters. The family and treasure lists are the stuff of theology here.

According to the heading in 8:1, the list which follows in 8:2–14 is of the 'heads of the fathers' which seems to be heads of families who went 'with me' to Jerusalem in the time of Artaxerxes king of Babylon. This is a strange heading for an official list which would be expected to say 'with Ezra'. This looks more like a list in a personal diary or like the statement of someone simply making up a narrative which includes a list of peoples. The first-person account which began in 7:27 in fact continues until 9:15, so 8:1 is not out of character unless one argues for the insertion of an official list here.

The list is organized according to families in which a remote ancestor is named and then the immediate head of family. After that the number of the males going with the head of family is often given. In 8:2 the names Phinehas and Ithamar look like the names of priestly ancestors, while David could be the famous king. Phinehas was a grandson of Aaron, but Ithamar was one of his sons. Strangely, no numbers are given for these three names. Of the list in 8:3–14, there are several strange aspects which suggest textual corruption. The 'sons of Shecaniah' in 8:3 breaks off without representation or number; similarly, the 'sons of Shecaniah' in 8:5 has no named representative, though a number is given. This still leaves eleven names in 8:3–14; of these, nine occur in 2:4–17 (all except Joab and Shelomith). By emendation on the basis of 1 Esdras, some make the agreement more exact, even to an exact twelve names (e.g. Blenkinsopp 1988: 158–62). If the number twelve is correct, this seems a strange coincidence since this is a significant number in the OT. Ignoring that, the content of the list still suggests that Ezra's groups could have been borrowed from the list in Ezra 2, or vice versa. The numbers with each are different, of course, but this does not resolve the query of whether this is an artificial creation.

Ezra, still speaking in the first person, found that there were no Levites. As the lower clergy, the Levites were a part of the temple personnel but could not preside at the altar. Therefore, they were usually designated separately from the 'priests'. This agrees with the picture we find in the P document (Leviticus and parts of Exodus and Numbers), Ezekiel 40–48, and the books of Chronicles. It differs from Deuteronomy which speaks of 'the priests the Levites' or 'Levitical priests', apparently as an undifferentiated group. All our sources for the Second Temple period seem to see the Levites as a group separate from the priests. Therefore, for Ezra the fact that there were priests as well as ordinary Jews among his group of emigrants was not sufficient, and he sent messengers to try to persuade some Levites to join them (8:14–20). The eleven men sent as messengers were apparently people of some stature in the community (8:16).

They went specifically to Iddo, the head of a settlement in Casiphia. This is very interesting because it suggests several things. First, this seems to be a settlement specifically of Levites. It is headed by a figure called Iddo, who seems to include a group of Netinim (8:17) under his jurisdiction. Up until now the Netinim have been considered a particular group of the temple personnel, a group whom David and his officials had appointed to help with the work of the Levites (8:20), but here it is possibly a more generic term for temple servants in general. This community seems to be considered as a part of the Levites. Especially interesting is Ezra's reason for asking for Levites to accompany him: so they could be 'ministers (*mĕšārĕtîm*) for the house of God'. Considering that the temple had been functioning for at least sixty years, why did he suddenly need 'ministers'? Since he needed Levites, he apparently thought that the temple lacked personnel at the lower end of the scale.

A variety of individuals responded. Some of these are listed: an astute man named Sherebiah and some of his relations from the Levitical family of Mahli, eighteen individuals; Hashabiah, with Isaiah and relatives from the Levitical family of Merari, twenty. These were presumably Levites proper since there are also an additional 220 Netinim. This was apparently enough, which makes one ask how many Levites were supposedly available in Jerusalem.

Having got his group of emigrants together Ezra now relates a strange situation (8:21–23). He calls a fast in order to pray for

God's favour and protection during their journey. Ezra claims that he was ashamed to ask the king for an escort because he had already said that God's protection would be on those journeying. It sounds almost as if at this point he regrets what seems a case of braggadocio, that he had emphasized too much how God was on his side and now it was difficult to request help. But this explanation does not fit the context very well. It is unlikely that Ezra is being criticized here; on the contrary, the point is that he trusted in God who brought him safely to Jerusalem. Part of the evidence of his trust was in calling a fast to show the sincerity of their purpose and mission.

Yet, while this theological point fits the context of the book of Ezra well, it does not fit the situation as laid out in the data given. First, if Ezra had such powers as delegated to him in Ezra 7 an armed military escort would surely have been normal. Either the king would have granted one without any request on his part or, more likely, Ezra himself had the authority to call for one without further reference to the king. Secondly, we need to consider that it was not just a caravan of people which would be making its way to Jerusalem. As will be shown in chapter 6 below, an enormous amount of silver and gold was being transported for this long distance. A good portion of this wealth had been donated by the king and his entourage. Far from Ezra's having to ask for an escort, it would rather more likely be the case that the king would *insist* on an armed guard. The laissez-faire approach of the king described here is totally unrealistic.

In 8:24–30 Ezra makes provision for the transport of the precious metal. He appoints twelve officers of the priests and, apparently, an additional twelve Levites led by Sherebiah and Hashabiah (the two prominent Levites mentioned in 8:18–19) for safe-keeping and carriage of the valuable cargo. The astonishing amount of this wealth is recounted (8:26–27): 650 talents of silver and 100 talents of gold, not to mention 100 silver vessels, 20 gold ones worth 1,000 gold *daric*s (Persian coins) each, and others of bronze as precious as gold. These are given to the twelve individuals to look after until they can deliver them in person to the temple when they would hand them over to the 'officers of the priests, the Levites, and the Israelite heads of families (*śārê-hā'āvôt lĕYiśrā'ēl*) in Jerusalem'.

The journey to Jerusalem was successful (8:31–36). They left on the 12th day of the 1st month (Nisan), and God protected them from the hand of enemies. They arrived in Jerusalem and, after resting three days, they weighed out the silver and gold to Meremot the priest, an individual named Eleazar (a priest?, since he is son of

Phineas), and two named Levites. The chapter concludes with a list of the sacrifices offered up to thank God for their safe arrival, including 'twelve bullocks for all Israel' (v. 35) and twelve he-goats for a sin (purification) offering. Finally, they gave the mandates of the king (*dātê hammelek*) to the satraps and governors of the Ebir-nari province. This last statement raises many questions: Was this done in Jerusalem? If so, why were the satraps and governors there? Had they been called together? Many of them would have been most easily informed during the journey itself, when Ezra was near their geographical area of jurisdiction. Is this what is in mind in v. 36? There was only one satrap over the whole province of Ebir-nari, so who were these 'satraps'? The term 'satrap' was sometimes used loosely to mean 'governor', but if so, how did these 'satraps' relate to the 'governors' who are also named? We are not told.

The genealogical concerns of this chapter need to be set alongside those of Ezra 2//Nehemiah 8.

Ezra 9

Ezra 9 and 10 form a unit relating to the marriage of the 'people of Israel' with the 'peoples of the land' (9:1). Thus, half the Ezra story is taken up with this one incident, which also seems a rather negative one with which to end the book. The figure of Ezra in these two chapters seems a great contrast with the Ezra who is given such sweeping powers in Ezra 7.

According to 9:1 all are involved – the people, the priests, and the Levites. Since Ezra and his band have just arrived, surely the problem cannot be theirs. This indicates that a large group of Israelites, priests, and Levites are already settled around Jerusalem. The 'peoples of the lands' are not identified, but they are immediately branded with the 'abominations' of the original inhabitants of the land, the Canaanites, Hittites, and the Perizzites, as well as the surrounding peoples of the Ammonites, the Moabites, the Egyptians, and the 'Amorites'. The text is difficult and may not exactly say that the 'peoples of the lands' are these various groups, but the implication is there. Yet most of these names are of traditional enemies of Israel and represent groups which had long since disappeared (assuming they ever existed). It is doubtful if any group identified itself as Hittite, Perizzite, or Amorite at this time. 'Canaanite' seems to have been used mainly as a term for 'trader' (cf. Job 40:30 [ET 41:6]; Prov. 31:24; Zech. 14:21).

The people of Israel have given their daughters to them and their sons, mixing 'the holy seed' with the 'peoples of the lands' (9:2). What is more, the leaders – the officials (*śārîm*) and the administrators (*sĕgānîm*) – were foremost in doing this (9:3). Ezra's reaction is that which we would have expected of a pious man shocked at this behaviour of his people, but it is also the reaction of a leader without powers: he tears his clothing, pulls hair from his head and beard, and goes into mourning until the evening sacrifice (9:4–5). A group of 'all those who tremble at the words of Israel's God' come to him. Having mourned all day, Ezra ceases this and drops to his knees, spreads his hands, and prays (9:6). What follows is a typical prayer of confession (9:6–15).

Ezra begins by saying that he is ashamed to raise his face to God, for the iniquities are great and our guilt reaches to heaven. We are in great guilt, from the days of the ancestors until now. In our iniquities our kings and priests were given into the hand of the kings of other nations, to suffer the sword, captivity, despoiling, and shame until now. Finally, for a little time we experience favour from Yhwh our God who let a remnant escape and gave us a toehold in God's holy place, to bring light to our eyes and a little renewal of life in our servitude. For we are servants, yet in our servitude God did not forsake us but extended his mercy before the king of Persia to give us a wall in Judah and Jerusalem. Now we have forsaken your commandments, given through your servants the prophets who said that the land to be inherited is a land polluted by the pollution of the peoples of the land in their abominations, completely filled with uncleanness by them (*bĕṭum'ātām*). Do not give your daughters to their sons and vice versa, and you shall never seek their welfare so that you will be strong, eat the good of the land, and possess it for your sons forever. After all which came upon us for our evil deeds and great guiltiness, you refrained from extending our iniquities and provided an escape to now. Shall we return to breaking your commandments by intermarrying with the people of these abominations? Would you not be angry with us to complete destruction so that no remnant or single person is spared? Yhwh, God of Israel, you are righteous, for we were spared to be here today. Behold, we are before you in our guilt; there is no one who can stand in your presence.

Ezra's prayer is a significant piece of theology. Like all such prayers, a great deal of emphasis is placed on the past and present sins of the people. That sin and guilt are acknowledged can be taken for granted, but several points are peculiar to this prayer.

The cause of their sin is placed on the shoulders of the 'peoples of the land' and their 'abominations' which made it ritually unclean. Thus, even though the sins of the ancestors and the present peoples are freely admitted, they are laid squarely at the door of the inhabitants of the land with whom Israel should never have mixed. Ezra thus labels the 'mixed marriages' as not just a sin but as a gross violation which could make them lose the land in which they had recently gained a toehold, just as it caused their ancestors to lose it.

Ezra 10

The narrative now switches to the third person. Ezra had been praying and weeping in front of the temple. A large crowd gathered around him – men, women, and children – and also took up the mourning (10:1). Shecaniah from the family of Elam acted as spokesman for them. He acknowledged their rebellion against God for taking foreign wives from the 'peoples of the land'; nevertheless, there was hope: he proposed that they make a covenant with God to send away their wives and also the children born from them, at the advice of the Lord and 'those who tremble at the commandment of God', to be done according to the Torah (10:2–3). He called on Ezra to get up, to be strong and do it. Ezra arose and made the chiefs of the priests, Levites, and all Israel swear to act according to this advice. Then he went from in front of the temple to the chamber of the Yohanan b. Eliashib, where he continued to fast in his mourning at this great rebellion (10:6).

A message was sent out to everyone for all the returnees from exile to assemble in Jerusalem in three days, under threat of confiscation of goods and excommunication from the community (10:7). All the men of Judah and Benjamin naturally complied, assembling in the rain in front of the temple on the 20th day of the 9th month. Ezra had set out from Babylonia in the 1st month. According to Ezra 7:8–9 they arrived on the 1st day of the 5th month; thus, a period of four months had elapsed between Ezra's arrival and this crisis over the marriages. Ezra wasted no words on preliminaries (10:10–11): he told them immediately that they had committed a guilty offence by marrying 'foreign wives' and that they should thank the God of their fathers (for what?) and do God's will by separating from these 'foreign wives'. The people responded immediately with one voice that they would comply. However, because of the cold rain and the size of the job, which would take days, they asked that a system be set up to deal with the matter

(10:13–14): let officers be set up and those who have contracted marriages with 'foreign wives' should then come at appointed times, with the elders and judges of their individual cities.

The next verse (10:15) is rather enigmatic. Somewhat literally it reads: 'Only/indeed Jonathan son of Asahel and Jahzeiah son of Tikva stood upon this, and the Levites Meshullam and Shabbetai supported them.' The Greek text of the Hebrew Ezra (Esdras B) reads: 'Only Jonathan son of Asael and Iazias son of Thekoe (were) with me concerning this.' 1 Esdras 9:14 states: 'Jonathas son of Azael and Iezias son of Thokan accepted this upon themselves.' Similarly, the Authorized Version translates it fairly literally: 'Only Jonathan the son of Asahel and Jahaziah the son of Tikvah were employed about this matter.' The REB, NRSV, and the commentaries of Blenkinsopp (1988: 191, 194) and Williamson (1985: 140, 156–57) read it: 'Only Jonathan son of Asahel and Jahzeiah son of Tikvah opposed this.' It is too bad that the verse is not clearer since a frank admission of opposition in the face of such strong pressures would tell us an interesting story. Even if it is translated 'opposed', this could take one of two forms: opposition to separating from the 'foreign' wives or opposition in the sense of wanting a stricter approach to the matter. We cannot rule out, though, that Jonathan and Jahzeiah were actually being engaged to do the work of carrying out the proposal.

The situation was handled as suggested. Ezra and family heads divided the people up according to family and sat to make decisions on individuals for two months, from the 1st day of the 10th month to the 1st day of the 1st month (10:16–17). This last date is significant. Not only is it the beginning of the year but it was also the day on which Ezra began his journey from Babylon a year earlier (7:8). Thus Ezra's mission was accomplished in exactly a year.

The rest of the chapter lists those who had offended (10:18–44). The 'offence' started at the top since four of the sons (descendants?) of Joshua b. Josadak and his brothers were involved. Joshua the high priest was, of course, one of the 'founding fathers' of the *golah* community (Ezra 3; Hag. 1:1, 12, 14; 2:2; Zech. 3–4). They agree to separate from their wives and offer a ram for a guilt (reparation) offering (10:19). According to Lev. 4:1–12, if a priest sins inadvertently, the offering is to be a bullock rather than a ram, though a ram is allowed (without specifying the person, whether lay Israelite or priest) in Lev. 5:14–19. But these four were not the only priests: another thirteen names are given by family (10:20–22). This means that seventeen priests in all were involved. In addition, other temple groups were implicated: six Levites, one singer, three gatekeepers (10:23–24).

The rest of the list is of those from 'Israel', listed according to family ('phratry'). There are sixty-six names in all (though one or two problems suggest textual corruption, such as the listing of Bani twice, vv. 29, 34). This small number is extremely surprising, given the amount of fuss made and the indication that it took two months to sort out. What are we to make of this? Was this the entire number, which had simply been exaggerated out of all proportion by the author? Was this only the 'upper classes'? Or had many more taken 'foreign wives' but simply refused to co-operate when it came down to actually having to separate from their wives and children? The silence of the author is very interesting at this point.

The book ends on a sombre and, from a modern point of view, cruel note: not only had they married these women but there were also children involved, children who were being sent away as well as their mothers. (The Hebrew text is difficult and is usually emended, but the main point still seems obvious from the context.) The text is strangely silent on how these women and children were supposed to live. The common practice was for a divorced wife to return to her father's house, but this was not always possible. The resentment and ill-will – not only among the women and children but also among the husbands – is not even hinted at. The reason is that the author is presenting an example of repentance and piety. To have focused on the hurt caused would be to detract from the main issue according to his way of thinking. On the other hand, the author may have taken it for granted that the pain and suffering of those involved would be plain evidence of their piety in obeying God rather than following their natural inclinations.

Summary and conclusions

The book of Ezra is made up of a narrative which is both clear and forceful. It begins with a resolution of the exile: the first king of a new empire – the man who destroyed and punished the Babylonians who had sacked Jerusalem – decrees the rebuilding of the temple and the return of those who wish to go. The exile comes to an end with the return of Jews to their homeland. The continuity with the pre-exilic temple is established by the return of the temple vessels. We know that representatives of the people and the temple personnel returned because Ezra 2 lists them. The altar is restored and rebuilding begins in Ezra 3, but 'enemies' cause difficulty in Ezra 4. Because of the work of prophets and the faith of the people and their leaders, the work resumes, and God sees that the Persian overlord supports the work until its completion in Ezra 6. The climax is reached with the celebration of the cult, re-organization of the cultic personnel, and the observance of the Passover.

The narrative continues with the story of Ezra, and although his mission is given a date, there is no consciousness of the passage of time in the story. The reader moves smoothly from the '6th year' (of Darius [6:15]) to the '7th year' (of Artaxerxes [7:7]). The compiler seems oblivious of the six decades (or more) which separate Ezra from completion of the temple. Ezra's concern is primarily with the law, and overall the impression is that his main activity is concerned with the law when he deals with the cases of inter-marriage. Yet one is struck by a more subtle message. This is that Ezra's arrival is in many ways a new beginning. He brings not just the law but more settlers, cultic personnel, and enormous wealth for the temple. He makes a special issue of getting Levites to come with him when he finds there are none. With a few minor changes to the text, Ezra could be the refounder of the temple and cult.

The book of Ezra, then, is made up of two 'episodes': the initial return in Ezra 1–6 and the Ezra story in Ezra 7–10. The first episode is dominated by the leaders Joshua and Zerubbabel, while Ezra clearly overshadows the second. The episodes are parallel in many ways, especially if one takes into account the continuation of the Ezra story in Nehemiah:

1: decree of Cyrus	7: decree of Artaxerxes
1: delivery of wealth/temple vessels	8: delivery of wealth/temple vessels
2: list of immigrants	8: list of immigrants
3: sacrifices offered	8: sacrifices offered
4: foreigners raise opposition	9: problem because of foreigners
6: opposition overcome	10: problem resolved
6: temple completed Neh.	8: mission completed (law read)
6: Tabernacles celebrated	8: Tabernacles celebrated

What strikes one at the completion of reading Ezra is that it ends rather unsatisfactorily. The resolution of the mixed marriages issue has formed a sort of denouement. Yet the last verses of Ezra 10 are rather negative, ending in a final verse which seems to talk about the plight of the wives and children of those who repudiated their marriages. To an ancient pietist, this willingness to sacrifice one's family could be taken in a positive sense as a sign of repentance and obedience, but the negative effect still hovers over the passage. It is like an unresolved chord which needs something to follow to relieve the tension created by the episode, such as the celebration of a festival. The overall impression is that the book of Ezra is incomplete in its present form. Its present inclusion in the Bible as part of a combined book of Ezra-Nehemiah resolves that incompleteness and confirms the view that the books of Ezra and Nehemiah form a single unit among the Hebrew biblical books in their present form. (1 Esdras does not have this problem because it is followed by a passage corresponding to the Hebrew Neh. 8:1–12, though there is reason to believe that it originally ended with the celebration of Tabernacles, as in the Hebrew Neh. 8:13–18. See further in chapter 4 below.)

Within the overall unity of the narrative in Ezra, there are many dissonances, some small and some not so small. One can expect to find some disharmonies even in the most well-constructed narrative, but these go beyond the failings of an individual. As one looks closer and closer at the seemingly straightforward narrative, the more peculiarities and incongruities present themselves. Some of these are internal to the narrative, where one section of the narrative is undermined by another; others relate to what we know of external history (e.g. the order and dates of the reigns of Persian kings). Both these facts convey a message, whether it is the overall unity of the macro-narrative or the discrepancies at a lower level. The first is the vehicle of the compiler's theological message; the other alerts the historian to questions of source, reliability, and growth of the tradition. Both questions will be further discussed in chapters 5 and 6.

3

NEHEMIAH IN THE
HEBREW BIBLE

Analysis of the text

Nehemiah 1

The first verse immediately identifies the specific author of the book: 'the words of Nehemiah b. Hacaliah'. Unlike Ezra which is an anonymous narrative (except for Ezra 7–9 which are in the first person, with Ezra speaking), Nehemiah is presented as the work of an individual, one who was crucial to the events narrated in the book. Much of the book is also narrated in the first person, primarily 1:1–7:5 and 13. Neh. 8–9, in which Ezra reads the law, and 10–12, which are mainly lists and declarations, are in the third person (except for 12:31), but we are to understand this primarily as the story of an eyewitness and participant in the events described.

It was in the month Kislev (November/December) in 'year twenty', but the king is strangely omitted and does not appear until 2:1. But if one has been reading Ezra-Nehemiah as a block, the Ezra story would have immediately preceded Nehemiah 1, and the king in the Ezra story is Artaxerxes. Therefore, the 'year twenty' follows naturally on 'year seven' (Ezra 7:7). The place is Susa which, as we know from other sources, served as one of the capitals of the Persian empire. Hanani, a 'brother', and some other men arrive from Judah. The term 'brother' means more than just 'fellow Jew' here since he does not label the whole group as brothers. Is Hanani a literal brother? This seems likely in the light of Neh. 7:2, but 'brother' can also be used of more distant relatives as well (cf. Tobit 2:10; 5:6; 7:1). In any case, it seems that Nehemiah is concerned to know about the state of 'the surviving group who escaped the captivity' in Judah, as well as of Jerusalem. One might think he was asking about those who were not taken captive by the Babylonians but had been left in the land (2 Kings 25:12, 22–24), but the rest of the book indicates that it is the *golah* community (those who returned from captivity) who are in mind (cf. also 2 Chron. 36:20–21 which envisages the land as being left empty).

The answer to Nehemiah is that the people are in great evil and distress, with the city wall in ruins and the gates burned (1:2–3). For one reading the book in isolation, this reply makes literary sense because it sets the scene for Nehemiah's activities which follow in the rest of the book: Nehemiah has to go to Judah to sort out a dire situation. However, for one who had just read the book of Ezra – the majority of readers – the statement would come as something of a shock. Although Ezra has had his troubles, the matter had been sorted out, and the community is presumably happy and at peace. We might assume, from 1:2–3, that the walls and gates of Jerusalem were in the condition in which Nebuchadnezzar had left them well over a century before, though it would seem extremely strange that a community would allow such disrepair to remain; however, such an explanation would not address the question about the people's being in 'great evil and shame'. Are we to understand that something has happened in the meantime, between Artaxerxes' 7th and 20th years? If one reads Ezra-Nehemiah as a literary whole, such a conclusion seems inescapable.

Nehemiah's reaction to this is what we would expect from any pious Jew: he goes into mourning and begins to fast and pray (1:4–11). As elsewhere in Ezra-Nehemiah the God of Israel is given the title 'God of heaven', as well as the personal name Yhwh. In a parallel to the prayer of Ezra (Ezra 9:6–15) but with a different content, he prays concerning the 'descendants of Israel' (1:6). His prayer takes the form of a confession (in language well known from the book of Deuteronomy) that he, his extended family, and his fellow Israelites have sinned and have not kept the commandments, statutes, and judgements as commanded by Moses. God had warned that they would be scattered among the peoples if they failed to obey, but if they repented and turned to him, he would gather them even from the ends of heaven to the place where his name would dwell. He finally asks for mercy in the presence of 'this man', who is presumably the king since Nehemiah is cupbearer to the king.

Nehemiah 2

Nehemiah's prayer was not answered immediately because this chapter opens several months later in the month Nisan (March/April).

Strangely, even though Nisan is the 1st month of the new year, it is still said to be Artaxerxes' 20th year (2:1). Either the writer was being rather loose and approximate when he opened the book with the 20th year or no year change had taken place. Since Nisan was the 1st month of a new year in Babylonia and the Babylonian month name is used, the conclusion is that the Babylonian calendar is in the writer's mind. The Babylonian calendar was used by the Persians; however, it is possible that the Persian kings began the new year with the date of their succession to the throne rather than a fixed new year (Dandamaev and Lukonin 1989: 290–91). It is generally assumed that Jews began their new year with Nisan at this time, but the calendar of Israel and Judah is still being extensively debated by scholars. From a literary point of view, it is probably best to understand 'year twenty' in 1:1 to be a general indication of time setting for the whole story which is then delineated in more detail as the story goes on.

The resolution of the tension set up in Neh. 1 begins in an exchange between Nehemiah and the king (2:1–8). We are now given the king's name for the first time, Artaxerxes. Nehemiah is carrying out his duties as cupbearer to the king and serves him wine, apparently trying not to show his depressed state of mind. The king notices, however, and asks why he looks bad and whether he is ill. Naturally, this frightens Nehemiah, but he tells the king that he cannot help feeling that way when the city of his ancestors' tombs is desolate and the gates burned up. The king asks what he wants, and Nehemiah (uttering a silent prayer) asks to be sent to Judah to the city to rebuild it. The king asks (with the queen [*haššēgal*] sitting beside him) when he plans to go and return and then gives permission, including a letter to the governors of the satrapy Ebir-nari, one of whose constituents was the province of Yehud, for permission to pass through. He also received a letter to give to the 'keeper of the king's parkland' (*šōmēr happardēs*) for timber for the gates of the temple fortress, the wall, and 'the house'. This last is somewhat puzzling. One might think that it is a reference to the temple, the 'house' *par excellence*. It might be a reference to a governor's residence since we know that Nehemiah was given the office of governor (5:14).

Nehemiah's journey to Jerusalem is not described in detail, but two significant points are made about it which contrast in an interesting way with Ezra's journey (2:9–11). First, he has letters from the king to the governors of the satrapy Ebir-nari. The exact content is not specified, but apart from permitting him safe passage (cf. v. 7), they would also have indicated that he had been granted the office of governor of Yehud. Accepting this explains other things in the story: it explains why he was well received in Jerusalem even though no one knew his mission (cf. 2:12), and it explains why Sanballat and Tobiah were suspicious of Nehemiah's coming. They would not have worried about someone just visiting relatives, but if they had heard of or been given official letters about Nehemiah's office, they would have seen him as a potential rival (especially if Judah was governed from Samaria up until now; see chapter 7 below). The second interesting point about Nehemiah's journey is that he has an armed guard to accompany him. Ezra had a rather strange decree from Artaxerxes (unlike the normal official letters which we would expect), but he had no escort or guard even though he was taking an enormous sum of wealth with him. In both cases, Nehemiah's situation looks more realistic in comparison with Ezra.

Nehemiah's first action after arriving is to slip out of the city at night to assess the state of the wall (2:12–16). Although this was his reason for coming to Jerusalem, he apparently has told no one and, for some reason, does not want anyone to know of his interest in it. Why should it matter whether anyone saw him surveying the wall? Was Nehemiah just naturally a secretive individual? He apparently took a small entourage (2:12: 'ănāšîm mĕ'aṭ), presumably some of those who had come with him from Persia since he apparently tells none of the local people (2:16). The path of his night journey is an important indication of the topography around Jerusalem and the extent of the city at that time, but without knowing that topography, it is not always easy to determine the path. He apparently went out of a gate in the western wall which paralleled the Tyropoean Valley, rode south along the wall and around the south end heading east. When the wall turned north, paralleling the Kidron Valley, Nehemiah followed it as far as he could, but some parts were impassible, so he descended to the Kidron Valley floor. However, he evidently proceeded only a certain way north before retracing his steps, rather than going entirely around the city.

He now presents the plan to 'the Jews, the priests, the nobles, the community officials [sĕgānîm], and the rest' (2:17–18; cf. v. 16). He points out the bad state of the city, the wall, and the gates. He also 'confesses' that the king had already approved the task and, besides, it was God's will. With such backing, they naturally agreed to get on with it. Sanballat the Horonite (who is never referred to by what seems to be his official title of governor of Samaria; see chapter 7 below), Tobiah the 'Ammonite slave' (evidently from a Jewish family living in the area of Ammon and holding a Persian office), and Geshem the Arab (ruler) accuse him of rebelling (2:19–20). Nehemiah's reply does not evoke the imperial power he has been given but the claims that the 'God of heaven' will give success to the project. He also states that Sanballat and his colleagues have no 'portion, legal claim, or memorial' in Jerusalem. This last statement may be an allusion to a former authority over the city or perhaps to the fact that Sanballat was actually also a worshipper of Yhwh (for further information on Sanballat and the others, see chapter 7 below) and a fellow Israelite.

Nehemiah 3

This chapter describes the building of the wall, being mainly a detailed catalogue of the individuals and groups who built the various sections of the wall and city. A number of things are striking about what might otherwise be a dull list. First, the list may have been an official record of the building, kept in city archives. Many of its characteristics can be explained by this view. In other words, the list does not appear as simply a literary composition with a literary or theological aim. But if so, one must ask why it was taken up in the book of Nehemiah which clearly has a theological purpose – in its present context, the catalogue definitely has a literary and theological intent. One message seems to be to show that certain families deserve special praise for the work they did. If your family (or its ancestors) participated, it demonstrated civic rights in the city or province, not to mention the family honour and pride which might be implied.

Another message is that the project was not supported by a 'Nehemiah coterie' but by the people as a whole. The high priest Eliashib and his fellow priests head the list (3:1), and a significant number of priests participate in the work. This might suggest that the list was composed by priestly scribes. In some cases, the names of fathers and even grandfathers are given, which could suggest that it legitimated the families of those who participated; in other cases, it is simply the men of a certain town or region who do the work. The former tells the reader that prominent leaders of the community were involved; the second, that ordinary people even from the outlying villages and cities helped (e.g. from Jericho, v. 2). In one case a man's daughters were involved (3:12). The 'throne of the governor of Ebir-nari' was responsible in some way for one section (3:7). The men of Tekoa undertook work, even though their local nobility would not take part (3:5). This is not explained, and there are many possible reasons. It may be that the nobles disagreed with the project. More likely is that, since Tekoa was some distance from Jerusalem, they saw no need to get involved in a project which would not benefit their local area. Or perhaps they disdained getting their own hands dirty.

Many of those who worked are said to repair the section of the wall near their own homes, which makes a good deal of sense since there would be a considerable degree of motivation in such circumstances. There are suggestions that the text has been corrupted. For example, a 'second section' is sometimes mentioned without a first section (e.g. 3:11, 30) and several 'second sections' are even mentioned in a row without any first sections (3:19–21). The first part of the list (3:1–15) is characterized by the expression 'next to them/him' (*'al-yādām/yādô*), and the second part (3:16–32) by 'after him' (*'aḥărâv*). This might indicate a connection between this differentiation and the topographical line of the wall, with the first half referring to the repair of the old wall and the second half to the new line of the wall established where the old one was abandoned (Williamson 1985: 200; Gunneweg 1987: 71).

The opposition of Sanballat and Tobiah continued (3:33–37), and Nehemiah pronounced a curse on them (3:36–37). However, their opposition seems to be no more than simple ridicule. How wide would their mocking of the rebuilding reach? If this is all Nehemiah had to contend with, it seems curious that he should be so exercised about Sanballat's 'anger' (3:33). True, Sanballat apparently spoke about it to the army, but how much weight does public mockery carry outside the territory? One wonders whether Nehemiah was not being unduly thin-skinned about the matter. Despite the supposed opposition, the chapter ends with the wall built to half its required height.

Nehemiah 4

This chapter describes the opposition to work on the wall and the measures taken to protect the workers. Just as the 'enemies of Judah and Benjamin' hindered the work on the temple in the book of Ezra (Ezra 4:1), so enemies fulfil the same function here – creating a necessary narrative tension. Nehemiah writes that the 'enemies' were planning to launch a surprise attack against the workers on the wall (4:2, 5). He hears of this from Jews who were living among the enemies (4:6). So he put armed guards behind the lower points on the wall; then when he thought the initial attack had been thwarted, he returned to the work but with the workers armed (4:7–11). This created problems, not least because there was a considerable distance between the gangs of workers. So he kept a trumpeter by his side, with instructions that when the repairers heard the trumpet, they were to converge on the spot indicated because that was where the attack was coming from (4:12–14). So they continued with the work from dawn until dark, working with half the workforce armed; Nehemiah and 'his brothers' and servants spent each night in Jerusalem, and they and the guard slept in their clothes (4:15–17).

The reader takes all this in with an undoubted frisson. The danger is described in an immediate way, and the work which would have been arduous at the best of times is now hampered by the workers having to keep watch and to carry weapons along with their tools, even while transporting heavy basketloads of rubble. The perceived threat from scurrilous enemies – not only to the workers but even to the lives of their families (4:8) – is a worrying one, and the measures taken by Nehemiah make eminent sense in the circumstances. The dedication and the tireless persistence under difficulties and hardships arouse the reader's admiration.

However, we must not forget that we have only one side of the story here. Nehemiah is giving everything from his own perspective and liberally flavouring the account with his particular interpretation. We know what he wants us to believe, but we do not always know that what he wants us to believe is actually what happened. There are several reasons to wonder whether another scenario may not have been the correct one. After all, no attack came, and the statement that one was planned was based on the interpretation of particular reports, apparently by fellow Jews (4:6 is difficult and probably corrupt). The idea that the builders were in danger of being attacked may have been entirely a creation of Nehemiah's own mind. (The question of Nehemiah's bias here will be looked at in more detail below, in chapter 7.)

The picture of the 'opponents' is also highly coloured by Nehemiah's tendentious description. He labels them as 'Sanballat, Tobiah, and the Arabs, Ammonites, and Ashdodites' (4:1). We may compare this with 'Sanballat the Horonite, Tobiah the Ammonite slave, and Geshem the Arab' (2:10, 19). At no point does he give us the real rank of Sanballat or the others. We get the impression from a careful reading of the text that Sanballat must have had a fairly prominent position, and external evidence confirms that he was governor of Samaria (Cowley 1923: no. 30). Tobiah seems to have been head of a prominent Jewish family with an ancestral home on the other side of the Jordan. Geshem is known to be king of an Arab tribe or group. What Nehemiah's account emphasizes, however, is the low and reprehensible character of these individuals (Tobiah is called a 'slave') and, especially, their foreignness. They are Horonites, Ammonites, Arabs, and Ashdodites. They are not Israel; they have 'no portion, legal claim, nor memorial in Jerusalem' (2:20). They are outsiders and they are enemies.

Nehemiah 5

This chapter focuses on the plight of the poor who are having to sell their property and even their sons and daughters to pay the taxes. Although it breaks into the narrative about the rebuilding of the wall, the end of the chapter indicates a time later in Nehemiah's governorship, even at the end of it (see below). It opens without preamble by a statement that 'the people and their wives' cried against 'their brothers the Jews' (5:1). They say that they need grain to eat to prevent starvation (5:2); that they had pawned their fields, vineyards, and houses for food (5:3); that they had borrowed money against their fields and vineyards to pay the imperial tax (5:4). Is not our flesh the same as that of our brothers, they ask, our sons like theirs, yet we are having to sell sons and daughters as servants and are left destitute (5:5).

In typical fashion, Nehemiah is incensed at this injustice and he calls the nobility and community officials to berate them (5:6–7). He accuses them of oppressing their fellows and calls an assembly (5:7), apparently to put pressure on them. He reminds them that he has bought Jews enslaved to Gentiles out of slavery but attacks them for then continuing to sell their own brothers into slavery, and they have no reply (5:8). Reminding them that they were in danger of disgrace before the 'Gentiles our enemies' (5:9) and that he, his brothers, and servants had also lent money and food (5:10), he proclaims his intent to cancel the debts and calls on them to do the same by restoring the people's fields, vineyards, olive groves, and houses to them and forgoing the claims (usury?) of silver, grain, wine, and oil (5:11). This was, of course, a very effective means of shaming them into accepting his measures, so naturally they agree to this. Then Nehemiah calls the priests and makes them swear to do as they agreed (5:12), and finally in front of the assembly he pronounces a public curse on anyone who does not abide by this (5:13).

The next section of the chapter at first appears to move to a different subject because Nehemiah discusses his activities as governor of Judah (5:14–19). But this section is relevant to the earlier part of the chapter because the question of the burden of debt imposed by the central administration lies behind Nehemiah's statements. In essence, he is defending his conduct in office by saying that he did not impose unnecessary burdens on the populace during his twelve years as governor. Unlike previous governors who had laid heavy burdens on the people, he did not take the governor's food allowance (5:14–15), even though he had 150 people eating at his table, requiring one ox, one sheep, and assorted other items each day (5:17–18).

There is no doubt that Nehemiah appears at his noblest in this chapter, at least to modern eyes. Some of his other activities are likely to be seen as of little consequence or even as examples of bigotry to a modern reader, but his measures to relieve the burden of debt will be read with approval by most today. Those crying out seem either not to have enough to eat in the first place or to have had some property but to be losing it because of taxes. In either case, they are presented as 'deserving poor', not as those who had become destitute because of mismanagement or being wastrels.

But perhaps things were not quite this simple. It seems to be a common assumption in a context like this that anyone owed money is automatically rich, grasping, and greedy. But the poor are only a portion of the community because they complain against their 'brothers' (5:1). Also, Nehemiah may have found it much easier to forgo his interest or repayment of the debt than some others who may have had their own livelihood tied up in loans to their fellow Jews. To cancel repayments of loans might well mean that some creditors would have to pawn their own property. Also, some Jews had been sold as slaves, but Nehemiah's buying them back does not mean that he has given up his own servants (cf. 4:10, 17; 5:10, 16; 13:19), though these might be employees associated with his office. In any case, *someone* had to pay for the upkeep of the 150 who ate at his table daily. If he did not impose this on the people, it was because he had the necessary means. Where did that come from? Did he have a private income? Did he have sources of income from the province besides the governor's food allowance? Nehemiah certainly feels no solidarity with the previous governors, dismissing them all as oppressors. Did he mean to include Zerubbabel?

A final question about this chapter is why the story of the debt outcry comes here. It breaks the narrative about building the wall and is clearly from a rather later time (*pace* Williamson 1985: 235–36). Nehemiah states that he had bought various Jews out of captivity. This would hardly have been when he was fully engaged in repairing the wall but must talk of a time after the wall was finished. (The last part [5:14–18] presupposes writing at the end of his governorship, but it could have been added to a pre-existent narrative.) According to Eskenazi's model (1988: 78), it represents 'obstacles within', parallel to the 'obstacles without' in Neh. 4. That would explain the location of this chapter, though much of Neh. 6 seems as much about 'obstacles within' as this chapter, yet her model does not note this fact.

Nehemiah 6

This chapter resumes the story of the wall. The efforts of the 'enemies' to disrupt the work continue. At the beginning of the chapter much of the work is done, with the breaches all repaired to full height; it only remains to set up the doors of the gates (6:1). Sanballat and the other 'enemies' send a message asking Nehemiah to meet them in Kephirim (6:2). Nehemiah knows that they are only intriguing against him and plan to do some injury to him if he agrees to their proposal (how he knows this is not stated). He replies by messenger that he is doing a great work and it will come to a halt if he leaves it to meet with them (6:3). Four further invitations are refused (6:4). Finally, Sanballat sends a message bringing an unsealed letter with the rumour that Nehemiah and the Jews are planning to rebel by rebuilding the wall and making Nehemiah king. Not only that, Nehemiah has instigated certain prophets to stand up and proclaim him king. This would be reported to the Persian king, so they need to discuss the situation. The implication is that a bad report would go to Susa unless they could come to some arrangement in a meeting (6:5–7). Nehemiah's reply is short and to the point: Sanballat is simply making this all up (6:8).

Nehemiah's version is that they were simply afraid of him and were wanting to weaken the ability and resolve to get the work on the wall done, and he calls on God to strengthen his hands (6:9). But then he relates a strange incident. He visits the house of an individual named Shemaiah son of Delaiah, who is evidently a prophet because he warns Nehemiah through the medium of a prophecy (cf. 6:12) that he should seek refuge in the temple because they are seeking to kill him (6:10). Nehemiah replies that it is not in him to flee, and he cannot go into the temple and expect to live (6:11), presumably because he is not a priest. In any case, he recognizes that this prophecy did not come from God but was hired by Sanballat and Tobiah so that he would become frightened and do something foolish, and gain a reputation which would bring ridicule on him (6:12–13). Nehemiah then calls on God to punish the deeds of Sanballat and Tobiah and also the words of the prophetess Noadiah and other prophets who were trying to make him afraid (6:14).

Despite all this supposed opposition, the wall was finished on the 25th of Elul (August/September) after only fifty-two days (6:15). This was a blow to his 'enemies' and all the nations surrounding them who lost confidence because they saw that the work was from God (6:16). Despite this there were many in Judah, especially among the nobles, who communicated with Tobiah and kept up a regular correspondence with him, reporting Nehemiah's activities (6:17). This was a natural alliance because Tobiah and his son had in fact married the daughters of prominent Jewish nobles, and the nobles as a whole would speak well of Tobiah to Nehemiah; Tobiah himself wrote letters to intimidate the Jewish governor (6:18–19).

This is quite a remarkable chapter in the book of Nehemiah. Ostensibly it reports the completion of the wall in a surprisingly short time despite determined opposition from without (Sanballat, Tobiah, and the surrounding nations) but also from within (various prophets and a prophetess, and also many from among the nobles of Judah). It is the nature of this opposition which excites curiosity. Neh. 3–4 contain not one hint of anything but full support for the building, with the possible exception of the elders of Tekoa (3:5), though why they do not help is not spelled out. The external opposition is taken for granted throughout these chapters, but Nehemiah seems to have the support of the community, including the nobles and the priesthood. Yet suddenly in Neh. 6 we find a significant fifth columnist element, according to Nehemiah's own account, including no less than several prophets and a prophetess and a number of the aristocracy.

We have to keep in mind that this is a very personal account from Nehemiah. He is suspicious of the meetings which Sanballat attempts to arrange. At this point, we cannot be sure that they were anything but genuine, however; Nehemiah's interpretation that they were meant to endanger him may have been groundless. Having assured us of plans to harm him and to kill some of the workers on the wall (cf. 4:2, 5), he strangely dismisses the prophecy which confirms that there is a plot to take his life. He also rejects what seem to be overtures towards a reconciliation from the associates of Tobiah, who is (as we know from external data) head of a prominent Jewish family. Is Nehemiah making all this up or does he have a solid basis for his suspicions and actions? There is the further fact that he emphasizes and even names some prophets who oppose him. No doubt there were such individuals, as he claims, but he skips over what also seems to be a fact: there were prophets supporting him. He puts in Sanballat's mouth the charge of having his own prophets (6:7) and makes a blanket denial (6:7), but it is prima facie likely to have been true. Nehemiah had his supporters as well as his opponents, and there is no reason why this did not include prophets on both sides. He would naturally emphasize the one and de-emphasize the other. All this will be further discussed in chapter 7 below.

Nehemiah 7

The theme of the perceived threat continues into this chapter. The wall has been completed, the gates hung, and the gatekeepers, singers, and Levites assigned their duties; nevertheless, there are still those who want to overthrow the new city (7:1–3). Nehemiah puts trusted men in charge over the city – Hanani his 'brother' (the context suggests a literal brother) and Hananiah the captain of the citadel (who feared God). He orders them not to open the gates until the sun is hot and then to close them while the guards are still on duty (the precise connotation is a guess; the Hebrew text is unclear). He also assigns guard duty to the inhabitants of the city, apparently both at the gates and also to each at his own house.

The city is naturally difficult to defend, however, because there are few people living there (7:4). Surprisingly, it is also said that no houses had been built, which seems very strange for a city supposedly resettled seventy-five years earlier but supports the view of some recent unspecified destruction. But how were people living there without houses, and how did people repair the wall opposite their own houses, as stated at several points in Neh. 3 (vv. 10, 20, 21, 23, 24, 28–31)? This is usually explained as a hyperbole and not to be taken literally. Nehemiah gathers the nobles, the officers, and the people to enrol their genealogy (7:5). In the process he finds the register of the original return which is then given in the rest of the chapter (7:6–72). The text repeats almost word for word the text already seen in Ezra (2:1–70), there being only minor differences between the two (mainly in Neh. 7:69–72//Ezra 2:68–70). The question of which (if either) is original in its context has been much discussed, with no overall consensus; however, from a literary perspective this is irrelevant since the list is a part of the text here and must be interpreted in its context. (The general question of the genealogies and lists will be discussed in chapter 6 below.)

The genealogical list does not pretend to be something different from that in Ezra 2 but claims to be a record of those who first returned. Why should it be repeated here since the information is already available earlier in the book of Ezra-Nehemiah? In this context it serves to connect the present inhabitants of the land with their original settlement, including their obligations in the province. The people had been settled in their cities and presumably continued to live there. Yet their settlement had been the consequence of a decree about the rebuilding of the temple (Ezra 1:1–4), for which large donations had been made (Ezra 2:68–69//Neh. 7:69–71). The safety and welfare of Jerusalem the capital city was intimately bound up with the settlement of the people. Thus, in this context the list implies that the measures Nehemiah is about to take with regard to increasing the population of the city are entirely justified by the original intent of the settlement.

Yet Nehemiah can be read in two ways. It can stand alone as an independent tradition, as indeed some other Nehemiah traditions do (see chapter 4 below). If so, then one might be reading it without the presence of the book of Ezra. In such a situation, the list would not be a repetition of material already given earlier but a rehearsal of vital data for the immediate context of bringing more people into Jerusalem. Thus, this chapter makes most sense if it is seen as part of the narrower literary context of Nehemiah alone rather than the broader context of Ezra-Nehemiah (but see the structure of the two books according to Eskenazi 1988, as discussed in chapter 5 below).

Contrary to the views of some scholars, however, a literary analysis does not have to overlook what might be clumsy editing or a slip on the part of the writer. Or to put it another way, without invoking questions of author or editor a literary analysis can still recognize that the construction of a text may have flaws or problems. In this case, the list fits its context in general, but the expected implications of the list are not then spelled out in the next chapter (Neh. 8) as we would expect. Instead, the story abruptly moves on to a reading of the law, and the important matter of increasing the population of Jerusalem is not resumed until Neh. 11. From the point of view of narrative construction, this cannot be considered ideal. From a traditio-historical perspective it suggests that an editor has inserted Neh. 8–10 into a narrative which arguably once went from the end of Neh. 7 immediately to the beginning of Neh. 11.

The significance of this chapter for the Nehemiah tradition is that it makes Nehemiah the restorer of the city. In Ezra 1–6 the restorers of the city are Joshua and Zerubbabel. Although the emphasis there is on rebuilding the temple, it implies that the city is settled as well. One of the so-called Persian documents, although quoted in the wrong context, mentions the rebuilding of the city (Ezra 4:12–16, 21). In the literary context, not only the temple but also the city is rebuilt. The Ezra story (Ezra 7–10) also presupposes the existence of the city of Jerusalem as well as the temple, though the emphasis is on the restoration of a proper Jewish community. Yet when we come to Neh. 1, the province is in trouble and the city has been damaged greatly; it is even described by Nehemiah as 'lying in ruins' (Neh. 2:3), and his task is to rebuild the city. In other words, Nehemiah is the restorer of the city in his tradition and no less worthy of honour for this task than Zerubbabel and Joshua in their particular tradition.

Nehemiah 8

In this chapter the attention suddenly turns from Nehemiah to Ezra. In the combined writing Ezra-Nehemiah this would cause no problem for the reader since Ezra was already the subject of an extensive section of the book a few chapters earlier; nevertheless, the appearance of Ezra without warning or preparation, with the almost non-mention of Nehemiah, still looks rather abrupt. The subject of the chapter is the reading of the law. Again, the focus on this makes some sense in the context since the completion of the wall allows the people to gather together, and the wall was finished on the 25th of Elul (6:15), the 6th month, while this chapter begins on the 1st day of the 7th month (8:2). In the context, one might expect that the people would gather, the law be read, and then the wall be dedicated in a mainly religious celebration. This is not what happens, however, for the dedication does not come until rather later (12:27–43, though no date is given), after the question of mixed marriages is dealt with. This is difficult to explain from a purely literary analysis (see further in chapter 5), as is the thirteen-year wait from the time of Ezra's first coming during which time he supposedly did nothing about the law.

The reading of the 'book of the law of Moses [*sēfer tôrat Mōšeh*] which Yhwh commanded Israel' (8:1) is the natural follow-on from Ezra 7–10. Ezra had brought the book of the law with him (whatever it was precisely), but so far he has done nothing about it except allow himself to be used in the issue of mixed marriages. He can hardly be said to have 'laid down the law' in that situation. Now, however, he finally does something with it by reading it to the people. If the law is to be used in judging them (Ezra 7:14, 25), it is natural that they should have it made known to them. Also, the command that Ezra is to teach and make known the law and to establish it as the law of the land (Ezra 7:10, 25–26) is here fulfilled.

The people, both men and women, are gathered on the 1st day of the 7th month (the Festival of Trumpets according to Lev. 23:23–25) in the space before the Water Gate, which was probably the main open square of the city (8:1–2). Ezra reads from early morning to midday, with various individuals standing on both sides of him (8:3–4; see below on these men). Ezra begins by pronouncing a blessing on Yhwh, to which the people respond (8:5–6). Then various individuals (presumably priests) and Levites clarify the reading to the people (8:7–8). The nature of this clarification (8:7: *mĕvînîm*; 8:8: *mĕfôreš*, *śôm śekel*, *yāvînû bammiqrā'*) has been much discussed. Was it a translation of the Hebrew text, whose language was no longer well known, into Aramaic? Or was it, rather, a clarification or explanation of the meaning of the law?

The meaning 'translate' for *prš* seems to be based on the analogy of the later synagogue service and the supposed translation of the Hebrew reading into Aramaic, but the use of that analogy is anachronistic (see Grabbe 1988). Also, it is assumed that Hebrew was no longer being used but had been replaced by Aramaic. There is in fact no evidence that such was the case by this time; on the contrary, we know that Hebrew continued to evolve and develop as a living language for many centuries after this. Aramaic did apparently become the dominant language of some Jews in Syro-Palestine, especially in Galilee and further north, but the evidence for this is much later. The assumption that the people of Jerusalem would have needed an Aramaic translation of a Hebrew text is based on an unproved hypothesis.

The other two clauses of 8:8 indicate giving sense and making to understand. The context suggests that the Levites were supposed to give a clarification. From a practical point of view, it does not seem feasible for disparate groups of Levites to be giving individual spontaneous explanations to a particular part of the audience at periodic intervals during the reading. This fact might seem to give weight to thinking of a simple translation. However, we need not assume that an actual event is being described; rather, we more probably have an idealized picture of a single reading and explanation to all the people all at one time (comparable to Deut. 31:10–13 which envisages the law being read and expounded to all the people at the Festival of Tabernacles every seven years). It is a nice image, but teaching and explanation would be more practically delivered over a period of time to smaller groups. Furthermore, no law of any length – even the book of Deuteronomy, much less the whole Pentateuch – could have been delivered in such a manner to all the people in a single morning.

The day is made into a festival day for eating, drinking, and rejoicing (8:9–12). The initial response is for the people to weep when they hear the words of the Torah, but Ezra, Nehemiah, and the Levites have to tell them to rejoice rather than mourn. Although the people have been read the Torah, nothing is said about this day as the Day of Trumpets. It is said to be a holy day but not because of the instructions given to Moses; on the contrary, the day is apparently declared holy because 'they made them understand all the words which they taught them' (8:12). The reason that the people originally wept is not discussed, but this is the expected reaction of one who hears God's words for the first time (cf. 2 Kings 22:11–13).

Having celebrated the 1st day of the 7th month, the people now know to celebrate the Festival of Tabernacles (Sukkot) or Booths (8:13–18). A great deal is made of gathering foliage to build temporary booths which are set up in the various courtyards and squares, including the courtyard of the temple itself. The Festival of Trumpets has been ignored, but at least the eight-day Festival of Sukkot is given the prominence envisaged by the Pentateuch (Lev. 23:33–36; Deut. 16:13–15). Indeed, it is said that no such celebration had taken place since the days of Joshua who succeeded Moses, but this is a standard hyperbole about a great celebration of a festival; it ignores the monumental celebration credited to Solomon in 1 Kings 8. It also ignores the celebration of Tabernacles in Ezra 3:2–5 and, again, what have the people been doing for thirteen years since Ezra came?

This chapter has focused on the renewal of the community by propounding the law and observing the commanded Festival of Sukkot.

This comes about by Ezra's reading of the law; however, a great deal is ascribed to the people: they weep and have to be told to rejoice. The heads of the families then come back for more (8:13) and find out about Sukkot. The implication is that the people themselves decide to celebrate Sukkot rather than being so ordered by Ezra. Ezra himself is the main figure. He has some of the priests and Levites alongside him. Nehemiah is also supposed to be beside him at 8:9, but there are some textual problems here. Nehemiah is designated the Tirshata (something like 'governor'); however, it seems strange to give him a title only a few verses after he has been the focus of the text. Also the verb is in the singular, as if Ezra's name was originally alone and the name of Nehemiah later inserted to make him a part of the proceedings. This chapter looks very much like a part of the Ezra tradition, as indeed part of it is in 1 Esdras (see chapter 4 below).

Nehemiah 9

This chapter begins abruptly. The people had just finished celebrating the Festival of Tabernacles at the end of Neh. 8. Nothing is said about a violation of the law being recognized by them or pointed out to them. Furthermore, before Tabernacles would have occurred the Day of Atonement on the 10th day of the 7th month. This day, the most solemn in the year, is strangely overlooked, despite its importance in the Pentateuch. This would also have been the logical time to fast and repent of sin and lawbreaking, yet it is completely ignored. Instead, in the very first verse of Neh. 9 – after Tabernacles, on the 24th day of the 7th month – they are fasting and separating from the 'sons of the foreigner' (*běnê nēkar*). One feels as if one has come into a film part way through. This is also the problem already dealt with a few chapters earlier by Ezra. What is happening? If Ezra-Nehemiah is read as a unit, then one can only assume that two parallel but separate incidents are in question: what happened under Ezra has arisen again and needs correcting under Nehemiah. However, it needs to be noted that the leaders in this are Levites, not Ezra or Nehemiah (9:4–5), though two separate lists of leaders are given in the space of two verses, with some differences. Why have Ezra and Nehemiah so suddenly disappeared from the scene? The immediate impression is that this episode is separate from the main Ezra and Nehemiah traditions.

Much of the chapter is taken up with a lengthy prayer of confession in which Israel's history is recited in outline. As far as this goes, it appears to agree with the present form of the biblical text, suggesting that by the time that this chapter was written the Pentateuch (and perhaps the book of Joshua) were by and large in the form known to us now in the Hebrew Bible. Specific details are the following:

Choosing Abram and bringing him from Ur of the Chaldees (9:7)
Changing Abram's name to Abraham and making a covenant with him (9:8)
Plans to give the land of Canaan and other tribes to his descendants (9:8)
Affliction of the fathers in Egypt; miraculous crossing of the Red Sea (9:9–11)
The cloud by day and pillar of fire by night in the wilderness (9:12)
Giving of the law on Sinai, including the Sabbath, by the hand of Moses (9:13–14)
Manna, and water from the rock (9:15)
Becoming disobedient and desiring to return to bondage (9:16–17)
The golden calf incident (9:18)
Clothes and shoes not wearing out in the wilderness (9:21)
Possession of the lands of Sihon, king of Heshbon, Og (9:22)
Possession of the land of Canaan (9:23–25)

But most of the prayer is a recital of past and present sins, interspersed with praise of God for his greatness and mercies.

Despite the often alleged beneficence of the Persian rule, this prayer asserts that they are still 'servants' (9:36: *'ăvādîm*) in their land and in great distress because they are still under the rulership of a foreign power which reaches down to their cattle and even their own bodies (9:37).

Nehemiah 10

This chapter appears on the surface to be a continuation of Neh. 9, though it can be read as an independent tradition as well, suggesting that it could have been attached to Neh. 9 after being more or less complete (see further in chapter 5 below). However, what is 10:1 in the Hebrew text is 9:38 in the English editions (and Esdras B 19:38 in the LXX). The chapter is made up of two complexes, a list of signatories (10:2–28) and a pledge to observe certain laws and regulations (10:29–40). In its present context the signatory list and the pledge mark the culmination of the task for separating from 'foreigners' begun in Neh. 9:1. The pledge itself does not focus particularly on mixing with foreigners (though that is included) but with a variety of issues relating mainly to the temple.

The chapter is headed by a formulaic verse that the pledge was a covenant or contract in writing and sealed by the officials, Levites, and priests (10:1). Then follows the list of those who signed the document, beginning with the governor Nehemiah (10:2). First is a list of priests (10:2–9), then a list of Levites (10:10–14), and finally a list of heads of families (10:15–28). These lists have names in common with some of the other lists in the book, surprisingly with that in Nehemiah 12 which is said to be a list of those coming with Zerubbabel and Joshua at the beginning of the return. The names Nehemiah and Zedekiah which head the list are not found in Neh. 12. The first list of names after Nehemiah and Zedekiah has no heading but is a list of priests (10:3–9). Seraiah, Azariah, Jeremiah (10:3) are the same as the first three names in 12:1. Then follows a middle section of names in 10:4–8 in which Neh. 10 has the same names as in Neh. 12:2–4 but an additional six. Finally, the last names in the priestly list (10:8: Abijah, Mijamin, Maaziah, Bilgai, Shemaiah) are the same as or similar to those in 12:4–5, but the names in 12:6–7 are missing. The result is that Neh. 10 has six names not found in Neh. 12 and vice versa. One can only conclude that a basic core list of names has been used in each case, with some additions later made to each one.

The list of Levites has seventeen names (10:10–14). Four of these (five if Judah is a variant of Hodiah) are found in 12:8–9. Of the names in 9:4–5 all but two (Chenani, Pethahiah) are found in 10:10–14 (if Bunni is a variant of Binnui or Beninu). Of the names of family heads, the first eighteen (10:15–20) can almost all also be found in Ezra 2:3–17//Neh. 7:8–24 (with the exception of Bunni, Azzur, and Hodiah), if one allows for slight differences between Ezra 2 and Neh. 7 and some slight variation in names. Those in 10:21–28 are paralleled almost entirely by names in Neh. 3 which is the list of the wall builders (again with some slight variations in spelling). Once more this suggests a list compiled from several sources rather than a genuine list of signatories.

The next few verses include the rest of the people, but they are in narrative form and do not include names. Neither are they clearly a part of the agreement (10:29–30), though they may be. The use of the participle instead of the finite verb (10:30: *maḥăzîqîm* 'joining') may indicate that it is a part of the document. The rest of the people and temple personnel (priests, Levites, gatekeepers, singers, Netinim) cut their ties with the 'peoples of the lands' for the Torah of God, including their wives, sons, and daughters (10:29). They join 'their brothers the prominent people' to undertake a curse and an oath to live according to the 'Torah of God which was given by the hand of Moses God's servant' (10:30). The next verse continues the thought but in the first person: 'we will not give our daughters' in marriage to the 'peoples of the land' (10:31). This looks more like what one would expect in a public pledge, and the actual text may begin here. However, it is always possible that 10:29–30 is envisaged as a part of it, as some translations and commentaries indicate.

The rest of the chapter (10:31–40) is a series of pledges. Many of them relate to the temple and its upkeep, though others deal with particular points of religious observance, such as the Sabbath. At the head is a pledge not to intermarry with the 'peoples of the land' (10:31); however, it does not dominate the pledge as one might have expected from Neh. 9:1–2. The concern about the 'peoples of the land' does continue into the next clause, though, for it pledges not to buy from them on the Sabbath and holy days; the sabbatical year is also to be observed by leaving the land fallow and remitting debts (10:32). Next follow a series of regulations relating to the temple and its service (10:33–40). First, a third of a shekel is to be given each year for the service of the temple and the various offerings (daily, weekly, monthly, annually) to atone for Israel (10:33–34). Next, they would also assign by lot the duty of bringing in the wood offering to burn on the altar, dividing it between the priests, the Levites, and the people (10:35). They would bring the first-fruits of the soil and the trees to the temple and the first-born of the livestock to the priests (10:36), and the dough offering, the 'heave' offering, and the fruit of every tree, vine, and olive to the priests at the entrance of the temple, and the tithe of the soil to the Levites serving in each city (10:37–38). An Aaronite priest is to be with the Levites when they collect the tithe, because the Levites would give a tenth of the tithe to the temple to the treasury storehouses; for the Israelites and Levites were to bring the heave offering of grain, wine, and oil to the storehouses where the holy vessels, the ministering priests, the gatekeepers, and the singers are so that the temple (and its personnel) would not be neglected (10:39–40).

This pledge list is very interesting because it seems to be based on actual temple practice. Although many of the points are probably based on long-standing usage, it also seems to be one of the first attempts to base practice on specific written instructions. An appeal is made in general to the commandments, judgements, and statutes of God (10:30) and to what is written in the Torah (10:35). A number of its regulations are paralleled in Leviticus or other passages in the Pentateuch or elsewhere in the biblical text, such as the various offerings to be offered on a regular basis on the altar, the Sabbath, and the seventh year. Others are completely new, such as the one-third shekel tribute laid on all Jews. Exodus 30:11–16 records a one-off payment at the time of a census, but the payment in Nehemiah is annual. In later Second Temple sources the payment is one half-shekel annually for all Jews (Josephus, *War* 7.6.6 §§216–18; *Antiquities* 18.9.1 §312). This is also the first mention of a wood offering, though we know it was brought in on a particular day which was treated as a festival day (Josephus, *War* 2.17.6 §425; 11Q *Temple Scroll* 19–25). The emphasis on the priestly dues, while not new, is quite understandable in the light of Neh. 13:10–13 where the Levites are not doing their duties because they are not receiving their dues. In fact some of the main points in this list have parallels in Neh. 13, though a number of the details found here are not found in the later chapter.

Nehemiah 11

This chapter is another list. The first verses (11:1–2) relate to 7:4–5 in which it is stated that, as the wall was finished, the city was too large for the number of inhabitants in it. Not only the officials but also one tenth of the general population is asked to come and settle in Jerusalem. They cast lots to decide who this should be.

The rest of the chapter looks like a settlement list, focusing on but not confined to Jerusalem and the heads of families or officials (11:3, 16, 17). The total number of about 3,000 is perhaps not different from the expected population of Jerusalem at this time. The largest group is the Benjaminites who number just under a thousand (11:8). As so often in this book, the number of Levites is much smaller than that of priests (11:12–14, 18). The priests are divided into three groups (11:10–14): those who did the work of the temple, the heads of families, and 'men mighty in war'. Similarly, the Levites seem to be divided into those who did the external work of the temple and those who praised in the liturgy, though they are not given separate numbers (11:15–18).

The settlers are divided into the 'sons of Judah', 'sons of Benjamin', the priests, the Levites, gatekeepers, and the Netinim, according to the heading (11:3), but the Netinim are not given a number and also appear in 11:21 which looks almost like an addition rather than part of the original list. Also mentioned in the heading are the 'sons of Solomon's servants', but these do not appear in this list itself anywhere. Singers are named in 11:23 but as a part of the Levites. Priests and Levites occur in more than one passage (11:20, 22), while the last part of the list does not pertain to Jerusalem but to various cities and their suburbs (11:25–36). All this suggests the lists have a heterogeneous origin and are not a simple listing of those who agreed to come to settle Jerusalem in the time of Nehemiah, an impression supported by the fact that Neh. 11:4–19 has many parallel points with 1 Chron. 9:2–17.

One of the most puzzling aspects of the list is that many of the place-names in 11:25–30 are in areas that would not have been in the province of Judah but rather were under Edomite control or in the Shephelah. They do not occur in other lists in Ezra-Nehemiah, but they are found at various points in Joshua. A number of suggestions have been made as to what this list is. The one which seems the most plausible is that these place-names mark the southern and western boundaries of Judah, though there is still an idealized aspect to the list, drawing on the Exodus-settlement pattern (Blenkinsopp 1988: 328–30).

This chapter gives a brief insight into the conduct of the temple service since singing, praise, and music are envisaged as a part of the temple liturgy (11:17, 22–23); indeed, some of the duties of singers are stipulated by royal decree (11:23). The inclusion of names of some officers in charge of certain parts of the city (11:9) gives some hints towards the city organization and administration. It is also noted briefly and intriguingly that a man named Pithahiah advises the king about the people; unfortunately, no explanation is given as to how this worked in practice. It is not clear that he reported to the king directly; he may have been only a local man used by the official Persian administration.

Nehemiah 12

The fondness for lists in the book reaches a ridiculous point with this chapter. The chapter begins with a list of the priests and Levites who came up with Zerubbabel and Joshua (12:1–26), even though Nehemiah 7 has already given such a list only a few chapters earlier. From a literary point of view, it seems to make little sense; however, if one thinks of someone trying to compile an archive, it looks more reasonable. Although a number of the names are the same, there is information here which is not found elsewhere. Thus, the content makes more sense than the literary form.

First is given a list of priests associated with the time of Zerubbabel (12:1–7), but it has hardly any agreement with Neh. 7:7//Ezra 2:2. However, Neh. 12:1–7 is mostly in agreement with 12:12–21, which lists the priestly clans with their heads, and is also mainly parallel with the supposed list of signatories in Neh. 10:2–8 (Eng. 10:3–9). The name Hattush (10:5; 12:2) is missing from 12:14, but apart from some variations in spelling, the names of 12:1–7 are all found in 12:12–21. Neh. 10:2–8 has six names not found in Neh. 12 but also lacks the last six in the lists of 12:6–7 and 12:19–21. This suggests that a common source was drawn on for the lists of both Neh. 10 and 12, but then the lists were later filled out in different ways. It also makes the alleged historical events with which the events are associated problematic in each case. That is, if the priests came up with Zerubbabel, why are they not listed in Neh. 7, and if they came with Zerubbabel, how are they signing a document in the time of Nehemiah almost a century later? The source may indeed have been in an official archive of some sort, as often speculated, but it seems not to have been very clear what exactly it was a list of. Of the twenty-two names in 12:1–7, nine are found in 1 Chron. 24 as part of the twenty-four priestly courses.

Similarly puzzling is the brief list of Levites (apparently including singers and gatekeepers) which is found in 12:8–9. Of the eight names, four are also found in 12:24–25. Four of the names (five if Judah is a variant of Hodiah) in 12:8–9 are also found in 10:10–14, and two (three if Hodeiah is a variant of Judah) are found in 7:43. Four of the names (five if Meshullam is a variant of Shallum) in 12:24–25 are found in 7:43–45, including two (or three) not found in 12:8–9. These variations indicate independence of the lists, but they do not inspire confidence that we have genuine historical data.

Of particular interest is 12:10–11 which seems to give a list of high priests: Joshua, Joiakim, Eliashib, Joiada, Jonathan, Jaddua. It is paralleled by a similar but slightly different one at 12:22: Eliashib, Joiada, Johanan, and Jaddua. The second is the same as the first (though omitting the first two names) except that it has Johanan instead of Jonathan. Some have wanted to emend Jonathan to Johanan, but one should be cautious about this. These may be lists with different data rather than the same lists with a textual corruption in one. The names Johanan and Jonathan are not that similar; a textual corruption is always possible, but there is no reason to think of one here. The name Joshua (Jeshua) is well known from Ezra 1–5 and the books of Haggai and Zechariah. Eliashib is probably the priest mentioned in Neh. 13:4–9. A Johanan is known as high priest from the Elephantine papyri (Cowley 1923: Nos 30–31). The lists are said to extend to the rulership of Darius the Persian, but which Darius is not stated: is it Darius II or Darius III? The books of Ezra and Nehemiah show no knowledge of more than two kings by the name Darius nor more than one (or possibly two) by the name Artaxerxes.

A large section of the chapter is given over to the dedication of the wall (12:27–43). This would have followed on naturally from the end of Nehemiah 6, which mentions the completion of the wall (6:15), or the beginning of Nehemiah 7 which speaks of setting up the doors and assigning duties. The matter may come up here partly because it contains a list of people who participated, and this section of Nehemiah (7–12) has been made up mainly of lists; however, there is also good reason to think that the compiler has deliberately delayed reporting on the dedication of the wall until the end of the book. However, the chapter shows no knowledge of the episode concerning reading the law in Neh. 8, an event which would naturally have been associated with dedication of the temple. Most of the narrative on the dedication is in the third person and makes no pretence of being Nehemiah's own version of the event (but see on 12:31 below); it is not dated in any way. It speaks impersonally of the Levites being brought to Jerusalem from the surrounding areas for the dedication and the general rejoicing, including singing and playing on musical instruments (12:27–30). The celebrations included the singers who had been lodged in settlements round Jerusalem. The priests and Levites purified themselves and then the people and the gates and wall.

The next section describes in the first person the procession that took place (12:31–43). The officers and temple personnel were divided into two groups or choirs giving thanks and led up to march on top of the wall. The first group went to the right or south towards the Dung Gate (apparently beginning on the west wall in the region of the Valley Gate). A man called Hoshaiah and half the officials are with this group, along with priests with trumpets and others with musical instruments. Ezra the scribe is said to lead them, though his name actually comes at the end of the list. Having reached the Dung Gate, this group apparently then turned north and proceeded to the Water Gate. The second group included

Nehemiah himself and the other half of the officials. No priests or Levites are mentioned as going with them in 12:38; however, the group listed in the temple contains seven priests and eight others, presumably Levites, along with 'half the officials' (12:40–42). If these are the rest of the second entourage, as seems likely, they form an exact parallel to the first (except for Ezra who seems out of place, as already noted). This group went north towards the Sheep Gate and eventually ended up at the Watch Gate. Then suddenly both groups are in the temple (without any description of how they got there), with priests trumpeting and singers singing. The consecration ends, as expected, by a large number of sacrifices, and the women and children joining in the rejoicing.

When one thinks about it, this ceremony is strange. A religious celebration marks the completion of the wall. One can expect the temple to have a special consecration ceremony, but a city wall? What immediately strikes the reader is how parallel this section is to Ezra 6:15–17: the wall in this chapter is being treated exactly like the temple in Ezra 6. The repair of the wall is a sacred task whose completion is marked by a procession of priests and Levites, as well as dignitaries, and with singing and sacrifices in the temple.

The last part of the chapter deals with the organization of temple gifts and dues (12:44–47). Men are appointed to be over the storehouses for the offerings, first-fruits, and tithes to gather the portions from the fields of the cities according to the Torah. This represents the expression of the people's gratitude to the priests and Levites who were on duty to keep God's charge and purity, including the singers and gatekeepers, as commanded by David and Solomon. In the days of David, Asaph was in charge of the singers, and of songs and praise to God. Thus, in the days of Zerubbabel and of Nehemiah gifts were given for the singers and gatekeepers, plus sacred gifts went to the Levites, and the Levites gave in their turn to the priests. It is interesting that in this chapter, the dedication of the wall is followed by organization of the contributions to the temple personnel, just as in Ezra 6:18 organization of the temple personnel immediately follows the dedication of the temple. This suggests that the arrangement of material here is not accidental.

This chapter has been made up of a diversity of material. The first part (12:1–26) contained lists of priests and Levites, some of which were allegedly from the time of Zerubbabel and Joshua. Included are two lists apparently of high priests, but even though they overlap, they do not precisely agree. Then came an undated account of dedicating the wall (12:27–43). The first part is an impersonal statement about gathering Levites for the dedication, but a first-person account of two processions marching in opposite directions on top of the walls takes up the second part. This means that 12:31–43 could be taken as Nehemiah's own account of the ceremonies to dedicate the walls. If so, it seems to have been supplemented by other material. The final section on organizing the storing and distribution of gifts to the temple personnel is described, impersonally and mentioning both Zerubbabel and Nehemiah, as if one or both have been brought artificially into the narrative. The idea that gifts went to the Levites who then gave a portion to the priests agrees with Num. 18:21–29.

Nehemiah 13

Apart from the first few verses, most of this chapter is in the first person and thus ostensibly from Nehemiah himself. The first part of the chapter (13:1–3) says that the passage of the 'book of Moses' was read which states that Ammonites and Moabites should not enter the congregation of God (Deut. 4:4–9). When the people hear 'the Torah' (13:3), they respond by separating the 'mixture' ('ērev) from Israel. The passage is undated and seems to be a fragment of text which has been placed somewhat awkwardly here. It would seem to fit best at the beginning of Nehemiah 9 or perhaps in Nehemiah 10, but since it does not occur there, it was probably seen as a separate tradition. It gives a slightly different basis and content to the 'separation' from the surrounding peoples, suggesting it is not a part of that specific tradition. Perhaps it is a variant tradition or version of the same incident. Since this passage is almost a word-for-word quotation from Deut. 4:4–9, it seems to presuppose the book of Deuteronomy or even the whole Pentateuch.

The next section (13:4–9) is an extremely interesting comment on the relationship between Nehemiah and the Jewish leadership. Although it is dated in the 32nd year of Artaxerxes (433–432 BCE) and thus long after the initial events of Nehemiah's governorship, it shows that the differences of opinion relating to the local leadership were still in existence. The high priest Eliashib had apparently participated willingly in the building of the wall (3:1, 20, 21), but he seems to have agreed with those who continued to have contact with Tobiah, the head of a prominent Jewish family in the Transjordanian area (6:17–19); indeed, Eliashib and Tobiah were relatives (13:1). As noted above in the discussion of Neh. 6, this did not mean hostility to Nehemiah, though the latter interpreted it as such.

For whatever reason, 'Eliashib the priest' made available one of the storerooms in the temple for Tobiah to use. This happens while Nehemiah is away in Babylon reporting to the king. When he returns and finds out that a chief opponent is installed in the heart of Jerusalem itself, he is livid and throws Tobiah's stuff out of the chamber and has it purified and returned to its former use. In so doing, Nehemiah is using his powers as Persian governor to overrule the temple personnel themselves. Since Eliashib is called 'high priest' and not just priest in Neh. 3, some argue that this is a different individual. We cannot be certain, of course, but it seems unlikely that a priest not high up in the temple administration could have made a decision in this way. There seems to me nothing in the way of understanding this as Eliashib the high priest (the term 'the priest' sometimes seems to be a way of referring to the high priest, for example Zadok in 1 Kings and Joshua in Ezra, though there is always necessarily an ambiguity when so done).

The next episode (13:10–14) may be connected with Nehemiah's return to Jerusalem after an absence (unless it occurred at the beginning of his governorship). The Levites and singers have left their posts to work in their fields (according to Num. 18:19–20 and Deut. 14:27–29 they had no fields) because their temple contributions were not being given. Nehemiah gathered them back to their temple duties and set up a commission consisting of a scribe, a priest, and a Levite to oversee the collection and distribution of the agricultural tithes. On the surface, it seems a case of neglect: the people had stopped paying their tithes and other temple duties, and the temple personnel had had to go elsewhere to find a living. However, we may be seeing the last phase of a rivalry among priests that probably goes back well into First Temple times. Only the Levites and singers are said to have left their posts, suggesting that the altar priests were still carrying on. Is it that the Aaronite priests judged that there were enough of them to do all the duties without need of help from the Levites? Were the tithes being collected directly by the priests rather than coming to them via the Levites? We do not know for sure but it seems unlikely that Nehemiah has given us the full story.

The next section (13:15–22) is designated vaguely as taking place 'in those days'; it could be connected with the previous episodes in the chapter but need not be. People were treading grapes on the Sabbath and bringing goods into Jerusalem and otherwise engaging in the commercial traffic of buying and selling on the Sabbath. Tyrian merchants are actually living in Jerusalem and selling to the Jews. This is being done with the approval of the Jewish nobility because Nehemiah takes his dispute up with them (13:17). He has the gates shut as the shadows begin to fall over them on Friday afternoon and they are kept shut until after the Sabbath. He makes sure this instruction is carried out by putting his own servants in charge of the gates (13:19). The merchants and sellers spend the night outside the walls once or twice, so Nehemiah warns them away. He then places ritually pure Levites in charge of the gates to hallow the Sabbath day.

Somewhat surprisingly, the issue of intermarriage with the people of the region comes up once again, this time in a very personal account (13:23–27). Nehemiah finds that some Jews have married Ashdodite, Ammonite, and Moabite wives, and some of their children did not speak 'the Jewish language' (*Yĕhûdît*). Or at least this is what he says, though his designation of Tobiah as an Ammonite might suggest that these women were actually of Jewish or Israelite origin. What is meant by 'the Jewish language' is not clarified, though it most likely refers to Hebrew. Interestingly, some are said to speak 'Ashdodite' but not Ammonite or Moabite. Nehemiah himself takes rather drastic action, not only psychological pressure but physical beatings and attacks on some. (Interestingly, in a similar situation Ezra is said to have torn his own hair [Ezra 9:3]!) He makes people swear not to intermarry – but such assurances and pledges were supposed to have already taken place earlier (Ezra 9; Neh. 9–10; 13:1–3). Nehemiah appeals to the example of Solomon whose 'foreign wives/women' caused him to sin.

The last section of the chapter continues the theme of marriage with the people of the region (13:28–31). In this case, one of the sons of Joiada (son of Eliashib) the high priest was married to the daughter of Sanballat, and Nehemiah drove him out. He then purified the priesthood and the Levites from every 'foreigner' and established the watches for the priests and Levites; also the wood offering in its times and the first-fruits. Although the general theme of this section fits well with some of the other sections supposed to be from Nehemiah's memorial (see p. 154 below), the vocabulary is unusual. Some have thought that it is the creation of a later writer imitating Nehemiah's personal style. It ends the book on a rather sombre note, as does the entirety of Nehemiah 13. Some feel that the logical ending of the book is at 12:43 with the rejoicing over the dedication of the wall, with the rest of Nehemiah 12 and 13 in the nature of appendixes. As the book now stands, it is somewhat open-ended, but the message is clear: the dangers of intermarriage with 'foreigners' are ever present and the people must be vigilant at all times. Even the priests are susceptible.

Summary and conclusions

When Nehemiah is read by itself, it contains a complete story; it does not really need the book of Ezra to be included with it. The only place the book of Ezra would be useful is in Neh. 8 and the few other odd verses where Ezra is mentioned without any background information. In many ways, the book of Nehemiah represents a different but parallel story about the restoration. The striking parallel structure of the books can be diagrammed as follows:

Ezra	*Nehemiah*
1: royal commission (Cyrus edict)	1:1–2:9: royal commission (by Artaxerxes)
3: task of rebuilding (altar/temple)	2–3: task of rebuilding (repair of wall)
4–6: hindrance by 'enemies'	4, 6: hindrance by 'enemies'
6: work completed with God's help	6: work completed with God's help
7–8: Ezra and the law	8: Ezra and the law
9–10: threat from intermarriage	9–10: threat from intermarriage
10: resolution by public pledge	10: resolution by public pledge

Other sections of Nehemiah are also parallel, even though the parallels do not fit the neat scheme just given:

2: list of returnees	7: list of returnees
2: list of returnees	11:1–12:26: list of returnees
6:16–17: dedication of temple	12:27–43: dedication of wall
6:18: organization of priests/ Levites	12:44–47: organization of priestly/Levitical dues
9–10: mixed marriages/threats from 'foreigners'/'peoples of the land'	13: mixed marriages/threats from 'foreigners'/'peoples of the land'

Thus, even though Nehemiah does not rebuild the temple in the same way that Joshua and Zerubbabel do, there is definitely a new beginning here. The task before Nehemiah is conceived of as a divine task, and when the wall is finally dedicated, it is done so with a religious ceremony which looks very much like a consecration.

One can see how such a tradition could develop into one in which Nehemiah became the builder of the temple as well as the repairer of the wall (cf. 2 Macc. 1:18–2:13, discussed in chapter 4 below).

In some ways the book ends negatively. One might think of Ezra which also ends negatively, with a list of those who had sinned by their marriages and a statement about the wives and children affected. My conclusion in the case of Ezra was that this demonstrates that the story is not ended, that the book of Nehemiah is necessary to complete what the book of Ezra began. The negative tone of Nehemiah 13 does not suggest incompleteness, however. It can be looked at in two ways. First, the climax of the book is the celebrations surrounding the dedication of the wall and the organization of the temple personnel in Neh. 12; therefore, Neh. 13 can be seen as a sort of epilogue. Secondly, Neh. 13 contains a powerful concluding message which parallels the preceding contents of the book. A number of negative episodes take place: the problem of mixed marriages (13:1–3); Tobiah's setting up of an office in the temple area (13:4–9); the lack of contributions to the Levites and singers so that they leave their service (13:10–14); the situation with the Sabbath (13:15–22); mixed marriages once again, including the son or grandson of the high priest who marries within the Sanballat family (13:23–28); and a summary (13:29–31).

Each of these, with one exception, occurs in some form earlier in the book. The mixed marriages were discussed in Neh. 9–10, Tobiah and Sanballat at various points (2:10; 3:33–35; 4:1), the Levites and singers (10:10–14; 11:15–18, 21–23). The one new topic is the Sabbath. Despite its supposed importance in the post-exilic period, it is interesting that it occurs only here and in 10:32 in the two books, yet is treated as a very serious issue at this point.

4

1 ESDRAS AND OTHER EZRA AND NEHEMIAH TRADITIONS

Although the books of Ezra and Nehemiah in the Hebrew Bible form the backbone of this study, a proper evaluation and understanding of them needs to take into account other Ezra and Nehemiah traditions, of which there are several. As far as length of text is concerned, the main other writing is 1 Esdras in the Septuagint. Yet there are a number of other traditions, albeit somewhat shorter, which must also be considered. All of them will be dealt with in this chapter and also considered in the overall analysis of chapter 5.

1 Esdras

The book of 1 Esdras is known only in a Greek version (and in translations of the Greek into Latin, Syriac, and some other languages); however, the style of the Greek strongly suggests a Semitic original even though no traces of an original Semitic text have so far been found. The relationship of 1 Esdras to Ezra-Nehemiah and portions of 2 Chronicles is very much debated. Although much of the book is parallel to one or another section of the Hebrew Bible, this does not mean that 1 Esdras was created simply by excerpting from pre-existing texts. In this chapter the book will be treated as an autonomous text in its own right (though parallel texts will be pointed out where appropriate). The question of the text's origin and its relationship to other OT texts will be discussed in chapter 5. Please note that the verse numbers below, which are given according to Hanhart's Greek text (1974), may differ slightly from those in some English translations.

1 Esdras 1

The book begins with the great Passover celebration under Josiah and continues to the destruction of Jerusalem under Nebuchadnezzar, king of Babylon. The story is otherwise known from 2 Kings 23:21–25:30 and from 2 Chronicles 35–36. 1 Esdras 1 closely resembles the account in 2 Chron. 35–36, paralleling it almost verse for verse, but with many minor differences.

The first part of the chapter (1:1–20) covers in detail how the Passover was celebrated by Josiah strictly according to the law, with emphasis on the organization and work of the priests and Levites (the singers are also mentioned [1:14]). Great quantities of animals were killed and eaten by the people, with Josiah supplying a large number from his own personal property (1:7), and various other officials also donating animals. The accompanying seven-day festival of unleavened bread was also kept (1:17). No such Passover had been held since the days of Samuel the prophet, for none of the Israelite kings had kept such a celebration of the Passover (1:18–19). It seems strange that this was all done according to the writing of David and the magnificence of Solomon (1:4), yet they had not celebrated such a Passover; neither is any such Passover described for the time of Samuel in the book of 1 Samuel. Tacked on to this section are a couple of verses about the righteousness of Josiah and the sins of the people (1:21–22).

The next section describes the death of Josiah at the hands of the king of Egypt (1:23–31). The unnamed king of Egypt (called Necho in 2 Chron. 35:20) is going up to fight on the Euphrates but is challenged by Josiah. The Egyptian king tries to avoid battle because his fight is elsewhere, but Josiah insists, ignoring the words of the prophet Jeremiah. Josiah is wounded in the battle (a statement about the actual act of wounding is missing, for some reason, though this might be due to a mistranslation) and brought back to Jerusalem, where he dies and is buried. All Judah mourns, including Jeremiah the prophet and the great men and women. It is decreed that this mourning for Josiah be an annual occasion for the people of Israel (1:30). The deeds and acts of Josiah are written in the story book of the kings of Judah. His fame, his understanding of the law, all those things reported about him are recorded in the book of the kings of Israel and Judah.

Several kings now reign in succession (1:32–46). The people make Josiah's son Iechonia (Jeconiah? 1 Chron. 36:1 has Jehoahaz) king, but he is replaced after only three months by the king of Egypt who puts a tribute of a hundred silver talents and one gold talent on the country. He also set up Joakim as king. But Joakim did evil in God's sight, and Nebuchadnezzar came and bound him, taking him in chains to Babylon and also taking away some of the temple vessels. The account of Joakim's uncleannesses and impieties are written in the royal chronicle. His son Joakim reigned in his place for three months and ten days and did evil in God's sight. After a year (*sic!*) Nebuchadnezzar sent and had him brought to Babylon, along with temple vessels, and appointed Zedekiah king of Judah and Jerusalem. Zedekiah also did wickedly and paid no attention to the words of God through Jeremiah the prophet.

The wickedness of the people and their ultimate punishment is now recounted (1:47–55). The leaders of the people and the priests committed impieties and the uncleannesses of the nations and profaned the sacredness of the temple. God sent messengers to warn them and spared them, but they mocked his messengers and ridiculed his prophets. Finally, God sent the kings (*sic*) of the Chaldeans who spared neither young nor old but removed the temple vessels, the ark, and the king's treasures and took them to Babylon. He then burned the temple, breached the city walls, burned the gate towers, and took captive those of the people who were not slain. They served him and his descendants until Persian rule in fulfilment of the words spoken by God through the mouth of Jeremiah that until the land enjoyed its Sabbaths, all the time as it lay deserted, it would have a Sabbath rest for seventy years.

A comparison of 1 Esdras 1 with 2 Chron. 35–36 strongly suggests a literary relationship of some sort. The two generally agree sentence for sentence and even word for word. Yet, as already noted, there are many minor differences, usually affecting detail, but sometimes more important. For example, the summary of Josiah's reign in 1 Esdras 1:21–22 has no parallel in the MT. 2 Chron. 36:22–23 and Ezra 1:1–3a are virtually the same word for word. 1 Esdras 1, which had been parallel up to 2 Chron. 36:2, has nothing corresponding to this, though 1 Esdras 2:1–5, which parallels Ezra 1:1–3, has this passage. In other words, the end of 2 Chron. 36 and the beginning of Ezra 1 have the same passage twice; 1 Esdras has it only once.

1 Esdras 2

The first part of this chapter (2:1–14) parallels Ezra 1 very closely. It is quite different from the LXX of Ezra and Nehemiah (sometimes

known as Esdras B) which is a fairly literal translation. Where Ezra
1:2 has 'Yhwh God of heaven', 1 Esdras 2:3 has 'the Lord of Israel,
the Lord most high'. 1 Esdras seems to have a preference for 'lord'
(*kurios*) where Ezra and Esdras B have 'God'. It has 'horse' (probably
from Hebrew *rekeš*) where Ezra has 'property' (*rĕkûš*) (1 Esdras 2:6,
8//Ezra 1:4, 6). Although the total number of temple vessels
delivered to Sanabassaros (5,469 [2:12–13]) is roughly the same as
given to Sheshbazzar in Ezra 1:9–11 (5,400), the numbers of the
individual types are often quite different.

The rest of the chapter (2:15–25) is roughly paralleled by Ezra
4:7–24, though there are many minor differences. (It should be
noted that Ezra 4:6, which mentions Ahasuerus [Xerxes?], is not
found in 1 Esdras.) The individuals of Samaria who write to the
king about the Jews claim that they are building 'the marketplace,
repairing the walls, and laying the foundations of the temple'
(2:17). The satrapy of Ebir-nari ('Across-the-River [Euphrates]')
is referred to as Coele-Syria and Phoenicia (2:16, 20, 21, 23). The
work in Jerusalem is halted until the 2nd year of Darius the Persian.

The story of the chapter can be summarized as follows: Cyrus
issued his decree allowing the return to Judah and the rebuilding
of the temple. He also brought out the temple vessels from Jerusalem
and gave them to Mithradates who, in turn, gave them over to
Sheshbazzar (Sanabassaros) who brought them to Jerusalem along
with those returning there from captivity. In the days of Artaxerxes
the king, some individuals in Samaria wrote to the king and claimed
that the city was being repaired and fortified. If this goes on, the city
will rebel and refuse to pay tribute. If the king will read the record, he
will find that the city has a history of such behaviour. The king sends
back a message that he has investigated and found that this is true.
He therefore tells them to hinder the rebuilding, which they do,
and the work stops until the 2nd year of Darius.

1 Esdras 3–4

These two chapters contain an element found in a number of
wisdom tales from this period in which the wisdom of a particular
individual is demonstrated by winning a contest of wits. In this
case, each of three bodyguards of the king Darius presents an argument for what entity is the strongest, the winner to be rewarded
handsomely and made the king's counsellor. One chooses wine; a
second makes it the king; the third says it is woman but the highest
is truth. The third guard is Zerubbabel (4:13). He first makes the

case for the woman as is expected by the story, but he then goes on to argue for the truth. His discourse meets with great approval, and he is promised even more than he originally asked (4:42). He requests that Darius fulfil the vow made before he became king to rebuild Jerusalem and the temple (4:43–46). In response, the king writes letters to all the satraps, governors, and the like to help him on his journey. He also writes to the governors in Coele-Syria, Phoenicia, and Lebanon to supply cedar wood for the temple (4:47–48). Furthermore, twenty talents (of silver?) are to be given towards the building of the temple until it is completed; in addition ten talents per year are to be set aside for sacrifices, of which seventeen are commanded (4:51–52). The priests and Levites and their vestments are also to be maintained at public expense until the temple is rebuilt (4:54–55); likewise, the guards should receive land and wages (4:56). The temple vessels, set aside by Cyrus before he destroyed Babylon, are to be returned (4:44, 57).

These chapters have no counterpart in the Hebrew Bible. The banquet of the king (3:1–3) has a resemblance to Ahasuerus' banquet in Esther 1, but only the general theme is the same rather than the details. Both mention 127 satrapies or provinces in the Persian empire from India to Ethiopia, but the content of the banquet account is otherwise somewhat different. Rather than borrowing from Esther, it seems more likely that 1 Esdras has used the common motif of the sumptuous banquet of the Oriental king (cf. also Daniel 5). Darius' solicitude for the Jerusalem temple also resembles the letter of Darius in Ezra 6:6–10 as far as making provision for the expenses of the temple to be defrayed at government expense (cf. also the vast amount of resources Ezra has in Ezra 7:21–24). Again, though, this is a motif of general Persian solicitude for the Jerusalem temple and is not necessarily a direct borrowing.

As has long been recognized, Zerubbabel's choice of topic indicates that an original story has been embellished by a pious redactor. The account of the three arguments as to which is strongest fits well the topics of wine, the king, and women, but the subject of the truth is clearly added on and goes against the ground rules which is to find which one thing is strongest. The author of 1 Esdras has taken over a traditional story but either has a version already expanded by the addition of the element truth or has done the expansion himself. 1 Esdras still has the problem that Artaxerxes precedes Darius, but Ezra's problem of Zerubbabel coming in the time of Cyrus does not exist in the 1 Esdras account because Zerubbabel is not associated with the first wave of immigrants.

1 Esdras 5

This chapter is mainly a list of those going up to Jerusalem, supposedly in the 2nd year of Darius, and is thus parallel to Ezra 2 and Nehemiah 7. The first few verses of the chapter prefacing the list are different, however, and there are many small differences in the lists.

The chapter begins with an introduction (5:1–6). The leading men by family and tribe go up with their families and property, being given an escort of 1,000 horsemen by the king, and arrive safely in Jerusalem to the sound of music. The names who went up according to their families were the priests, Joshua son of Jozadak, Joachim son of Zerubbabel from the house of David and the tribe of Judah who spoke wisely before Darius the king. This mention of Zerubbabel's son instead of Zerubbabel himself is puzzling. From 4:63 we expect Zerubbabel himself to go to Jerusalem.

The next section of the text gives a list of those returning from the captivity of Nebuchadnezzar and settling in their own towns (5:7–45). It parallels Ezra 2 very closely, usually verse by verse and even word for word, though there are some differences in the names given and the numbers. Without begging the questions of priority or origin, one can say there is definitely a literary relationship between this passage and Ezra 2:1–70.

The following pericope (5:46–62) describes the first assembly of the people, the offerings made, the celebration of the Feast of Tabernacles, and the commencement of work on the temple. 1 Esdras 5:46 mentions that the people assembled in the open space to the east in front of 'the first gate'. This is not found in Ezra 3:2 but is very similar to Neh. 8:1. Particularly interesting is 5:49 which states that some of the 'other peoples of the land' gathered together with them (*episunēthēsan autois*, though some translate 'against them') in founding the altar. The following sentence seems to say that the 'people of the land' were enemies to them, though one translation gives the surprising rendering, 'even though they were at enmity with them, all the people of the land supported them' (Myers 1974: 62). However, no explanation is given, and it is difficult to find evidence to support this understanding. 1 Esdras 5:55 has no counterpart in Ezra. Otherwise, the text is very closely parallel to Ezra 4, even to a reference to Cyrus the king (1 Esdras 5:53), despite the fact that the events in question have been dated to the time of Darius.

The final section of the chapter (5:63–70) tells how the 'enemies of the tribes of Judah and Benjamin' sought to help them in building the temple. They are turned down with the statement that Cyrus king of Persia had commanded those returning with Zerubbabel and Joshua to do it. Therefore, the 'peoples of the land' hindered the work of rebuilding all the lifetime of Cyrus, for two years until the reign of Darius.

1 Esdras 6

The subject here is resumption of the work of rebuilding, the investigation of the Persian governor over the region, the correspondence with Darius, the latter's investigation of the command to build the Jerusalem temple, and the king's reply. It parallels the Hebrew text of Ezra 5:1–6:12, with no major differences. It seems mostly word-for-word the same, though here and there minor differences suggest an underlying Aramaic textual variant from the MT. For example, 1 Esdras 6:23 (//Ezra 6:3) for the difficult MT 'where sacrifices are offered and its foundations laid' (or something similar) has 'where offerings of fire are offered'. Interestingly, the LXX text of Ezra also has only 'where the sacrifices are offered'. This suggests that both Greek texts used an Aramaic text which omitted part of the sentence found in the MT. Similarly, both 1 Esdras 6:31 and the LXX of Ezra 6:11 speak of the miscreant's having his property confiscated (rather than being turned into a dungheap as the MT does). For the MT form śāvê 'elders of' the Jews in Ezra 6:8, 1 Esdras 6:27 has 'captivity' of Judah. This is probably not a textual difference but simply reading the unpointed Aramaic text as šĕvî 'captivity' (though 1 Esdras 6:5 seems to have a double translation of both 'elders' and 'captivity' for this word). The anonymous governor of the Jews of Ezra 6:7 is named as Zerubbabel in 1 Esdras 6:26. These differences are relatively minor, though, and do not detract from the general conclusion that the underlying Aramaic text of 1 Esdras was generally very close to the MT.

The work of rebuilding having been stopped at the end of 1 Esdras 5, the prophets Haggai and Zechariah now prophesy, and Joshua and Zerubbabel respond by resuming the building (6:1–2). Then Sisinnes the governor (*eparchos*) of Syria and Phoenicia and Sathrabouzanes and the other companions come to Jerusalem and ask who gave permission to build the temple. But the elders of the Jews received favour because the Lord watched over the captivity, and they did not cease work while waiting for a decision from Darius (6:3–6).

Sisinnes, Sathrabouzanes, and the rest wrote a letter to Darius (6:7–21). They report that they visited the Jews. The work was progressing rapidly, and they asked the elders with what authority this was being done and took the names of the workers. The Jews replied that they were servants of the Lord who created heaven and earth. A great king of Israel had built the temple, but when their father sinned, the Lord of Israel delivered them into the hands of Nebuchadnezzar who destroyed the temple and took the people captive to Babylon. In his 1st year king Cyrus wrote that the temple should be rebuilt and the temple vessels returned. Cyrus took the vessels from a temple in Babylon and gave them to Zerubbabel and Sheshbazzar (Sanabassaros) the governor to place in the Jerusalem temple. (Some manuscripts read 'Zerubbabel who is Sanabassaros', but the identification of Sheshbazzar and Zerubbabel does not seem a standard part of the tradition.) This Sheshbazzar laid the foundations of the temple in Jerusalem, and it has been in the process of building ever since but not completed. Therefore, if it is pleasing to the king, let a search be made for the decree of Cyrus.

Darius has a search made in the archives, and a document is found with Cyrus' decree given in his 1st year (6:22–33). It commands the rebuilding of the temple (even giving some of the dimensions), payment from royal funds, and the return of the temple vessels. Therefore, Darius orders Sisinnes and company to stay away and let Zerubbabel, the Lord's servant and also the governor of Judah, and the elders get on with the building (though, somewhat inconsistently, Sisinnes is also apparently to assist the Jews in completing the project). The king also decrees that public funds from the income of the province of Coele-Syria and Phoenicia are to be given regularly to the Jews to buy animals and agricultural products for the temple cult. Offerings and prayers are to be made on behalf of the king and his sons. Anyone ignoring the decree is to be impaled on a timber from his own house, and his property is to be confiscated for the king.

1 Esdras 7

The story of 1 Esdras 6 is continued. The king has commanded that the building is not to be hindered but supported. Sisinnes the governor of Coele-Syria and Phoenicia and his companions were careful to support the work of the elders and temple officers of the Jews. Because of the prophecies of Haggai and Zechariah, the work proceeded and the temple was completed in Adar (February/March) of Darius' 6th year. The temple was dedicated with a large number of offerings, and the priests and Levites took up their posts according to the book of Moses (7:9). The Israelites returned from exile now celebrate the Passover on the 14th of the 1st month, the priests and Levites purifying themselves ritually (though not all the exiles had been ritually purified). All the Israelites who had separated from the abominations of the peoples of the land and sought the Lord ate of the Passover (7:13). They went on to celebrate the Festival of Unleavened Bread for seven days with great joy because the Lord had turned the counsel of the king of Assyria (*sic*) to strengthen their hands.

This chapter has a close literary parallel in Ezra 6:13–22 with which it generally agrees basically word for word. There are three interesting differences. At 1 Esdras 7:6 the statement is made that the priests and Levites and ones from the exile 'acted according to the things in the book of Moses', whereas Ezra 6:16 states that they 'performed the dedication of this house of God with joy' (both texts have a reference to the 'book of Moses' a couple of verses later: 1 Esdras 7:9//Ezra 6:18). The very end of 1 Esdras 7:9 mentions that in addition to the priests and Levites taking up their posts, the gatekeepers were on each gate. Ezra 6:18 has nothing about the gatekeepers. The reference to some of the people being ritually impure (1 Esdras 7:11) has no counterpart in the MT (Ezra 6:20). The rather curious expression 'king of Assyria' for the Persian king is found in both texts (1 Esdras 7:15//Ezra 6:22).

1 Esdras 8

In an extremely long chapter of more than ninety verses, 1 Esdras 8 covers the same ground as is found in Ezra 7:1–10:5. Most of the time 1 Esdras is very similar to the text of Ezra, evidently word for word the same when allowance is made for the fact that one text is in Greek and the other in Hebrew and Aramaic. Differences include some small discrepancies in names and numbers of the list in 8:28–40 (//Ezra 8:1–14), the number of temple vessels in 8:56 (//Ezra 8:27), the name of one of the Levites in 8:62 (//Ezra 8:33), and the number of lambs sacrificed in 8:63 (//Ezra 8:35). What appears to be a damaged text in Ezra 8:3a has an intelligible counterpart in 1 Esdras 8:39. Ezra finds he has neither priests nor Levites in his company (8:42, whereas it is only Levites in Ezra 8:15). 1 Esdras 8:66 has 'Edomites' where Ezra 9:1 has 'Ammonites'.

1 Esdras 8:89 has Jechonias son of Jehiel speak to Ezra; the man is
called Shecaniah son of Jehiel in Ezra 10:2.

In the first section (8:1–27), Ezra is introduced as a priest whose
genealogy is traced back to Aaron and as a scribe of the law of Moses
and of the Lord. He journeys to Jerusalem in the 7th year of king
Artaxerxes, accompanied by Israelites, priests, Levites, temple
singers, gatekeepers, and temple servants. Artaxerxes had issued a
decree which allows all those who wish to go to Judah and Jerusalem.
They are vowed silver and gold by the king and his counsellors plus
'whatever is found in the area of Babylonia' plus what is given by the
nation for the temple, all to buy animals and agricultural products
for sacrifice. If they have other needs, they are to be paid out of
the royal treasury for Syria and Phoenicia, up to a hundred talents
of silver plus quantities of wheat, wine, and salt. No tax is to be
imposed on the temple personnel. Ezra is to appoint judges in all
Syria and Phoenicia to administer the law and is to teach it to
those who do not know it.

Having summarized the journey overall and quoted the decree of
Artaxerxes, the narrator now turns to a more detailed account of
Ezra's journey to Jerusalem. The leaders of families and divisions
are listed (8:28–40). When they reach the river Theras, he finds
there are no priests or Levites in his company, and remedies the
lack (8:41–49). He sends to a named group of officials and knowl-
edgeable men and tells them to go to Addaios (who is over the place
of the treasury) to provide temple personnel. As a result learned men
from priests as well as temple servants join Ezra. Having got his
group together, Ezra calls a fast to ask for God's protection since
he is ashamed to ask the king for an escort, having asserted how
God protects those who serve him (8:49–59). He then appoints
twelve of the chief priests to take charge of the silver, gold, and
temple vessels given by the king and his counsellors and the
people. This amounts to 650 talents of silver, a hundred talents of
gold, plus vessels of various sorts. They make the journey and
arrive safely in Jerusalem where they deliver over the precious
metals to the priests (8:60–64). They offer sacrifices, and Ezra finally
turns over his orders from the king to the royal stewards and to the
governors of Coele-Syria and Phoenicia who extol the people and
temple.

The rest of the chapter (8:65–92) begins a section (which continues into the next chapter) concerning the problem of intermarriage with 'the foreign peoples of the land' (8:66). The people
of Israel, the leaders, priests, and Levites have not separated from

the 'uncleannesses' of the Canaanites, Hittites, Perizzites, Jebusites, Moabites, Egyptians, and Edomites (this list is based on a traditional list of the inhabitants of the land whom Israel originally conquered, with some variation) but have mixed 'the holy seed' with the 'foreign peoples of the land'. Ezra acts according to the expected custom of tearing his garment, tearing his hair, fasting, and sitting on the ground. At the time of the evening sacrifice, he utters a prayer (8:71–87), confessing their sins and those of the ancestors. Although the Lord had given them into the hands of foreign kings to be exiled, he had extended mercy and given them a root and name in the holy place and favour before the king of Persia. Yet they have transgressed the commands of the Lord given by the hands of the prophets that they were not to mix with the 'foreigners' of the land who had polluted it with their impurities. When Ezra finishes his prayer, a great crowd gathers weeping to him before the temple (8:88–92). Jechonias son of Jehiel recommends that they swear to put away their foreign wives and children, and Ezra administers the oath to the leaders of the priests and Levites of all Israel.

1 Esdras 9

The final chapter covers the same ground as Ezra 10:6–44 and Nehemiah 8:1–12. There are some small differences, most of these in the lists in 9:18–35 (//Ezra 10:18–43), 9:43–44 (//Neh. 8:4), and 9:48 (//Neh. 8:7). Those who assist in sorting out the mixed marriages are Mosollam, Levis, and Sabbatai according to 1 Esdras 9:14, but Ezra 10:15 has 'Meshullam and Shabbetai the Levites'. An individual named Attharates declares a holy day in 1 Esdras 9:49, whereas Neh. 8:9 says it is Nehemiah the Tirshata (governor – see below).

The first part of the chapter (9:1–36//Ezra 10:6–33) carries forward the story of the mixed marriages to its conclusion. An order goes out to all the returnees of the exile in Judah to gather in Jerusalem in three days. When they do, Ezra calls on them to separate from the 'peoples of the land' and their 'foreign wives'. The people agree, but because of the numbers they propose that the matter be handled by having the people come over a period of time, with the elders and judges of their cities, to the leaders. A panel is appointed and the matter taken care of. A list of those separated from their wives – priests, Levites, temple singers, gate-keepers, and Israelites – is given (a rather short list in light of all the fuss preceding it). These separated from their wives and children.

The final part of the book (9:37–55) is parallel to Nehemiah 8:1–12 and describes the reading of the law by Ezra. The priests, Levites, and Israel are settled in Jerusalem and in the countryside. They gather before the temple in the 9th month and ask Ezra to read the law. (Ezra is, interestingly, called 'high priest' [*archiereus*] several times in this chapter [9:39, 40, 49].) He does so on a wooden platform, flanked by several named individuals. He reads to both men and women from early morning to midday. A group of named Levites teach the law and read it, making the people understand. Then Attharates (which seems to be a literal rendering of the Hebrew *hattiršātā'* 'the governor') tells Ezra that the day is a holy day. The people are not to mourn (for they wept when hearing the law) but to eat, drink, and rejoice. The people do this because they are happy that they now understand the law.

Summary regarding 1 Esdras

The book of 1 Esdras is not just similar or parallel to the Hebrew Ezra and Nehemiah but, except for 1 Esdras 3–4, clearly was translated from a Hebrew text almost the same as 2 Chronicles 35–36, Ezra 1–10, and Nehemiah 8. Any theory about the origins of the book and its relationship to the canonical Hebrew books must take account of this fact. The parallel texts can be summarized as follows:

1 Esdras	MT
1	2 Chron. 35–36
2:1–14	Ezra 1
2:15–25	Ezra 4:7–24
3–4	No parallel
5:1–45	Ezra 2
5:46–70	Ezra 3:1–4:5
6–7	Ezra 5–6
8:1–87	Ezra 7–8
8:88–9:36	Ezra 9–10
9:37–55	Neh. 8:1–12

There are, nevertheless, other small differences (apart from the main one in 1 Esdras 3–4 which has no parallel). Some differences are likely to be the result of a different underlying Hebrew or Aramaic text, though it is not always possible to be sure. The text is in relatively good Greek and is less literal than the Septuagint translation of the Hebrew Ezra and Nehemiah known as Esdras B; also the translator apparently had little in the way of other translations of the OT to use as a guide and was experimenting with finding appropriate language to express the original Semitic text (Pohlmann 1980: 378–80). All of this makes determining the Hebrew/Aramaic *Vorlage* more problematic; nevertheless, we can be sure that that text was mostly the same but occasionally slightly different from the MT. Most of the main differences have been pointed out above in comments on the individual chapters.

The precise relationship between 1 Esdras and the Hebrew Ezra and Nehemiah will be discussed in chapter 5. At this point, the close relationship has to be recognized; that is, there are more than parallel but independent traditions. Either 1 Esdras was made by editing Ezra-Nehemiah, Ezra-Nehemiah were produced by editing a text like 1 Esdras, or some other formal literary relationship pertains. The answer to the question of the relationship could be important for understanding how the Ezra tradition developed.

Josephus on Ezra and Nehemiah

It is almost universally accepted that Josephus' account of Ezra uses 1 Esdras as a source. He gives the story in his own words and makes many small changes and additions, and generally adapts it to fit his account; however, this is his normal procedure with his sources. There can be no doubt that he uses 1 Esdras for at least part of his account, and there is no passage where he has clearly used the Hebrew version of the book. He gives the entire story of Ezra before then going on to Nehemiah. The source for his information on Nehemiah is not clear, as will be discussed below, but he keeps the Ezra and Nehemiah traditions separate.

The initial return

Josephus discusses the initial return and also Ezra's mission in *Antiquities* 11.1.1–5.5 §§1–158. He omits all of 1 Esdras 1 which describes Josiah's activities and the fall of Jerusalem but begins his account with 1 Esdras 2:1–14. He has Cyrus acknowledge the God of Israel and allow the return of the Jews because of reading the book of Isaiah which the prophet had left behind 210 years earlier (*Ant.* 11.1.1–2 §§3–6). Josephus has Cyrus commanding the governors and satraps to make gifts of gold, silver, and sacrificial animals for the temple, rather than their being given by the people

(11.1.2–3 §§7–9). He then introduces Cyrus' letter to the satraps giving permission for the Jews to return and build their temple, drawing on 1 Esdras 6:23–31, except that he confuses (deliberately?) a portion of Darius' letter with part of Cyrus' letter and includes the list of temple vessels within it. He has thus created his own version of the Cyrus letter which differs in a number of details from that in 1 Esdras. The list of temple vessels differs from that in 1 Esdras (11.1.3 §§15–16) and also includes an enormous gift of 205,500 drachmas for cattle, wine, and oil and 20,500 measures of flour, all for the temple offerings (as opposed to being unspecified in 1 Esdras 6:28–29). It is to be paid from the revenues from Samaria (rather than Syro-Phoenicia [1 Esdras 6:28]). He then moves to 1 Esdras 2:15–25 and the correspondence with Artaxerxes halting the work on the temple, except that Josephus assigns it to Cambyses (*Ant.* 11.2.1–2 §§19–30). This seems an arbitrary alteration by Josephus but it resolves a major chronological discrepancy. Despite some deficiencies Josephus had a better knowledge of Persian kings and chronology than the biblical writer.

Josephus had already implicitly identified Sheshbazzar and Zerubbabel (cf. *Ant.* 11.1.3 §11 and 11.1.3 §13). He now gives the story of the contest of the three royal bodyguards (*Ant.* 11.3.1–9 §§31–67//1 Esdras 3–4). Since one of these is Zerubbabel, Josephus has him return from Jerusalem to see Darius with whom he had had a previous friendship. Josephus makes Darius the instigator of the contest rather than the guards themselves, but the general story is the same. When Zerubbabel wins, he reminds the king of his vow (made on condition of becoming king [*Ant.* 11.3.1 §31]) to return the temple vessels to Jerusalem. In this way Josephus does not resolve the problem of returning the vessels which had already been returned, but he does explain the reference to the king's vow of 1 Esdras 4:43–46 which appears there without prior anticipation in the story. In a slight discrepancy, the twenty talents of silver for the temple (1 Esdras 4:51) becomes fifty (*Ant.* 11.3.8 §61).

The list of returnees of 1 Esdras 5:1–45 is understandably omitted, though the totals are given (*Ant.* 11.3.10 §§68–74). The number of men is said to be 4,628,000 if read literally, though the text is often emended to something close to the biblical figure of 42,000. In addition, Josephus gives the number of women and children as 40,742, a figure not found in 1 Esdras. Josephus follows 1 Esdras 5:46–70 fairly closely about the celebration of the Feast of Tabernacles and the renewal of the rebuilding (*Ant.* 11.4.2–5 §§79–95) with some small but significant changes. First, contrary to all other sources, the Jews allow the Samaritans the opportunity to worship in the temple (though forbidding them to help with the rebuilding [*Ant.* 11.4.3 §87]). Second, Josephus inserts a section following 1 Esdras 5:68 (ET 5:71) about the opposition of the Samaritans who instigate the governor of Syria and Palestine to investigate (*Ant.* 11.4.4 §§88–94). This visit is described largely by drawing on the letter to Darius in 1 Esdras 6:7–21. Third, contrary to 1 Esdras 5:70 (ET 5:73), the work on the temple is not stopped, which eases a chronological problem found in both 1 Esdras and the Hebrew Ezra.

The prophets Haggai and Zechariah are introduced into the narrative (*Ant.* 11.4.5 §96), but here they only strengthen the resolve of the Jews (rather than urging them to resume the building [1 Esdras 6:1–2]). *Ant.* 11.4.6–8 §§97–110 follows 1 Esdras 6:3–7:15 reasonably closely, including Cyrus' letter (which Josephus had already used in part earlier in *Ant.* 11.1.3 §§12–17, as noted above). This section ends with the completion of the temple and the celebration of Passover. At the very end of the section, Josephus inserts some chronological figures for earlier periods in Israel's history and comments on the Jewish form of government (*Ant.* 11.4.8 §112). He then gives a further section on Samaritan opposition, including a further letter from Darius, which has no parallel in other sources (*Ant.* 11.4.9 §§114–119); although this is likely to be Josephus' own creation, it is just possible that it was a part of his version of 1 Esdras.

Ezra

The story of Ezra the priest takes up the rest of his account (*Ant.* 11.5.1–5 §§120–58). Again, Josephus adjusts the chronology to fit his own perception of Persian history by placing this in the reign of Xerxes rather than Artaxerxes (though no year is given until later in the account [*Ant.* 11.5.2 §135]). The account has been slightly reshaped to fit his aims and context, but it is by and large the same as 1 Esdras 8–9. He suggests that Ezra read out the letter of 'Xerxes' to the Babylonian Jews and also had a copy sent to those in Media, as well as noting that the majority of the Jews ('ten tribes') remained in Mesopotamia (*Ant.* 11.5.2 §§131–33). He omits the names of the families who accompanied him and the measures taken to ensure that Levites were in Ezra's company (1 Esdras 8:28–48), and shortens Ezra's long prayer to a few sentences (*Ant.* 11.5.3 §§143–44). He naturally omits the names of those who sent away their wives and children (1 Esdras 9:18–36). The reading of the law (1 Esdras 9:37–55//Neh. 8:1–12) is said to be at the Feast of Tabernacles (instead of the 1st day of the 7th month), and the account is slightly shortened, but it is otherwise parallel. The story concludes with a sentence that Ezra died an old man and was buried in Jerusalem about the same time as the high priest Ioakeimos (Joiakim) son of Eliashib (*Ant.* 11.5.5 §158). This could well be an invention of Josephus, including the synchronization with the high priestly line.

Nehemiah

Having come to the end of the information in 1 Esdras, Josephus now gives a version of the story of Nehemiah (*Ant.* 11.5.6–8 §§159–83). Following Josephus' own chronological scheme, this is placed in the reign of Xerxes rather than Artaxerxes. By and large this is parallel with sections of the Hebrew Nehemiah (and the Septuagint translation); nevertheless, many details are different and whole sections of the book are omitted. The first part of the story is roughly parallel to Neh. 1:1–2:8 (*Ant.* 11.5.6 §§159–67) but with a number of differences. Nehemiah overhears a group of Jews speaking Hebrew in the street (instead of hearing it from his brother). He prays only briefly (compared to the longer prayer in Neh. 1:4–11). He then immediately rushes off to serve the king where he is asked about his sadness (instead of several months later, as in Neh. 2:1–8). He carries letters to Addaios the 'eparch' of Syria and Phoenicia (instead of letters to the governors of Ebir-nari and also to Asaph the king's forester).

Nehemiah arrived in Jerusalem in Xerxes' 25th year (rather than the 20th of Artaxerxes). In what is probably Josephus' own creation, Nehemiah addresses the people (the night reconnoitring journey is not mentioned). They are harassed by the Ammonites, Moabites, and Samaritans (the Hebrew Nehemiah mentions the Arabs, Ammonites, and Ashdodites, as well as the leaders Sanballat and Tobiah [Neh. 4:1]) who kill many of the Jews (no one is killed in the Hebrew Nehemiah) and hire some foreigners to get rid of Nehemiah. The building of the wall took two years and four months and was finished in the 9th month (as opposed to taking fifty-two days and being finished in the 6th month in Neh. 6:15). They celebrated a festival of eight days (this sounds like the Feast of Tabernacles, but that is in the 7th month, and there was apparently no festival in the 9th month until Hanukkah was instituted to celebrate the restoration of the temple under the Maccabees). Because of the small number of inhabitants in Jerusalem, Nehemiah brought the priests and Levites into the city (as opposed to a tenth of the people chosen by lot [11:1]) and had the people bring them the tithes there. Nehemiah's death is also given, though it is only a generalized statement and could have been Josephus' own creation.

This account presents many puzzles. It is possible that Josephus has depended on the Hebrew Nehemiah or its Septuagint counterpart in Greek. Since a number of chapters consist of lists, he would have omitted those, as well as the events of Nehemiah 8 since this had already been covered in his paraphrase of 1 Esdras 9. Nehemiah 5 is not very flattering to the people as a whole and might have been omitted for this reason (just as Josephus omits the Gold Calf incident much earlier). However, this would not explain the many other changes of details already noted, nor why the dedication of the wall is not given, nor the omission of the events in Neh. 13. A version of the Sanballat story is given (*Ant.* 11.7.2 §§302–3), though it is set in the time of the last king of Persia, long after Nehemiah. According to it, the brother (not son) of the high priest named Manasses (he is nameless in Neh. 13:28) married the daughter of Sanballat. I have argued elsewhere (Grabbe 1987) that this is not a separate incident from that in Nehemiah 13 but rather only a version of it. On the other hand, it also seems clear that Josephus has not taken his information from the account in Neh. 13:28. All this suggests that Josephus did not take his Nehemiah material from the Hebrew Nehemiah (or its Septuagint counterpart) but had available a different version of the Nehemiah tradition. This tradition was in parts close to that in the Hebrew Nehemiah but differed in a number of details and may have been shorter. This means that Josephus may not have known the Hebrew Ezra-Nehemiah or its Septuagint version.

Summary on Josephus

Josephus' account in the *Antiquities* has 1 Esdras as the basis of its account of the return from exile. The parallels are roughly as follows:

Antiquities	*1 Esdras*
11.1.1–3 §§1–11	2:1–14
11.1.3 §§12–18	6:23–31

11.2.1 §§19–20	(cf. 5:63–70)
11.2.1–2 §§20–30	2:15–25
11.3.1–9 §§31–67	3–4
11.3.10 §§68–74	5:41–45
11.4.1 §§75–78	5:46–53
11.4.2–4 §§79–88	5:54–70
11.4.4 §§89–94	6:3–21
11.4.5 §§95–96	(cf. 6:1–2)
11.4.6–8 §§97–110	6:22–7:15
11.4.8–9 §§112–19	No parallel
11.5.1–5 §§120–57	8–9 (with some alterations)
11.5.5 §158	No parallel

Exact parallels are not possible because he makes changes and small additions. Some of the more significant additions and changes to 1 Esdras include the following: lists tend to be omitted; the names of kings are changed to fit Persian chronology better (at least, as Josephus understands it); a number of times the 'enemies' of the Jews are explicitly said to be the Samaritans (cf. 11.2.1 §§19–20); Sheshbazzar is explicitly identified with Zerubbabel; other minor changes to remove potential contradictions and smooth the flow of the passage.

His version of the Nehemiah story (*Ant.* 11.5.6–8 §§159–83) has some parallels with Neh. 1–6, but there are a number of differences. Some of these could be explained as his reshaping of the story to fit his aims (e.g. the omission of Neh. 5), but there are really too many differences for this explanation to be reasonable. More probable is the suggestion that Josephus had a source for the Nehemiah story other than our Hebrew Ezra-Nehemiah (or its Greek equivalent). That source may have included the NM or portions of it, but it was probably not the original NM, if the scholarly suggestions about its nature and contents are anywhere near correct.

Ben Sira 49:11–13

Writing some time around 200 BCE (probably a few years afterward but before 175) Jesus ben Sira gave an encomium on the great men (no women are listed) of ancient Israel in 44–50 of his work often referred to as Ecclesiasticus. Not only are the main figures in the biblical account of Israel's history given, but there are indications that they follow a text similar to Genesis to 2 Kings in our present Hebrew canon. For example, there is a reference to 'the Twelve

Prophets', a clear testimonial not only to the writings in the Minor Prophets but to a collection of them into a single body as we now have them (49:10). Relevant to our theme, Ben Sira mentions Zerubbabel, Joshua, and Nehemiah in 49:11–13. The Hebrew text of the first part of the verse is partially broken but reads as follows:

> How shall we [magn]ify [. . .], and they raised up the holy temple, established for eternal glory; Nehemiah – may his memory be honoured – who raised up our ruins, and he repaired our breaches and set up the gates and bar.

The Greek text is slightly different:

> How shall we magnify Zerubbabel who is like a signet ring upon the right hand, and also Joshua son of Jozadak, who in their days built the house and raised up the holy temple to the Lord, prepared for eternal glory? And Nehemiah, whose memory is great, raised up for us the fallen wall and erected the gates and bars and raised up our buildings.

Ben Sira knew the tradition about the founding of the altar and temple by Joshua and Zerubbabel. Whether he knew it in a version which was similar to or the same as that in Ezra 1–6 is difficult to say. This is possible, but the reference to Zerubbabel as a signet ring is found not in Ezra but in Haggai 2:23. It is possible that everything in Ben Sira's tradition is from Haggai or inferred from that book, but it seems more likely that a fuller tradition was available to him; however, we cannot be sure that it came from the Zerubbabel-Joshua tradition as we know it in Ezra 1–6. Nehemiah's deeds are also not different from what we read in the Hebrew book of Nehemiah. On the other hand, they could have been taken from a tradition about building the wall and resettling Jerusalem. That is, they could be taken from the NM or another version and do not imply the extant form of the Hebrew book of Nehemiah.

Thus, Ben Sira's statements as we have them show a knowledge of the Zerubbabel-Joshua traditions and the Nehemiah tradition, but they do not require a knowledge of our present Hebrew books. The most significant point of Ben Sira's passage, though, is the omission of Ezra. This omission has often been discussed over the centuries. Many have attempted to explain that Ben Sira knew of Ezra but was not attempting to be complete, or deliberately omitted him for some reason or other. Two statements can be made with some force. First, Ezra would not have been omitted simply because Ben Sira was not bothered to include him, because he makes a point of including the major characters of the biblical narratives. The only other significant omission is Daniel. Daniel 7–12 would not have been written at this time, of course, but the tales of Daniel 1–6 were probably in circulation in some form or other. If his source was the Hebrew Ezra-Nehemiah, it is inconceivable that he would have skipped from Zerubbabel and Joshua to Nehemiah without mentioning Ezra. Second, Ben Sira would not have omitted reference to a work which had major authority by his time. If the Hebrew Ezra and Nehemiah were authoritative works when he wrote, there is no question that he would have mentioned Ezra (and the same could be said for Daniel). His non-mention shows either that he did not know the Hebrew Ezra-Nehemiah or, if he knew it, he did not regard it as significant. This is clear evidence that for the Zerubbabel-Joshua and Nehemiah traditions, he was not using the Hebrew Ezra-Nehemiah, nor was he using 1 Esdras or a form of it.

2 Maccabees 1:18–2:15

Here is one of the best examples of the pure 'Nehemiah tradition' and a vital key to the development of the Ezra and Nehemiah traditions. The Nehemiah tradition in 2 Maccabees appears to be completely independent of the book of Ezra since it assigns to Nehemiah various activities which in Ezra are associated with other individuals. Nehemiah is said to have built the temple and the altar (1:18), rather than Zerubabbel and Joshua. This does not appear to be just a reference to an additional repair job when he repaired the city wall, as some have suggested, because of the episode with the fire on the altar (see below) which indicates the first renewal of sacrifices after the exile. Nehemiah is also credited with instituting the Feast of Tabernacles (the wording is ambiguous, but this is one possible meaning) and 'the Festival of Fire' which is said to have arisen from the following incident. At the time of the destruction of Jerusalem, the priests had hidden some of the fire of the altar (1:19). When Nehemiah sent the descendants of these same priests to get the fire, they found a thick liquid. A bit of this was sprinkled on the altar wood and sacrificial parts, and when the sun came out, it burst into flames (1:20–23). This was reported to the Persian king who declared sacred the area where the 'liquid fire' was found (1:33–34). The substance was called 'naphtha' (Greek *nephthai*), though Nehemiah called it *nephthar* ('purification', apparently from the *niphal* form of *ptr* 'be freed, dismissed').

A Jeremiah legend not found in the biblical text is next related (2:1–12). In the 'records' (*apographai*) it is stated that Jeremiah had been the one to order that the priests take some of the altar fire. He gave the law to those about to be deported and commanded them not to forget it. In the 'document' (*graphē*, the same as the 'records'?) it is stated that Jeremiah, instigated by an oracle (*chrēsmatismos*), had the tabernacle, the ark of the covenant, and the altar of incense secreted in a cave in the mountain from which Moses had viewed the land. They were to remain hidden and undiscovered until God gathered his people again and showed them mercy. Both Moses and Solomon had prayed and fire came down from heaven and consumed the offerings. Solomon had kept the eight-day festival. The narrative now returns to Nehemiah with a surprising statement which is quoted in full (2:13–14 NRSV):

> The same things are reported in the records [*anagraphai*] and memoirs [*hupomnēmatismoi*] of Nehemiah, and also that he founded a library [*bibliothēkē*] and collected the books about the kings and prophets, and the writings of David, and letters of kings about votive offerings. In the same way Judas [Maccabeus] also collected all the books that had been lost on account of the war that had come upon us, and they are in our possession.

Nothing like this is found anywhere else. The 'records' and 'memoirs' of Nehemiah are said to report about what Jeremiah did, and also Moses and Solomon. They also allegedly report that Nehemiah collected a group of books which we might call 'canonical'. After the Maccabean revolt, when many books had been lost, Judas Maccabeus did the same thing. There is no parallel to this elsewhere, certainly not in the Hebrew (or Septuagint) book of Nehemiah. Especially significant is the fact that Nehemiah is here credited with doing something similar to Ezra. In the Ezra tradition, Ezra brought a book of the law and promulgated it. Here it is Nehemiah who makes an authoritative collection which has a similar function. Nehemiah has thus also taken over the tradition of the book which elsewhere is associated with Ezra.

Apocalypse of Ezra (4 Ezra or 2 Esdras)

The Apocalypse of Ezra or 4 Ezra is known as 2 Esdras in general English nomenclature (there is no uniform usage; the term 2 Esdras is sometimes confusingly used of the LXX translation of Ezra-Nehemiah [Esdras B], in which case this work is called 3 Esdras). It is conventionally analysed as consisting of chapters 3–14 (a Jewish work known as 4 Ezra), chapters 1–2 (a Christian work known as 5 Ezra), and chapters 15–16 (a Christian work known as 6 Ezra). Our concern here is with the Jewish work 4 Ezra.

Most of the book of 4 Ezra seems to be an original writing which simply uses Ezra as a vehicle for its message. In other words, it is difficult to see a true Ezra tradition behind much of the book beyond the use of a name known from the OT (indeed, he is even said to be named Salathiel though also called Ezra). The apocalyptic material in 4 Ezra 3–13 naturally has many parallels in other apocalyptic books and traditions, but none of these are particularly associated with Ezra elsewhere. Since the book is dated thirty years after the fall of Jerusalem (3:1), it might be thought that the author was using a tradition in which Ezra's activities were during the exilic period. That is possible, but given that this is more likely a reference to a time thirty years after the destruction of the *Second* Temple, we should be careful about inferring any dating of the Ezra tradition from this verse. So whatever traditions the writer of 4 Ezra is drawing on for the most part are not *Ezra* traditions. There is one exception to this generalization, however: 4 Ezra 14 does look like a possible version of an earlier tradition associated with the Ezra of Jewish history and tradition.

4 Ezra 14 is no doubt the author's particular version and interpretation of an earlier tradition; nevertheless, the core of it looks like a tradition parallel to the book of Ezra, suggesting the author is drawing on something passed down from long before. The central concept of 4 Ezra 14 is that the law had been lost but is restored by divine intervention. The law was destroyed by fire, and Ezra asks permission to receive it again (14:20–22). God agrees and tells him to isolate himself for forty days with five men trained as rapid writers. He does as commanded and is given a draught to drink which puts understanding in his heart (14:37–40). He dictates without stopping for the forty days. The result is ninety-four books, seventy of which are esoteric and thus not available to the people generally. But twenty-four are exoteric and constitute the present books of the Hebrew Bible (14:41–47).

How much of this picture is due to the creative talents of the author is difficult to say, but it seems considerable. What does look like a genuine tradition is that Ezra restored the law after it had been destroyed, and that he was the instrument for making available the books of what became the Hebrew canon. Given the tradition in the Hebrew book of Ezra that he brought the law to Jerusalem, it would hardly be surprising if there was a variant form of the tradition in which Ezra actually restored the law which had somehow been lost. Whether the version that Ezra restored the law (instead of just bringing it to Palestine) is a development from the tradition in the Hebrew Ezra or whether it is an independent but parallel tradition is not of great concern. It illustrates the richness of the Ezra tradition over the centuries.

Summary and conclusions

This chapter has looked at a variety of other Joshua-Zerubbabel, Ezra, and Nehemiah traditions beyond those in the Hebrew book of Ezra-Nehemiah. The most extensive of these was 1 Esdras, but it is very close to portions of 2 Chronicles and the Hebrew Ezra-Nehemiah. How to account for this relationship has not been discussed here but will be taken up in the next chapter. What 1 Esdras does demonstrate is that the three complexes of tradition do not necessarily always go together. Nehemiah is conspicuous by his absence in 1 Esdras. Whatever the origin of this book, Nehemiah was either unknown to the author or was deliberately omitted from the story. Either way this is quite significant.

Josephus' account is derivative since he has clearly made use of 1 Esdras for his story of the return from exile. As he usually did with his sources, he has rewritten it to suit his own purposes, omitting bits and occasionally adding material, but his account is too close to 1 Esdras for him to have used any other source for the narratives about Joshua-Zerubbabel and Ezra. However, he also has an account about Nehemiah even though the latter does not occur in 1 Esdras. Some have suggested that he used 1 Esdras because of its better Greek but then turned to the Hebrew Nehemiah for the rest of the story. This seems quite unlikely, however, because the Hebrew Ezra-Nehemiah would have suited his purposes very well and would have saved the effort of using two separate sources. Also, even though the Nehemiah pericope has parallels with portions of Nehemiah 1–7, there are significant differences. It seems unlikely that his source was the Hebrew Nehemiah. So what is his source here? It seems to have been an unknown version of the Nehemiah tradition. Was it the original NM? Probably not, because he would likely have given a more extensive account if he had had the full NM before him. He could well be drawing on an oral tradition.

Ben Sira mentions Zerubbabel, Joshua, and Nehemiah but not Ezra. Again, a number of suggestions have been made as to why Ben Sira omits Ezra from his account, but the simplest explanation is that he did not know of him or at least did not consider the Ezra tradition as having authority. Although statements about Zerubbabel, Joshua, and Nehemiah could possibly have come from the Hebrew Ezra-Nehemiah, this is unlikely to be the source. In his 'praise of the fathers' Ben Sira lists most of the main figures in the biblical history. It would be extremely strange for him to take a book which he regarded as part of the authoritative tradition (viz. Ezra-Nehemiah) and leave out one of the central characters in it. Ezra is, after all, given greater prominence in the Hebrew Ezra-Nehemiah than either Joshua or Zerubbabel. It is clear that Ben Sira has not used what became the canonical Ezra-Nehemiah. If he knew of it, he did not treat it as having special weight.

2 Maccabees, on the other hand, seems to know of neither Ezra nor Joshua-Zerubbabel. Instead it credits Nehemiah with the founding of the temple and altar, which are elsewhere associated with Joshua and Zerubbabel. Nehemiah is also associated with collecting the sacred books together, in a manner parallel to the bringing of the law by Ezra in the Ezra tradition. Nehemiah is clearly the hero of the return-from-exile tradition in 2 Maccabees and has displaced Joshua-Zerubbabel and Ezra.

4 Ezra is more difficult to evaluate since Ezra seems to be mainly a vehicle for apocalyptic views. In 4 Ezra 14, though, the story of how Ezra restored the law which had been burnt looks like the use of a tradition about Ezra and the law which has developed in a particular way. Whatever the source of this story it is unlikely to have been taken directly from the Hebrew Ezra-Nehemiah.

From the material in the other Zerubbabel-Joshua, Ezra, and Nehemiah traditions we can come to two significant conclusions: (1) the three complexes of tradition (Zerubbabel-Joshua, Ezra, Nehemiah) did not automatically go together but seem to have existed and developed independently even after they were brought together in various combinations; (2) the Hebrew Ezra-Nehemiah or its Greek version (whenever it was written, which was probably no later than 200 BCE) was not always known or, if known, was not regarded as authoritative by some noteworthy Jewish writers.

5

THE TRADITIONS FROM
A LITERARY POINT
OF VIEW

The studies in chapters 2–4 above threw up a good deal of material relating to the aims, composition, structure, and growth of the various books and traditions relating to the books of Ezra and Nehemiah. This chapter will now bring together the scattered analytical comments arising from the close reading and produce a synthesis.

Among the results of the studies in chapters 2–4 are included two important and closely related conclusions: first, the books of Ezra and Nehemiah are based on independent traditions – that is, the main traditions of the two books originally grew up separately; second, they have been brought together by a compiler of some skill and are now meant to be read as a single unit. Both these factors – which in some way are two sides of the same coin – have to be taken into account in any use of the two books, especially for historical purposes. The Hebrew tradition that the two form a single book recognizes the present nature of the two books in their final textual and canonical form. This chapter will bring together the scattered evidence and provide support for the conclusions just mentioned.

My study did not consider the question of whether the two books are part of a larger work by the 'Chronicler' (or *das chronistische Geschichtswerk* 'the Chronicler's history' in German). This view has long been argued. It was challenged in recent decades by Japhet (1968) and Williamson (1977), but their views have not always been embraced in subsequent studies (e.g. Blenkinsopp 1988: 47–54). One could always argue that even if not the product of a common compiler, the two books occur in the Hebrew canon contiguous with 1–2 Chronicles. This may be true, but it goes beyond the scope of my investigation and will not be further considered here.

Structure of the Hebrew Ezra and Nehemiah

Arguments for the unity of the canonical Ezra and Nehemiah

There are a number of elements in the present form of the books which link them together. The most obvious is the list of returnees which is almost identical in Ezra 2 and Nehemiah 7. Such a repetition is not likely to have happened by accident (see below on the separate traditions). In the present structure of the books a settlement list fits naturally in Ezra 2, but Nehemiah 7 is in many ways redundant. The list in Nehemiah 7 is introduced by the statement that Nehemiah, while organizing a genealogical registration of the people, 'found the genealogical register of those who were the first to come up' (Neh. 7:5). There is no reason for him to repeat this register since the context is interested in those about to be registered in his own time. So why repeat it? There is no particular reason in the immediate context, but when the two books are seen as a whole, the repetition is a powerful tie holding the books together in a unity. Whatever other function the repeated genealogy may have had, its utility as a link joining the two books together is an important one.

A second set of joining elements are the passages mentioning the person of Ezra in the book of Nehemiah. Because Nehemiah is supposed to come after Ezra according to the chronology of the books, we would not expect to find Nehemiah in Ezra 7–10. But the reading of the law in Nehemiah 8, in which Ezra is the leading figure, unites the book of Nehemiah with Ezra. Nehemiah himself has no role in the proceedings (his name occurs in 8:9, though the Hebrew construction is awkward), but the placing of the chapter implies that this public reading takes place in the Jerusalem controlled by him. Ezra also appears in connection with the ceremony celebrating the completion of repairing the wall, a ceremony in which Nehemiah is clearly the leading figure (Neh. 12:27–43). The procession is divided into two parts. After one group is listed (Neh. 12:31–36), the text suddenly says that Ezra preceded it (12:36). As with Neh. 8:9 the verse is awkward and looks like a later addition, perhaps by the final editor of the two books. Finally, Ezra is listed alongside Nehemiah and the high priest Joiakim son of Joshua as rough contemporaries (Neh. 12:26). Whatever the evidences of editing, then, the final form of Nehemiah is irrefutably joined together with the Ezra tradition by means of these passages.

Third, Ezra 10 ends quite awkwardly. Those who have sinned by marrying 'foreign' women are listed. Although this is positive evidence of their 'repentance', the final verse mentions the 'foreign' wives and (apparently) their children. The ancient reader may not have reacted like the modern one by seeing this tearing apart of families as tragic; nevertheless, the book ends awkwardly and on a down note. Such an ending is not unparalleled (note Jonah, for example), but it is not what we would have expected of a skilled editor in this instance. On the other hand, it leads naturally into Nehemiah 1. This indicates that Ezra in the present context is not to be read independently but with the book of Nehemiah.

Fourth, several common themes are found in both books. Central to both books is the return of people from the 'exile', even from the Mesopotamian administrative centre, to rebuild or restore things in Jerusalem. This happens to Joshua and Zerubbabel and those with them in Ezra 1–6; it occurs with Ezra who restores the law and meta-phorically rebuilds proper worship; and a similar achievement is made by Nehemiah who repairs the walls. In each case it is the Persian king himself who decrees the Jewish expedition and makes provision for it to take place with care and generosity. A second theme is the threat to the community by intermarriage with the 'peoples of the land', a threat removed by a common oath and physical separation from the 'foreigners' (Ezra 9–10; Neh. 9–10; 13:1–3, 23–31). In both books the activities of the Jews are hampered and harassed by the surrounding peoples, especially those in the area of Samaria (Ezra 4–6; Neh. 4:1–2; 6).

Finally, the two books show a parallel narrative structure, at least with regard to content. Both begin with a royal commission, the Cyrus edict (Ezra 1) and the official permission of Artaxerxes granted to Nehemiah (Neh. 1:1–2:9). They each begin a major task of rebuilding (Ezra 3; Neh. 2–3). The work in each case is hindered by local 'enemies' who are in part associated with Samaria (Ezra 4–6; Neh. 4, 6). Nevertheless, the great work is finished because of God's oversight and favour (Ezra 6; Neh. 6). This is followed by Ezra and the law in each book, with Ezra arriving with the law in Ezra 7–8 and reading it publicly in Neh. 8. The new blissful order is then disturbed by the threat posed by intermarriage with the 'foreigners'/'peoples of the land' (Ezra 9–10; Neh. 9–10) which is resolved in each case by a public pledge by the 'sinners' (Ezra 10; Neh. 9–10).

There are also other correspondences on an individual level even though they do not fit the overall parallel structure noted above. Although Neh. 11–13 have no parallel in the overall pattern just described, individual elements parallel portions of Ezra. Neh. 11:1–12:26 forms a parallel to the settlement list in Ezra 2. The dedication of the wall in Neh. 12:27–43 corresponds to the dedication of the temple in Ezra 6:16–17. The dedication of the wall is immediately followed by a re-organization relating to the cultic personnel (Neh. 12:44–47); in exactly the same way the dedication of the temple is followed by a re-organization of the priests and Levites (Ezra 6:18). Finally, the theme of mixed marriage and the threat from 'foreigners'/'peoples of the land' is prominent in the last chapter of Nehemiah, just as it is in Ezra 9–10.

This section has considered some of the major indications of unity for the books of Ezra and Nehemiah. Some of the points made need further consideration. Especially in need of additional elucidation are the matters of structure and theological themes.

Structure of Ezra-Nehemiah

The question of the overall structure of the Hebrew Ezra-Nehemiah is an important consideration in determining the message of the books and how it is conveyed to the readers. An overall message of the two books together is quite easily discerned. There is a progression through the two books which, despite the diversity of material, is coherent and intelligible.

The most detailed investigation of the structure of the book has been done by Tamara Eskenazi (1988). Following the structuralist model of Claude Bremond, she sees a threefold structure in the two books (1988: 37–42):

I Potentiality (objectives defined): decree to the community to build the house of God (Ezra 1:1–4)
II Process of actualization: the community builds the house of God according to the decree (Ezra 1:5–Neh. 7:72)
    A. Introduction: proleptic summary (Ezra 1:5–6)
    B. First movement (Ezra 1:7–6:22)
    C. Second movement (Ezra 7:1–10:44)
    D. Third movement (Neh. 1:1–7:5)
    E. Recapitulation: the list of returnees (Neh. 7:6–72)
III Success (objective reached): community celebrates the completion of the house of God according to Torah (Neh. 8:1–13:31)
    A. Consolidation according to Torah (Neh. 8:1–10:40)

B. Recapitulation: lists of participants (Neh. 11:1–12:26)
C. Dedication of the house of God (Neh. 12:27–13:3)
D. Coda (Neh. 13:4–31)

This model works quite well for the most part and has a number of attractive features. Perhaps one of the most admirable is its interpretation of the lists of Ezra 2 and Nehemiah 7 as in some sense forming an *inclusio*, which also helps to explain the apparent duplication of the lists. That the decree of Cyrus at the beginning of the book sets the context for the rest of the book is certainly a valid assumption.

It is true that some aspects are not so convincing or fit somewhat artificially. For example, where Eskenazi's threefold structuralist model does not work so well tends to be in the more detailed analysis, particularly in the third section, Neh. 8–13. The assumption that this signals success is problematic in the light of some of its contents. Success is indeed found in part of Neh. 8–13 but there is significant material of a different sort. Neh. 8 marks a culmination with the reading of the law and the celebration of Tabernacles, but it is then immediately followed by the problem with mixed marriages (9–10). Although this episode ends satisfactorily, it does not fit the theme of 'celebration' very well. Neh. 13 is also not a celebration but an indication of difficulties and setbacks: mixed marriages, Tobiah in the temple area, the Levites leaving the altar, the breach of the Sabbath, mixed marriages (again!), and finally a curse on those causing difficulties. It is true that each of these issues is addressed and some sort of solution found, but the negative tone of the last chapter remains. Its message is not celebration but the importance of eternal vigilance because the forces of evil are always ready to insinuate themselves into the community (as indeed Eskenazi seems to acknowledge [1988: 126]). She has labelled it a 'coda', which might seem to obviate criticism, but why is it so labelled? Is it precisely because it does not fit her scheme? Also problematic is her view that Ezra 6:14 summarizes and encapsulates the central event of the book. This may fit its content, but there seems to be no structural reason to focus on this particular verse, and its choice looks arbitrary.

Therefore, Bremond's model, as applied by Eskenazi, works well enough to illustrate the literary unity and the overall message of the two books as they now stand. Nevertheless, it is not the only possible analysis of the structure; there may be other structural outlines which would be equally convincing or at least will highlight other structures within the literature which may provide further insight into the writings. Also, the presence of one particular structure may be perfectly compatible with finding additional structures of another sort.

One structural element often overlooked, even though it was clearly important to the compiler, is that of chronology. A glance at Ezra and Nehemiah leaves one in no doubt of its significance in the combined books. Events are usually given dates according to a particular Persian king. Even when no specific date is given, the event is often associated with the reign of a particular Persian king (as, for example, with the Persian decrees of Ezra 4–6). Some of these dates are nonsensical in that they show no knowledge of the correct sequence or relationship of the various Persian kings. Either the compiler had a particular scheme in mind which happened to be wrong, or he had no idea of when the kings reigned and did not really care. In the former case, the compiler could have been trying to give authenticity to the events but simply got them wrong. In the latter case, however, the chronological data have a function other than dating events; that is, they have an ideological function in which they aim to convey a particular message about events.

Ezra 1:1: Cyrus, year 1
   3:1: month 7, year 1 (of return)
   3:4: Feast of Tabernacles (month 7, days 15–22)
   3:6: month 7, day 1 (altar begins to be used)
   3:8: year 2 (of return), month 2
   4:5: all years of Cyrus until Darius of Persia
   4:6: reign of Ahasuerus (Xerxes?)
   4:6: time of Artaxerxes
   4:23: Artaxerxes
   4:24: Darius, year 2 (work on temple stops until then)
   (5:13: Cyrus, year 1 [order to rebuild temple])
   (6:3: Cyrus, year 1 [order to rebuild temple])
   6:14: temple completed under Cyrus, Darius, Artaxerxes
   6:15: Darius, year 6, month 12, day 3 (temple finished)
   6:19: month 1, day 14 (Passover celebrated)
   (7:8: Artaxerxes, year 7, month 5 [arrived in Jerusalem])
   7:9: Artaxerxes, year 7, month 1, day 1 (journey began)
   7:9: Artaxerxes, year 7, month 5, day 1 (arrived in Jerusalem)
   8:31: month 1, day 12 (set out for Jerusalem from Ahava River)
   10:9: month 9, day 20 (people assemble in Jerusalem)

10:16: month 10, day 1 (task of investigation begins)
10:17: month 1, day 1 (task of investigation ends)

Neh. 1:1: (Artaxerxes) year 20, month (9) Kislev
  2:1: Artaxerxes, year 20, month (1) Nisan
  5:14: Artaxerxes, year 20 to year 32
  6:15: wall finished on day 25, month (6) Elul
  8:1: month 7
  8:2: month 7, day 1
  8:13–18: month 7 (days 15–22: Feast of Tabernacles kept)
  9:1: (month 7), day 24
  13:6: Artaxerxes, year 32

Apart from the fact that the chronology in relationship to the Persian kings is sometimes nonsense, the chronology in Ezra is very interesting in showing a sequence of events according to months and years. That is, if one ignores the years in relationship to the reigns of kings and looks only at the numbers of the years, months, and days, an interesting sequence takes place. The year numbers are progressive, moving from the first year (of Cyrus), to second year (of Darius), on to the seventh year (of Artaxerxes), and ending with the twentieth and thirty-second years (of Artaxerxes). It is clear that any attention to Persian chronology would show that a gap of many decades separates Ezra 6 from Ezra 7, yet it moves smoothly from year 6 to year 7 with no indication that the one did not take place shortly after the other. Particular attention is paid to festivals, and the majority of months mentioned are those with one or more holy days in them (months 1 and 7 are especially frequent). A full study of chronology is beyond my purpose, but it is another indication of the unity of the two books.

There is no doubt that with regard to content, there is a progression of narrative in the books which delivers a consistent theological message. Although this could be dealt with under this section on structure, it would probably be better to deal with it under a section on the theological message. This leads us naturally to the next section.

Theological themes and message

Eskenazi (1988: 40–42) has pointed to three major themes in the two books which she sees as structural: (1) the centrality of the community as a whole accompanied by a shift away from the actions of the 'great men'; (2) the expansion of the house of God to encompass not just the temple but also the city as a whole; and (3) the centrality of written texts as the source of authority. All three themes are very much in evidence in various parts of the book. For example, as was noted in chapter 3 above the dedication of the wall (Neh. 12:27–43) takes on the trappings of a ceremony of sanctification, much as the dedication of the temple (Ezra 6:15–17). As will be pointed out in the next section, the first theme is evident in Ezra 1–6; however, it does not fit so well in other parts of the books, especially Neh. 1–6. But even without accepting Eskenazi's assertion that the themes are consistently present in all sections, one can say that a number of important common motifs are still clear.

A theme central to both books is the return of people from the 'exile'. They came even from the Mesopotamian administrative centre of Babylon to rebuild or restore things in Jerusalem. Joshua and Zerubbabel are presented as leading the first returnees and thus formally ending the exile (Ezra 1–6). In the case of Ezra he restores the law and metaphorically rebuilds proper worship. Nehemiah came with another building project, the repair of the walls, which allowed the Jewish state to have its identity and defend itself from enemies. In each case it is the Persian king himself who issues a decree authorizing and even commanding the Jewish expedition, and he makes provision for it with a degree of generosity undreamt of.

Another theme is the threat to the community by 'foreigners' or 'peoples of the land'. It first surfaces with the building of the temple (Ezra 4–6); it comes in the form of a threat through intermarriage with 'foreign wives' under Ezra (Ezra 9–10). In the case of Nehemiah his work is opposed by a coalition led by Sanballat, Tobiah, and Geshem, but the book also mentions the threat in the shape of intermarriage with the 'peoples of the land' (Neh. 9–10; 13:1–3, 23–31). The counter-theme is that only the returnees were true members of the community, the true Israelites; anyone who had not gone into captivity had no claim on the God, temple, and community of Judah.

An element central to the two books is the various lists. To the reader they may seem tedious and a disruption to the story, but they were plainly extremely important to the composition of the whole. Eskenazi emphasizes how they contribute to her first theme by creating a focus on the community away from the prominent individual leaders. This applies up to a point, depending on the particular section of the two books (though this happens in some cases more than others). However, they seem to me to make a significant contribution to Eskenazi's third theme, that of the centrality of written texts. They anchor the story in formal documents and make legitimation dependent on being written down in an official list. To be a part of Israel, one had to have an appropriate genealogy (Ezra 2:59–60//Neh. 7:61–62). Those who participated in the wall building self-evidently claimed some sort of debt from the rest of the community on behalf of themselves or their descendants (Neh. 3). The various groups of the people bound themselves to keep the law, including to remain pure from marriage with outsiders, laying themselves open to public ridicule or censure if they defaulted (Neh. 10). Where the people lived in Jerusalem or in the land entitled them to membership in the community (Ezra 2; Neh. 7, 11). Those who came up as part of the original immigration (or with later important leaders) would have had a special claim to being part of the community (Ezra 2; 8:1–14; Neh. 7; 12:1–25).

These various themes are an important contribution to the overall message of the book. The story the books of Ezra and Nehemiah together have to tell us is a simple one – one can hardly accuse the compiler of being overly subtle. The narrative progresses to a climax and then ends on what might seem an anti-climax but is actually a skilful additional message. By saying that the story is simple is not to suggest that there is only a single message or that the message does not have its complexity; rather, the message lies on the surface of the narrative.

The story is how God takes a people, defeated and exiled for their sins, and returns them to their land and creates a nation once again, a nation with a restored temple and cult. The achievement of this goal did not run smoothly; there were difficulties and setbacks caused by enemies who were labelled as 'foreigners', but by God's help (working through the Persian regime) they prevailed. In the next episode Ezra came with the law which is identified in context as the book of the law of Moses. A new problem had arisen, again caused by 'foreigners', in the form of unlawful marriages. This problem was also sorted out. In the final episode Nehemiah came to restore the city by repairing the wall and settling it with an adequate population. Again, he is opposed by enemies in the form of Sanballat, Tobiah, and Geshem – labelled by implication as foreigners. When the wall is finished, the law is read by Ezra and the Festival of Tabernacles celebrated. But the problem of the 'peoples of the land' still continues and ends in a pledge of the people; only then is the wall dedicated. In the last chapter of the book the threat from the surrounding peoples, indirectly by intermarriage and more directly by deliberate insinuation of themselves into the community and even the temple, warns of the need for eternal vigilance.

This is the message in a nutshell; there are several strands to it: God's providence, the Persian empire as an instrument in God's hands, the importance of the temple and cult, the continual threat to the nation and religious community by the surrounding peoples. The message is blatant and, consequently, quite effective.

Ezra and Nehemiah as separate books

The present unity of Ezra and Nehemiah just described is an editorial unity. It has been created by a compiler taking separate traditions and putting them together with some care and intelligence to effect a whole. Curiously, some of the elements which unite the books are also some of the indicators of a secondary unity rather than of a single literary creation from the beginning.

First, there is a clear indication of the use of diverse material. Some of this material may be seen only as sources used by an author, but some of the material breaks the narrative in such a way that it is difficult to think of an author creating a single literary unit from the beginning. The main list of returnees (Ezra 2; Neh. 7) is the sort of thing that an author might use with little change. However, Nehemiah 10–12 contains a number of different lists which do not always fit easily together. These lists are also only tangential to the narrative as such. The book of Ezra forms a somewhat coherent narrative with two main parts, the initial return and rebuilding of the temple (Ezra 1–6) and the mission of Ezra (7–10). The same is not true with Nehemiah. The first four chapters form a narrative about events leading up to and surrounding the repair of the walls. In Neh. 5 Nehemiah is himself the principal character but the events are not clearly dated and have nothing to do with the repair of the wall.

Nehemiah 6 goes together with Neh. 1–4 to complete the narrative about the wall, but this is not followed by the dedication which one might expect. Instead there is a reading of the law (Neh. 8), a community repentance and oath about intermarriage and obedience to the law (Neh. 9–10), and a series of lists of various types (Neh. 11:1–12:26). Only then is the ceremony of dedication described (Neh. 12:27–43). Another couple of miscellaneous sections occur (Neh. 12:44–13:3). A narrative of sorts resumes in Neh. 13:4, but the various episodes which follow have the feel of diverse examples to illustrate Nehemiah's activities without really giving a coherent narrative (13:4–31). The chronological relationship between them is uncertain, and we have no way of knowing whether they relate directly to each other. The diversity of the material in the book of Nehemiah is thus very evident.

Second, by and large the characters of Ezra do not occur in Nehemiah, and vice versa. Because Ezra 1–6 sets itself much earlier than Nehemiah, we would not expect any overlap. Whether there should be any overlap between Ezra 7–10 and Nehemiah depends on when one dates the activities of Ezra and Nehemiah. It is almost universally agreed that Nehemiah's work is to be dated to the time of Artaxerxes I (465–424 BCE) (a rare exception to this consensus is Saley 1978; for criticisms, cf. Grabbe 1992a: 88–89). If Ezra is dated to the time of Artaxerxes II, their period in Jerusalem would not have overlapped. However, the book of Nehemiah explicitly puts some of the activities of Ezra and Nehemiah together, specifically in Neh. 8:9 and 12:36. Yet these passages are also evidence that the traditions have been brought together artificially. Neh. 8 does not mention Nehemiah except in this one verse, and the grammar of the verse may indicate that the phrase 'Nehemiah the Tirshata (governor)' has been added to a verse which originally had only the singular 'Ezra the priest and scribe' (this explanation is queried by Eskenazi [1988: 98–99], however). Similarly, the two processions of Neh. 12 are parallel if Ezra is excluded; also it seems strange that even though Ezra is said to lead one of the groups, his name appears almost as an afterthought (12:36). The Ezra and Nehemiah traditions have been brought together in the present form of the two books, but the few connecting verses and the evidence of their editorial nature is clear testimony that the two traditions were originally separate.

Third, some of the common elements linking the two books look like doublets and are unlikely to have been included by an author creating the two books as a new composition. The most obvious are the common lists in Ezra 2 and Neh. 7. Although they serve to connect the two books in their present form, is it likely that an author would have included the same long list, word for word, at two separate points in his work? But even if he did, why include two slightly different versions? The structuralist model used by Eskenazi uses the two lists as an *inclusio* (1988: 88–93), as noted above; however, the logical place for the first list is directly after Ezra 1:4, whereas it is delayed until Ezra 2. In any case, the structuralist model only describes its function in the present combined books, not its origin. It seems to me that a more likely explanation is that the list (in two slightly different forms) found its way into originally separate traditions and was left by the compiler when the two books were brought together.

Similarly, the problem with mixed marriages appears in both Ezra 9–10 and Neh. 9–10. These are dated as being only a few years apart; however, Ezra is absent in Neh. 9–10. The two accounts thus appear to be two versions of the same event. Other references to mixed marriages occur in Neh. 13:1–3 (though Nehemiah is absent) and 13:23–27; this seems strange for a unified composition. On the other hand, a compiler might be reluctant to abandon an available tradition even if it looked somewhat similar to another, especially if it was not clearly the same one.

Fourth, 1 Esdras is a more logical arrangement of material relating to Ezra. If it represents to a large degree the Ezra tradition before it was incorporated into Ezra-Nehemiah, as will be argued below, it demonstrates that Ezra-Nehemiah was created by dividing the Ezra material between the two books.

Fifth, several common themes go through both Ezra and Nehemiah; however, one of these at least indicates the editorial nature of these themes. This is the theme of the community as the actor rather than individual leaders (cf. Eskenazi 1988: 40–41). The attempt to divert the emphasis away from the individual leaders and towards the community in Ezra has been well described by Sarah Japhet (1982, 1983). This also applies to portions of Nehemiah, in particular 9–10 in which the issue of mixed marriages is handled by the community, in 11 with the population of Jerusalem, and in 12 with the dedication of the wall. Yet in Neh. 1–7, 13 there can be no question that Nehemiah dominates everything. The de-emphasis on the leaders in Ezra 1–6, and to a considerable extent in Ezra 7–10, is absent from those sections of Nehemiah taken from the NM. (Eskenazi's argument that the compiler also attempts to de-emphasize Nehemiah and give the people more prominence [1988: 79–83] only indicates, if so, how unsuccessful the attempt was.) Furthermore, it seems clear that the endeavour to de-emphasize the Jewish leaders is an editiorial feature. The original tradition is likely to have given greater emphasis to them, as 1 Esdras indicates (cf. Eskenazi 1988: 170–74).

There is no doubt that the present book of Ezra-Nehemiah is a compilation of a number of originally separate traditions. The unity of the book is an editorial unity. It is a unity created with a good deal of dexterity, and it is perfectly legitimate to read the two books together as a unity. On the other hand, it is also perfectly legitimate to go behind the editor and to look at and interpret the traditions separately. Because the books have traditionally been read together does not mean that we must always do so. I cannot accept that 'the transmitted unity take [sic] precedence in the interpretation' (Eskenazi 1988: 13). Some other scholars have also taken the line that a unitarian reading is unnecessary. Both James Vander-Kam (1992) and David Kraemer (1993) have addressed the question, apparently independently, and have emphasized that Ezra and Nehemiah were separate compositions. They have both made well the general point of different emphases in the two books, and VanderKam has noted linguistic differences. They both also give some necessary correctives to Eskenazi's thesis. For example, Kraemer points out that her argument that the first section of Nehemiah describes the expansion of the 'house of God' to include all of Jerusalem goes contrary to Neh. 5:2 and 6:5 which make the 'house of God' not Jerusalem but *in* Jerusalem (Kraemer 1993: 75). VanderKam criticizes her attempts to extend certain themes cutting through Ezra into Nehemiah.

However, I think Kraemer's discussion makes the mistake of pushing the contrast between the two books too far and thus in the end considerably weakens his argument. For example, he states that 'the Temple, though possibly in disrepair, is ignored' (1993: 91) and speaks of the 'almost complete neglect of the Temple and sacrifice' (1993: 89). This is simply absurd. The priesthood and the maintenance of the temple and cult is the subject of a number of passages in Nehemiah: the daily (*tāmîd*) offering (10:34), the wood offering (10:35, mentioned for the first time in the Bible), the priestly dues (10:36–40), sacrifices at the dedication of the wall (12:43), the re-organization of priestly dues (12:44–47), the issue of support for the Levites (13:10–14), organization of the cultic personnel, etc. (13:29–30). The priests are called on to administer the oath about releasing debtors (5:12–13). The priests, Levites, and other cultic personnel form a conspicuous part of the group repairing the wall (Neh. 3) and feature prominently in a number of lists (7:39–60; 9:4–5; 10:2–14; 11:3, 10–23; 12:1–26) and in the dedication of the wall (12:27–42).

Kraemer has made the mistake of assuming that, because they do not have the same emphasis as in parts of Ezra, they are therefore ignored; on the contrary, their place is recognized and assumed. Nehemiah, especially in the NM, has his mind focused on things other than the temple, but the book of Nehemiah hardly ignores the priests and temple. Part of the problem is evoking the old opposition of priestly versus lay and priest versus scribe. Such a dichotomy often represents modern concerns rather than a careful study of ancient society. Priests themselves were concerned with the written tradition (cf. Grabbe 1995: 65, 170), scribes were often from the priests or Levites, and in the temple-centred religion of Israel and Judah (cf. Grabbe 1992a: 437–41) the place of priests was taken for granted until the destruction of the temple.

Kraemer has pointed out a difference in perspective between the traditions about Ezra in the book of Ezra and those in Neh. 8. He notes that the temple and sacrifices are emphasized in Ezra whereas at the celebration of Sukkot in Neh. 8 nothing is said about sacrifices. This is an interesting difference in emphasis and illustrates, once again, the many discrepancies in detail between the various parts of the books. Nevertheless, this would not suggest that Neh. 8 is to be separated from the Ezra tradition of Ezra 7–10 as Kraemer suggests ('the accounts of Ezra in the book of Ezra and in Nehemiah differ radically in their pictures of Ezra and his purported activities' [1993: 80–81]). Both Ezra 7 and Neh. 8 make Ezra both a priest *and* a scribe, and in both contexts he has the law (*dat, tôrāh*). As a priest he possesses the Torah, not just as a scribe. The emphasis on the temple in Ezra 7–10, noted by Kraemer, gives one aspect of Ezra, primarily his association with the cult, while Neh. 8 emphasizes his activity with the Torah which is both a priestly and a scribal function. Neither passage alone does justice to his titles. Yet it is also interesting that in Ezra he never actually *acts* as a priest, and Ezra 9–10 are taken up not with the cult but with the matter of inter-marriage which is a violation of 'the commandments' of Torah (9:10–14). The reaction is to pledge to be trembling 'at the commandment of our God' (*bĕmiṣwat 'ĕlōhênû*) and to let 'the Torah' be done (Ezra 10:3). Whatever the distinctions between Neh. 8 and Ezra 7–10, they are not sufficient to invalidate the view that they were both once part of a united Ezra tradition.

This section can be concluded by noting once again (see p. 67 above) how Ezra and the first part of Nehemiah are parallel in content. They do not just form a unit but also form two separate but parallel units in their present form. This parallel structure was, of course, created when the two books were combined since an original unified composition is not likely to have been arranged in such a way.

Ezra	*Nehemiah*
1: royal commission (Cyrus edict)	1:1–2:9: royal commission (by Artaxerxes)
3: task of rebuilding (altar/temple)	2–3: task of rebuilding (repair of wall)
4–6: hindrance by 'enemies'	4, 6: hindrance by 'enemies'
6: work completed with God's help	6: work completed with God's help
7–8: Ezra and the law	8: Ezra and the law
9–10: threat from intermarriage	9–10: threat from intermarriage
10: resolution by public pledge	10: resolution by public pledge

Other sections of Nehemiah are also parallel, even though the parallels do not fit the neat scheme just given:

Ezra	*Nehemiah*
2: list of returnees	7: list of returnees
2: list of returnees	11:1–12:26: list of returnees
6:16–17: dedication of temple	12:27–43: dedication of wall
6:18: organization of priests/Levites	12:44–47: organization of priestly/Levitical dues
9–10: mixed marriages/threats from 'foreigners'/'peoples of the land'	13: mixed marriages/threats from 'foreigners'/'peoples of the land'

The traditions in the book of Ezra

Up to now the focus has been on Ezra and Nehemiah as separate units, but this is not the whole story. The book of Ezra itself also incorporates two stories, even if in an overall sense they constitute a single narrative. The first is found in Ezra 1–6 and concerns the initial rebuilding of the temple. To a large extent it can be called a Zerubbabel-Joshua tradition, since they are the leaders in the work of rebuilding (even though they disappear in Ezra 6 and are not mentioned in the final stage of rebuilding and dedication of the new temple; however, Zerubbabel is mentioned in the parallel section in 1 Esdras [6:26, 28]). For convenience the term 'Zerubbabel-Joshua tradition' will be used for the basic tradition of rebuilding in Ezra 1–6. The other tradition is the 'Ezra tradition' proper, that relating to the person of Ezra, in Ezra 7–10. These have been welded together in the final form of the book of Ezra, yet this unity is as much editorial as that of the whole of the Hebrew Ezra-Nehemiah.

There is no direct connection between the initial rebuilding and the coming of Ezra. To what extent the original compiler was aware of a chronological gap is not clear (see next section), but to a modern historian Ezra is at least sixty years after the supposed completion of the temple, and possibly well over a century later. The parallels between Ezra 1–6 and 7–10 are rather striking. Both sections begin with a royal decree by the reigning Persian emperor, the Cyrus edict (in the first episode) and the Artaxerxes *firman* (in the second). Both decrees envisage a return of peoples, not just the leaders Zerubbabel and Joshua or Ezra. In both instances, a good deal of stress is placed on priests and Levites. In the case of Ezra, he makes a point of enlisting Levites when he finds he has none (Ezra 8:15–20; both priests and Levites according to 1 Esdras 8:42). Both traditions have a gift of temple vessels as a part of the return, even though it makes little sense in relation to Ezra (Ezra 1:7–11; 7:19; 8:25–34). In both cases, a difficulty is encountered which has to be sorted out with the help of God. The two traditions end somewhat differently in the present Ezra-Nehemiah, but a greater parallel to Ezra 6 can be found in 1 Esdras 9:37–55 where the downbeat incident of the mixed marriages is followed by a reading of the law and the celebration of the Feast of Tabernacles.

When one compares the Zerubbabel-Joshua story with the Ezra story, one looks suspiciously similar to the other in certain respects. If we accept Ezra 1–6 for what it says, some aspects of Ezra 7–10 are puzzling. Ezra almost seems to be coming to an empty Jerusalem with a non-functioning cult which he needs to set up and get going. The story does not quite say this, because it clearly follows after what has happened in Ezra 1–6. But then Ezra's mission becomes a puzzle. Granted, Ezra 7 focuses on Ezra as scribe and priest and his bringing of the 'law that is in his hand'. But when he makes his journey, he brings Israelites, priests, and Levites. He also brings much wealth and temple vessels. The question in all this is, *why*? The temple had been rebuilt at least six decades earlier and had been functioning ever since – with plenty of priests, Levites, and temple servants. Temple vessels had been returned for its service. Settlers from Judah and Benjamin had also come many years before to settle Jerusalem and the surrounding area. Ezra's mission seems unnecessary. The only immediate aspect which seems to be justified is the law he is supposed to bring. But what is this law? The people who came under Cyrus (and Darius) seem to have been able to undertake the temple cult and celebrate the Festival of Passover and Unleavened Bread (Ezra 6:19–22). So what law did they lack? Even Ezra's law looks superfluous!

The impression which strikes the reader is that Ezra seems almost to be the founder of the new order. With a few small changes to the text, Ezra would be coming to a Jerusalem in which there was no functioning cult or perhaps not even any settlers. Was that the original form of the story? If we compare the present Ezra story with other Ezra traditions, it would not be surprising to find a version in which Ezra, rather than Joshua and Zerubbabel, rebuilt the temple, much as Nehemiah rebuilds the temple in some of the Nehemiah traditions (2 Macc. 1:18). Once the Joshua-Zerubbabel tradition was attached to the Ezra tradition, alterations would have had to be made to integrate the two stories. Yet such integration is not usually complete, and some of the old message peeps through. One suspects that this is what has happened with the Ezra tradition in the present book.

Even with the alterations made by combining the traditions, there is still a clear parallel in content of the two. A common development of the narrative is found in both the Joshua-Zerubbabel and the Ezra traditions, especially when one includes Nehemiah 8 with the reading of the law and the celebration of Tabernacles:

1: decree of Cyrus	7: decree of Artaxerxes
1: delivery of wealth/temple vessels	8: delivery of wealth/ temple vessels
2: list of immigrants	8: list of immigrants
3: sacrifices offered	8: sacrifices offered
4: foreigners raise opposition	9: problem because of foreigners
6: opposition overcome	10: problem resolved
6: temple completed	Neh. 8: mission completed (law read)
6: Tabernacles celebrated	8: Tabernacles celebrated

Relationship of 1 Esdras to the Hebrew Ezra-Nehemiah

The relationship of 1 Esdras to the Hebrew Ezra and Nehemiah has long been a puzzle (cf. the survey of scholarly opinion in Pohlmann 1970: 14–26). The study of 1 Esdras in chapter 4 above was not intended to resolve the major problems relating to that book, but it was able to come to several conclusions which bear on our understanding of the development of the Ezra and Nehemiah traditions.

It is evident from a superficial study that 1 Esdras is closely related to sections of Ezra and Nehemiah, having an almost word-for-word correspondence for most sections. The presence of occasional differences, or of the long section on the contest of the guards (3–4) which has no counterpart, does not militate against that overall conclusion. Yet a comparison of 1 Esdras with the Greek translation of the Hebrew books, often known as Esdras B, shows the differences. Whereas Esdras B is clearly a fairly literal translation of a text the same as or very close to the present Hebrew Ezra and Nehemiah, 1 Esdras shows no literary or translation relationship to Esdras B. 1 Esdras seems the earlier translation whose translator in some cases was having to pioneer the choice of Greek vocabulary to render the words of the original. The Greek is more elegant and probably less literal than that of Esdras B. Although the text of the original was probably close to that of the Hebrew Ezra-Nehemiah, it seems to have differed from it at various points.

The close relationship between the text of 1 Esdras and the Hebrew Ezra-Nehemiah shows that there must be a literary relationship between the two and not just a relationship at the general level of common traditions. Either 1 Esdras was borrowed from Ezra-Nehemiah, Ezra-Nehemiah borrowed from 1 Esdras, or the two borrowed from a common third source.

The first possibility to consider is that 1 Esdras was created simply by editing the Hebrew Ezra-Nehemiah, cutting out all of Nehemiah except a portion of Neh. 8, prefacing it with 2 Chron. 35–36, and adding the story of the courtiers' contest (1 Esdras 3–4). This seems to be the view of some commentators (cf. Williamson 1977: 35–36; Blenkinsopp 1988: 71; Eskenazi 1988: 155–74). But why would someone do this? If the books of Ezra and Nehemiah were already a unit and already authoritative, why would someone go to the trouble of writing a partial account which more or less paralleled an existing account but was less complete? It might be argued that the Hebrew Ezra-Nehemiah was not yet authoritative and the creator of 1 Esdras was opposed to Nehemiah. Therefore, he felt free to redact Ezra-Nehemiah to fit his own views. The question then is: if he was opposed to Nehemiah, why use a source in which Nehemiah was prominent? Why not start with another source of the Ezra tradition? Furthermore, why include Neh. 8? Modern source criticism has concluded that Neh. 8 is indeed a part of the Ezra tradition, but why should we assume that an ancient author would have come to the same view? It seems to me that this option makes no sense and is, a priori, unlikely.

Eskenazi (1986) has argued that 1 Esdras is derived from the Hebrew Ezra-Nehemiah (and a bit of 2 Chronicles) on the analogy of Chronicles as a rewriting of 1 Samuel–2 Kings; in fact, according to her theory the author of 1 Esdras was also the author of 1–2 Chronicles. This would explain why a writer used an authoritative work to create something rather different. This thesis seems to me the most cogent of those arguing that 1 Esdras is derived from Ezra-Nehemiah. Nevertheless, it is not convincing. 1 Esdras' relationship to Ezra-Nehemiah is different from that of 1–2 Chronicles to Samuel-Kings. As usually explained, Chronicles rewrites Samuel-Kings to give his own emphasis to the deeds of the kings, focusing on the Judaean kings and generally ignoring the Israelite kings, all in aid of a particular theological message. But why would the writer of 1 Esdras ignore Nehemiah? This would be the equivalent of the books of Chronicles ignoring David or Hezekiah. And why would he take Neh. 8:1–13 from the book of Nehemiah but nothing else? This might make sense to a modern tradition critic, but why would it to an ancient writer?

It has long been argued that 1 Esdras is a fragment of the 'Chronicler', a work which once encompassed 1 and 2 Chronicles, as well as Ezra and perhaps eventually even part or all of Nehemiah (cf. Pohlmann 1970: 19–26 and the literature cited there). Is 1 Esdras then a fragment of the larger work of the Chronicler? Although this is possible, the arguments for it do not seem any more decisive than the opposite conclusion. A full examination of this view would require a good deal of space (see Pohlmann 1970 versus Williamson 1977: 12–36), but this also seems unlikely. The details of the argument are considered below, but 1 Esdras functions well as a self-contained unit. Of particular interest is the *inclusio* formed by the first and last chapters, 1 Esdras 1 and 9. The book begins with a significant Passover, the one celebrated by Josiah, which is said not to have been so celebrated since the days of Samuel the prophet, not by any of the Israelite kings (1 Esdras 1:18–19, a rather strange statement since Hezekiah only a century earlier had celebrated the Passover in a way not done since the days of Solomon [2 Chron. 30:26]). The book then ends with the celebration of a festival (the Feast of Trumpets? [Lev. 23:23–25]) during which Ezra reads the law (1 Esdras 9:37–55). If the book originally included the rest of what we now find in Neh. 8 (see below), the *inclusio* would be even more striking, because it would end with the last festival of the year, the Feast of Tabernacles, just as it began with the first festival of the year, the Passover in 1 Esdras 1.

Another possibility is that 1 Esdras is simply a version of the Ezra tradition which served as a source for the present Hebrew of Ezra (and Neh. 8). That is, if 1 Esdras did not use Ezra, then it might be the other way round. Several arguments have been adduced (albeit in more than one context) which may be relevant here. First, it is often said that the beginning and ending of the book show that it is a fragment of a larger work. It begins with the conjunction 'and' (Greek *kai* which probably translated the Hebrew *wĕ-*), suggesting that something preceded it. However, a few Hebrew books begin with *wĕ-* even though nothing preceded them (e.g. Ruth and Esther). Also, if 1 Esdras was created by prefacing the Ezra tradition with 1 Chron. 35–36 (see below), the book would naturally begin with 'and' because 1 Chron. 35:1 begins with 'and'.

More difficult is the last verse of the book which states, 'And they came together' (1 Esdras 9:55), apparently corresponding to the first few words of Neh. 8:13 which states, 'And in the second day the heads of families of all people, the priests, the Levites gathered themselves to Ezra . . .'. It does indeed look as if the text has been cut off here. However, it could easily be that the lost text continued no further than the present Neh. 8:18. It would make a good deal of sense that the celebration of the Feast of Tabernacles was once included in the book. Neh. 8:13–18 is a part of the Ezra tradition and would naturally find a place in 1 Esdras. Rather than 1 Esdras being a 'fragment', therefore, it is simply a text which had somehow lost its last few verses somewhere in early history.

Second, it has been argued that the text used by 1 Esdras presupposes a text in which Nehemiah 7 and 8 were already combined (Williamson 1977: 32–35). If so, this would argue that 1 Esdras was excerpted from the combined book Ezra-Nehemiah. The reason for saying that Neh. 7 and 8 were already combined lies in the fact that Neh. 7:72–8:1 (//1 Esdras 9:37–38) is very similar to Ezra 2:70–3:1 (//1 Esdras 5:45–46). This suggests that when the list in one text was copied into the other, the final verses were also copied with the list as if a part of it. Some argue that the original list was in Ezra 2 and was subsequently copied into Nehemiah 8 (e.g. Mowinckel 1964a: 31; Pohlmann 1970: 57–64), while others argue that the original list was in Nehemiah 8 and was then copied into Ezra 2 (Williamson 1985: 29–30). I believe that either the list was copied into both Ezra 2 and Neh. 8 from a common source or that Ezra 2 is the original, but in either case, the conclusions about Nehemiah 7 and 8 would still pertain. That is, it assumes that 1 Esdras had a text before it with the list in two places and then dropped the one that corresponded to Neh. 7 but retained the duplicated verse.

A variety of explanations have been given to account for this phenomenon, usually assuming a textual corruption (Mowinckel 1964a: 21–25; Pohlmann 1970: 66–71; cf. Williamson 1977: 32–35). Although it is an old assumption that the statement in question is a duplicate copied with the list (Mowinckel 1964a: 40–45), this is not a necessary conclusion. The two verses are indeed similar, but each is appropriate in its context in 1 Esdras. 1 Esdras 5:45 serves not only as a conclusion to the list of returnees and their places of settlement but also introduces the episode of erecting the altar at the beginning of the 7th month which makes possible the celebration of the Festival of Tabernacles (5:46–52).

1 Esdras 5:45–46	*1 Esdras 9:37–38*
[45]καὶ κατῳκίσθησαν	[37]καὶ κατῴκησαν
οἱ ἱερεῖς	οἱ ἱερεῖς
καὶ οἱ Λευῖται	καὶ οἱ Λευῖται
καὶ οἱ ἐκ τοῦ λαοῦ αὐτοῦ	καὶ οἱ ἐκ τοῦ Ἰσραὴλ
ἐν Ἰερουσαλὴμ	ἐν Ἰερουσαλὴμ
καὶ τῇ χώρᾳ,	καὶ τῇ χώρᾳ
οἵ τε ἱεροψάλται	—————
καί οἱ θυρωροὶ	—————
καί πᾶς Ἰσραὴλ	—————
ἐν ταῖς κώμαις αὐτῶν.	
[46]Ἐνστάντος δὲ	τῇ μουμηνίᾳ
τοῦ ἑβδόμου μηνὸς	τοῦ ἑβδόμου μηνὸς
καί οἴντων	– καὶ
τῶν υἱῶν Ἰσραὴλ	οἱ υἱοὶ Ἰσραὴλ
ἑκάστου ἐν τοῖς ἰδίοις	ἐν ταῖς κατοικίαις αὐτῶν –
συνήχθησαν	[38]καὶ συνήχθησαν πᾶν
ὁμοθυμαδὸν	τὸ πλῆθος ὁμοθυμαδὸν
εἰς τὸ εὐρύχωρον	ἐπὶ τὸ εὐρύχωρον
τοῦ πρώτου πυλῶνος τοῦ	τοῦ πρὸς ἀνατολῇ τοῦ
πρὸς τῇ ἀνατολῇ.	ἱεροῦ πυλῶνος

And the priests and the Levites and some of *his people* settled in Jerusalem and in the countryside; also the temple singers and the gatekeepers and all Israel in their villages. But *when arrived* the seventh month and were the sons of Israel each in (their) own (places), they came together in the plaza in front of the east gate.	And the priests and the Levites and some of *Israel* settled in Jerusalem and in the countryside. ⎯ ⎯ ⎯ ⎯ *In the new moon* of the seventh month – and the sons of Israel (were) in their dwellings – and they all came together in the plaza in front of the east gate.

The same applies to 1 Esdras 9:37–38. Recognizing that the contents of Neh. 8 are a part of the Ezra tradition suggests that some sort of linking passage had to connect its contents with the episode of the mixed marriages. We would hardly expect Ezra 10:44 (//1 Esdras 9:36) to be followed immediately by Neh. 8:1 (//1 Esdras 9:38); a link is demanded. The examination relating to the mixed marriages is completed, the 'sinners' are listed, and the suffering of the wives and children is generously mentioned. Then the statement is made that 'the priests, the Levites, and some of the Israelites were living in Jerusalem and in the countryside' and on the 1st day of the 7th month – with the Israelites in their habitations – all the people gathered in Jerusalem in front of the temple.

The reference to the 7th month in both contexts is natural (especially if 1 Esdras 9 originally ended with the Festival of Tabernacles, as Neh. 8 does). The statement in 1 Esdras 9:37 fits reasonably well in the context. What we do not know is how the compiler of 1 Esdras chose that particular link, if he contributed it, or the state of the tradition on which he drew. What we do know is that despite some similarities, there are some important differences between the two verses which militate against one being a borrowing of the other (underlined above, though many other minor differences are not indicated). Therefore, what we need not assume is that the author of 1 Esdras drew on a tradition which included a list of settlers preceding the episode on reading the law, as currently in Neh. 7–8. It may be that some of the suggestions about how the passage developed, as it now stands in the text of 1 Esdras, are correct, but there is much we do not know about the state of the original tradition.

I therefore conclude that 1 Esdras represents in some fashion an earlier stage of the Zerubbabel-Joshua and the Ezra traditions from which the compiler of the Hebrew Ezra-Nehemiah drew. However, it seems to me that 1 Esdras was not the specific source used but itself is also a development of that source. The tradition picked up by the Hebrew Ezra-Nehemiah apparently did not have the story of the guards' contest. I can see no reason why this story would have been omitted in the Hebrew Ezra, if it was extant in the source, so it was probably added at a later date to 1 Esdras. Similarly, 1 Esdras 1 which parallels 2 Chron. 35–36 could well have been added to give a more suitable introduction to the Ezra tradition. It seems to have been a simple copying out of 2 Chron. 35–36 with some minor changes. If so, the Ezra tradition used by the compiler of the Hebrew Ezra-Nehemiah was probably close to that now found in 1 Esdras 2, 5–9. The development of the traditions as I see them are diagrammed below in the last section of the chapter.

Eskenazi (1988: 170–74) has noted how 1 Esdras puts particular emphasis on Zerubbabel as a person and leader, in contrast to Ezra which tends to put more emphasis on the community. This conclusion seems to be valid, but it does not demonstrate that Ezra is more original than 1 Esdras. On the contrary, the community emphasis looks editorial; the original tradition was likely to have put particular emphasis on the 'heroic' qualities of Zerubbabel, in which case the compiler of Ezra-Nehemiah tried to de-emphasize Zerubbabel by certain editorial changes (as argued by Japhet 1982, 1983).

Place of other Ezra and Nehemiah traditions

The relationship of the other Ezra and Nehemiah traditions to the Hebrew Ezra-Nehemiah and 1 Esdras is a complex question. We cannot assume that a literary relationship exists in every case, but we also have to recognize where it is possible or even quite certain. An unravelling of the relationships could be very helpful in understanding the origin and development of the traditions.

Literary borrowing is clearly evident in the case of Josephus. He has used 1 Esdras for his story of Ezra. Although it was his custom to rewrite his sources rather than quoting them word for word, he nevertheless followed the text of 1 Esdras quite closely for the most part but making some interesting changes. He omits certain sections which he regarded as inessential or tedious for his readers (e.g. 1 Esdras 1 on the reform of Josiah, which he had already described earlier; the settlement list in 5:1–45). The most important change he makes is that, having a knowledge of the sequence of Persian kings, he tries to correct the text of 1 Esdras to fit the historical data. Finally, he ends with the death of Ezra. Although a tradition about Ezra's death may have developed by this time, there is nothing in Josephus' account to indicate he had anything specific to use: his account looks simply like his own invention to fill out the story.

When it comes to Nehemiah, however, Josephus has not clearly drawn on the Hebrew Nehemiah (or its Greek translation). Much of the story parallels Neh. 1–6, but there is nothing to correspond to Neh. 5 and many details are different, details which seem not just to be adjustments to the story made by Josephus himself. Whether Josephus is drawing on a written or oral source is not clear. The ultimate origin of his account could be the NM, but his immediate source was probably not the NM as such but a tradition which had developed from it. Some of the differences from the Hebrew Nehemiah could have been Josephus' own changes (e.g. Xerxes as the king rather than Artaxerxes), but the variety of differences (catalogued in chapter 4 above) suggests that they were already in Josephus' source. However, he may have invented the statement about Nehemiah's death as he probably did the one about Ezra's.

None of the other Ezra or Nehemiah traditions is clearly based on the Hebrew Ezra-Nehemiah or 1 Esdras. The oldest is that in Ben Sira who mentions Joshua and Zerubbabel and also Nehemiah. His statement is only brief and there are textual problems, which makes it difficult to determine its origin. From the little said it is theoretically possible that he took the information from the Hebrew Ezra-Nehemiah. This seems extremely unlikely. Ben Sira is citing the heroes of Israel, and he covers all the main ones known from the biblical text. The only two omitted are Daniel and Ezra. Although a Daniel tradition was almost certainly already around by his time, it was naturally not in the form of our book of Daniel (since Dan. 7–12 could not have been written until after 168 BCE). Any Daniel traditions known to Ben Sira would not be considered authoritative, but we have no reason to assume he knew such traditions. However, it is extremely unlikely that he knew the canonical Ezra-Nehemiah and then deliberately omitted Ezra. He missed no major figure in the Deuteronomistic History (Genesis–2 Kings) or in the Chronicler's History except Ezra; if he knew of Ezra in an authoritative tradition, he would have included Ezra. On the other hand, he would not have taken his information about Joshua, Zerubbabel, and Nehemiah from the Hebrew Ezra-Nehemiah if he had not considered it an authoritative source. The only logical conclusion is that he used some other source for his information.

The Nehemiah story in 2 Macc. 1:18–2:13 represents a considerable development from any known source. The writer seems unlikely to have used the Hebrew Ezra-Nehemiah as his origin; indeed, it goes quite contrary to the picture in Ezra-Nehemiah which makes Joshua and Zerubbabel the founders of the altar and the builders of the temple. One cannot imagine that the version in 2 Maccabees could have been derived from the canonical Ezra-Nehemiah, even allowing for a long period of development. Perhaps it ultimately goes back to the NM but with a considerable period of evolution. As found in 2 Maccabees, it looks like the recording of an oral tradition.

The image of Ezra in 4 Ezra also seems to derive from an Ezra tradition somewhat different from that in Ezra-Nehemiah. Of course, the author of 4 Ezra has used a traditional figure as a vehicle for his own message, but some elements look as if they came with the figure and are not just the author's creation. Ezra is placed in the period of the exile, thirty years after the fall of Jerusalem (4 Ezra 3:1). This date is widely believed to be a key to the actual author's time (i.e. thirty years after the fall of the Second Temple in 70 CE), and this probably is its origin, but the apocalypticist may have known an Ezra tradition which put him close to the fall of Jerusalem rather than more than a century later. The account of how Ezra restored the law and wrote another seventy esoteric books in 4 Ezra 14 does not seem to be simply adapted from either the Hebrew Ezra or 1 Esdras. It looks like a tradition which the author of 4 Ezra has taken over for his own use, but also a tradition which made Ezra more than just an interpreter of the law. The idea that the law had been lost and needed to be revealed again is not one easily taken from the two books relating to Ezra that we find in the canonical or deutero-canonical books. It looks like an independent Ezra tradition with a long history.

The picture we are left with is that there were once three complexes of tradition: the Joshua-Zerubbabel tradition, the Ezra tradition, and the Nehemiah tradition. There were certain parallels between these three traditions. They developed and interrelated in different ways as time went on, but from the information available the most likely conclusion is that they were once separate and only later brought together in various forms.

Summary and conclusions

This chapter has attempted to bring together some of the results of the studies in chapters 2–4 and also consider them in a wider context to ask about literary structure and development of tradition. The books of Ezra and Nehemiah taken as a single literary unit is the situation in the Hebrew Bible. This traditional reading is supported by a number of elements which unite the two books, including a common literary structure and major themes which cut across both books, and the presence of Ezra in both. A recent structuralist model (Eskenazi 1988) has received considerable attention and, despite some weaknesses in detail, provides a reasonably convincing analysis of the overall unity of the Hebrew Ezra-Nehemiah. But arguments for this unity are not new, and other models based on content or other criteria have also been adduced for the two books to be read together.

Of particular importance is the presence of a number of themes running through the two books and a storyline which moves from Ezra 1 to Nehemiah 13. One theme is the return of the people from exile. This is especially apparent in Ezra 1–6 but is also present in Ezra 7–10 and in Nehemiah. The legitimate community is the one made up of those whose ancestors had been taken from the homeland and exiled to Babylonia. A counter-theme to this is the danger of 'foreigners'/'peoples of the land' to the newly formed community. This latter theme is perhaps one of the most consistent through the two books, being found as strongly in Nehemiah as it is in Ezra. A further theme is the providence of God in shepherding his people in forming a new nation with a restored temple and priesthood. Associated with this is the Persian empire as a tool in God's hand, with the Persian government generally acting as a supportive and benevolent agent for the Jewish religion. Another theme is the importance of written documents to the community, including the many tedious lists (especially in Nehemiah) whose significance has frequently been overlooked.

The narrative line found in Ezra-Nehemiah is also a seductive one. It tells the compelling story of how God takes a people, defeated and exiled for their sins, and returns them to their land and creates a new nation with a restored temple and cult. During the process there were difficulties and setbacks caused by enemies who were labelled as 'foreigners', but by God's help – using the Persian regime as his instrument – they prevailed. In the next episode Ezra came with the law which is identified in context as the book of the law of Moses. A new problem had arisen, again caused by 'foreigners' in the form of unlawful marriages, and had to be sorted out. In the final episode Nehemiah comes to restore the city by repairing the wall and settling it with an adequate population. He also is opposed by enemies in the form of Sanballat, Tobiah, and Geshem who are understood in context as foreigners. When the wall is finished, the law is read by Ezra and the Festival of Tabernacles celebrated. But the problem of the 'peoples of the land' still continues and ends in a pledge of the people; only then is the wall dedicated. In the last chapter of the book the threat from the surrounding peoples, by intermarriage or by actual infiltration of the community, warns of the need for eternal vigilance.

Despite these persuasive arguments for unity, there are many indications that this harmony has been achieved by careful editing, and numerous hints still extant in the text show the presence of disharmonies and clashes with an organic unity. This fact invited us to look further at the various elements which might have come together and been combined to achieve the final form of the Hebrew text.

It quickly becomes obvious that the first major division is between the two books. This is not a neat division because Nehemiah 8 is obviously a part of the Ezra tradition. The mention of Ezra in a couple of other places in Nehemiah (12:26, 36) and Nehemiah's name in Nehemiah 8 are easily explained as due to redactional activity. But apart from Nehemiah 8 the two books can easily be read independently. Ezra ends abruptly, but Nehemiah 8 rounds it off quite nicely. The book of Ezra itself contains two complexes of tradition, one surrounding Joshua and Zerubbabel in Ezra 1–6 and one surrounding Ezra in Ezra 7–10. Just as Ezra has a parallel structure to Nehemiah, so Ezra 1–6 has a number of parallels to Ezra 7–10. Therefore, the literary structures lead one to see three complexes of tradition (despite the gross structure which serves to create the unity of Ezra-Nehemiah), one relating to Joshua-Zerubbabel, one to Ezra, and one to Nehemiah.

Ezra	*Nehemiah*
1: royal commission (Cyrus edict)	1:1–2:9: royal commission (by Artaxerxes)

3: task of rebuilding (altar/ temple)	2–3: task of rebuilding (repair of wall)
4–6: hindrance by 'enemies'	4, 6: hindrance by 'enemies'
6: work completed with God's help	6: work completed with God's help
7–8: Ezra and the law	8: Ezra and the law
9–10: threat from intermarriage	9–10: threat from intermarriage
10: resolution by public pledge	10: resolution by public pledge

Other sections of Nehemiah are also parallel, even though the parallels do not fit the neat scheme just given:

2: list of returnees	7: list of returnees
2: list of returnees	11:1–12:26: list of returnees
6:16–17: dedication of temple	12:27–43: dedication of wall
6:18: organization of priests/ Levites	12:44–47: organization of priestly/Levitical dues
9–10: mixed marriages/threats from 'foreigners'/'peoples of the land'	13: mixed marriages/threats from 'foreigners'/'peoples of the land'

The parallels between the Joshua-Zerubbabel story and the Ezra story can be outlined as follows:

1: decree of Cyrus	7: decree of Artaxerxes
1: delivery of wealth/temple vessels	8: delivery of wealth/ temple vessels
2: list of immigrants	8: list of immigrants
3: sacrifices offered	8: sacrifices offered
4: foreigners raise opposition	9: problem because of foreigners
6: opposition overcome	10: problem resolved
6: temple completed	Neh. 8: mission completed (law read)
6: Tabernacles celebrated	8: Tabernacles celebrated

The parallels between the books of Ezra and Nehemiah are not complete, partly because the presence of a genuine writing by Nehemiah disrupts the stereotyping to some extent. Real life is not as neat and patterned as literature! However, a comparison of the Ezra story

with the Joshua-Zerubbabel and Nehemiah stories reveals a remarkable scenario: there are hints that the tradition once made Ezra the
refounder of the cult and temple after the exile. This picture had
to be subverted once it was combined with the Joshua-Zerubbabel
tradition which made those two individuals the rebuilders of the
temple and the restorers of the cult. Ezra followed in their wake and
his story must now presuppose their work, but aspects of the Ezra
tradition still suggest that he was the original restorer without
precedent.

The other Ezra and Nehemiah traditions confirm this conclusion.
We find separate traditions or partial combinations in some cases,
such as Joshua-Zerubbabel and Ezra (1 Esdras), Joshua-Zerubbabel
and Nehemiah (Ben Sira 49:11–13), Ezra alone (4 Ezra), Nehemiah
alone (2 Macc. 1:18–2:13). Josephus' version is possibly the easiest
to sort out. He used a version of 1 Esdras for his story of Joshua-
Zerubbabel and Ezra. As was his custom, he rewrote the text, making
minor alterations and omitting what he thought would not suit his
purpose. He also has the death of Ezra, but this is probably his own
inference. He then has a story about Nehemiah which is unlikely to
come from the canonical book of Nehemiah, suggesting that his
Nehemiah tradition was a separate one. Although it is parallel in
many ways to Nehemiah 1–6, it has some significant differences
(including the omission of Neh. 5) which suggests an independent
tradition that perhaps developed directly from the NM.

1 Esdras has been long debated, and several recent scholars have
argued that it is simply a secondary compilation from the Hebrew
2 Chronicles and Ezra-Nehemiah. I find this very unlikely, though
there is clearly a close relationship between 1 Esdras and the
Hebrew books. My conclusion was that an Ezra tradition lies at its
core, in 1 Esdras 2, 5–9. This tradition was picked up by the
compiler of Ezra-Nehemiah, with a portion split off to form Nehemiah 8. But the original tradition continued to develop on its own,
with chapters from 2 Chronicles and a story about the contest of the
guards being added at some point. Also, it seems that the ending was
lost; that ending probably extended at least to the celebration of
Tabernacles (as known in Neh. 8:13–18).

The proposed growth of the tradition can be diagrammed as
shown in Figure 5.1.

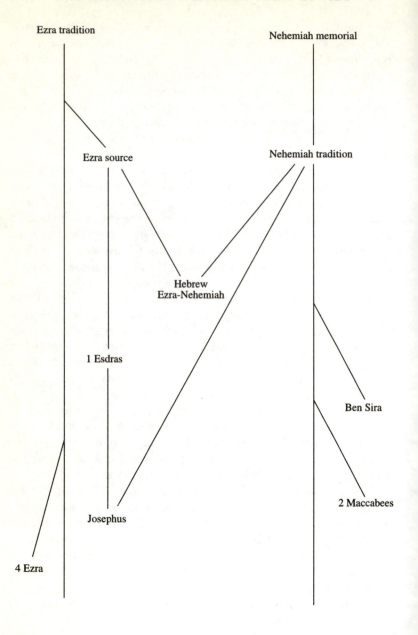

Figure 5.1

Part II

THE HISTORICAL QUESTION

The first section of the book focused on the question of the literary structure of the Hebrew Ezra and Nehemiah and the various other Ezra and Nehemiah traditions. It attempted to see how the literary versions were put together and how they related to one another. A close scrutiny was also given to matters of internal consistency, purpose, and message. These were all literary questions and could be undertaken regardless of the question of history or historicity, though at various points historical questions were raised with a cross-reference for further treatment. The purpose of this section of the book is now to address the questions of history and historicity. The literary analysis was necessary, nevertheless, as a foundation to discussing historical questions. In the chapters of this section, I apply the insights gained from the literary analysis along with data from other sources and the historical context to address the questions of historicity. Although there is some necessary overlap between the books of Ezra and Nehemiah (e.g. Ezra 2//Neh. 7), most questions relate to one book or the other; therefore, for convenience I generally take up the questions in the order of the text.

6

EZRA AND HISTORY

An analysis of Ezra-Nehemiah for historical purposes is quite different from that required for literary and theological purposes. The historical analysis must take into account the results of the literary and theological study, but the questions asked are different. A literary or theological investigation can be internal to the literature itself. It is concerned with what the literature says or implies. A historical study must go beyond this and ask about the relationship of the literature to external reality – to actual historical events. It must also make use of sources other than the literature, wherever they are extant. The aims of historical study and how they differ from those of literary and theological study have been discussed in chapter 1.

The problem of sources and ideological intent

The studies of Part I have shown that the Hebrew books of Ezra and Nehemiah and the Greek work of 1 Esdras are important theological works whose message is primarily an ideological one. Their literary structure is set out to advance this theological message. Whatever history they may contain is subordinated to telling the story of how God has acted on behalf of his people to show them mercy and further his own aims for them. A dispassionate description of events or a mere chronicle of what happened is clearly not the primary purpose of the author/editor. Any record of events is secondary to the theological clarification of what it all meant. Theological truth comes first in the story; the question is to what extent it has slanted, distorted, and supplanted historical truth.

This theological bias is an important factor in any study of history using the books of Ezra, Nehemiah, and 1 Esdras (the other Ezra/Nehemiah traditions are much briefer and harder to determine).

However well-intentioned the aim of the authors, they were not writing as historians. They were not exercising critical judgement in selecting their data as we would expect historians to do, but were using whatever advanced their ideological aim and were using it in ways which might go counter to good historical practice. They gave a version of events which suited their ideology, regardless of whether it would match the rigorous critical criteria required by historians. This inbuilt canalizing of the data cannot be taken at face value but must be detected and critically evaluated by the historian before the account is used to make any sort of historical reconstruction.

Any attempt to get at the historical data within the books must thus reckon with the theological and ideological bias of the author(s)/editor(s). But before the books become usable as sources, they must contain historical data in the first place. To determine whether they contain historical data we have to ask for the sources of the books in question. The historical value of the book is no greater than the sources used for its information. If the writer used good sources, the data in them may still be accessible despite the ideological purpose for which they have been used by the writer, but worthless sources remain worthless, however they have been used. A number of sources have been proposed, but they do not necessarily all stand up to scrutiny as trustworthy or even usable (Grabbe 1991). For Ezra 1–6, the sources seem to be the Cyrus edict (1:1–4), a list of temple vessels (1:9–11), a list of returnees (2:1–72), the prophetic books of Haggai and Zechariah, and several alleged Persian documents in Aramaic in 3–7 (Williamson 1983; cf. Williamson 1985: xxiii-xxiv). It has also been thought that some sort of 'Ezra memoir' lies behind Ezra 7–10. These sources will be looked at in the appropriate sections below.

Edict of Cyrus (1:1–4)

The most thorough study of the Hebrew edict of Cyrus which opens the Hebrew Ezra was done by E. J. Bickerman (1976). A number of recent commentators have accepted his arguments (e.g. Williamson 1985: 6–7, 11–14; Clines 1984: 36–39), but others have not been convinced (e.g. Galling 1964: 61–77; Blenkinsopp 1988: 74–76; Smith 1987: 78, 186 n. 16). The issues are the following.

First, Cyrus issued an edict at the beginning of his reign in which he allowed the 'exiled' divine images taken to Babylon to be returned to the native peoples and the peoples themselves to return to their homelands. A section of that edict reads as follows (ANET: 316):

> (As to the region) from . . . as far as Ashur and Susa, Agade, Eshnunna, the towns Zamban, Me-Turnu, Der as well as the region of the Gutians, I returned to (these) sacred cities on the other side of the Tigris, the sanctuaries of which have been ruins for a long time, the images which (used) to live therein and established for them permanent sanctuaries. I (also) gathered all their (former) inhabitants and returned (to them) their habitations. Furthermore, I resettled upon the command of Marduk, the great lord, all the gods of Sumer and Akkad whom Nabonidus has brought into Babylon (Šu.an.na^{ki}) to the anger of the lord of the gods, unharmed, in their (former) chapels, the places which make them happy.

A similar decree is related in the name of the god Sin (de Vaux 1971: 68–69). At first blush, this makes it plausible that Cyrus issued a decree on behalf of the Jews to allow them to return. It must be noted, however, that Cyrus' decree seems to have been a general decree, not one on behalf of a specific nation; in fact, nothing is said about the Jews or the other side of the Euphrates. The propagandistic nature of Cyrus' decrees has been made clear since Bickerman wrote (Kuhrt 1983). A more reliable source is the Babylonian Chronicles. One of these confirms that gods were returned, but only the Babylonian gods are specifically mentioned (*Nabonidus Chronicle* iii.21–22; quotation from Grayson 1975: 110):

> From the month Kislev to the month Adar the gods of Akkad which Nabonidus had brought down to Babylon returned to their places.

That Cyrus would have taken the trouble to issue a decree specifically on behalf of a small nation in the first year of his reign is not at all demonstrated by the parallels cited.

Second, Cyrus' decree is in Hebrew, whereas the normal scribal language of the Persian empire was Aramaic. We do find official texts in other languages (Akkadian, Elamite, Old Persian), but these were also languages central to the empire. Furthermore, a decree in Aramaic allowing the Jews to return is quoted in Ezra 6:3–5 (though there are also questions about its authenticity; see below). Bickerman (1976) suggests that 1:1–4 was an oral message and therefore in the language of the native peoples (Hebrew in this case), whereas 6:3–5 represents the official written decree. The only evidence offered is from the biblical text, however, and these are all examples which could easily be Jewish propaganda (e.g. Esther 1:22; 2:12; 8:9).

Third, the alleged decree, despite its short length, is full of biblical theology. The reference to a prophecy of Jeremiah in 1:1 may not be a part of the decree, though this is not certain. The decree refers specifically to the God of the Jews, namely Yhwh (even though he is also called 'the God of heaven'). Bickerman (103–4) defends even this theology, though others accepting the decree are more cautious (Williamson [1985: 9–10] admits this is probably the contribution of the editor). More suspect is the requirement that the local people (apparently even non-Jews) provide funds and provisions for anyone who wants to go to Jerusalem to build the temple (cf. Blenkinsopp 1988: 75–76). What is the likelihood that an official Persian decree would have such statements from Jewish theology? On the other hand, they are precisely what we would expect from a Jewish writer inventing a decree to support his theology (e.g. Williamson [1985: 16] sees an exodus motif here).

The detailed studies by Bickerman and others have answered the various objections to the authenticity of the Hebrew Cyrus decree; nevertheless, the question is not whether the objections can be answered or explained away but what is the most likely conclusion from the known data. The theological colouring of the decree, the fact that it is in Hebrew, the lack of a convincing parallel, and the fact that it so well fits the theological aim of the writer make it most likely that the decree is a creation of the author (or possibly another Jewish writer, from whom the writer took it, possibly in all innocence). The weight of the argument is against authenticity.

Lists of returnees

Since all the lists of Ezra-Nehemiah occur in Nehemiah except the list in Ezra 8 (including the duplicate of Ezra 2 in Nehemiah 7), these are all dealt with in chapter 7.

Aramaic Persian documents

The judgement above was that the Cyrus decree in 1:1–4 is most likely not an authentic document. There are a number of other documents quoted in Ezra 3–7, allegedly from the Persian administration, and these are all in Aramaic as we would expect of official documents. A slight query is raised by the fact that all but one of them are a part of an Aramaic narrative. One could ask why the narrative changes to Aramaic just to quote a Persian document. More like what might be expected is found in Ezra 7 in which the surrounding narrative is in Hebrew and only the alleged document is in Aramaic. This has been partly the basis of the argument that the writer of the narrative, whose language is Aramaic, has simply created the documents *a novo* when he felt the need for them (Torrey 1896; 1910).

It is difficult to believe that the writer of the narrative has created the documents, however, because in a number of cases they do not fit the narrative itself. In one instance, an introduction is given but no document is quoted (4:6). This is immediately followed by reference to a letter sent to Artaxerxes by Bishlam, Mithredat, and Tabeel (4:7), yet the letters quoted (4:8–22) relate to Rehum the commissioner and Shimshai the scribe. Also, as will be discussed below, the language of the documents sometimes differs from that of the surrounding narrative. Furthermore, these letters in the name of Artaxerxes are used to stop a work being built in the time of Cyrus, a strange invention for the writer of the narrative. Thus, the most likely situation is that the compiler actually had some alleged documents before him and made use of them, even when they did not fit very well.

Concluding that the writer had actual documents does not thereby demonstrate their authenticity. A range of issues must be taken into account. One of the most neutral of these is the question of language. Although our documentation of the ancient Semitic languages is inevitably incomplete, we have a range of texts in Aramaic from the Achaemenid period which allow us to document the varieties of language and their development towards the later form of the language commonly referred to as Middle Aramaic (cf. Fitzmyer 1979: 57–84). This includes a set of letters from an Achaemenid official (Driver 1957) even if, sadly, we have no royal decrees comparable to those alleged in the book of Ezra.

An investigation of the language of the supposed decrees turns up some remarkable sets of data (Grabbe 1992b). Older features of a language may survive and turn up in language of a later age (deliberate archaisms, survival in a dialect, learned usage, and the like), but later characteristics will not be found in the earlier stages of the language. Some features of Aramaic common in Middle Aramaic do not seem to have developed until late in or after the Achaemenid period. Cataloguing these may help in determining the authenticity of the Aramaic letters and documents.

The invention of documents and the editing of documents to give greater support for a particular position is well known from antiquity. A good example of documents as literary inventions to spice up a narrative can be found in the Greek text of Esther where various decrees are not just said to be issued, as in the Hebrew text, but are also 'quoted' in full (13:1–7; 16:1–24; 8:13). It would be difficult to find a scholar willing to defend these as authentic decrees from a Persian king. One of the best examples of Jewish scribes taking a genuine decree and altering it to fit their own propaganda is found in a passage of Josephus relating to citizenship for Alexandrian Jews (cf. the discussion in Grabbe 1992a: 407–8). Josephus quotes a decree allegedly from the Roman emperor Claudius which states that the Jews have 'equal civic rights' with the Greeks (*Ant.* 19.5.2 §§280–85). Fortunately, an authentic decree of Claudius on the subject has been found among the papyri from Egypt (Tcherikover, Fuks, and Stern 1957–64: 2.36–55 [text No. 153]), and it says something quite different, making it clear that most Jews did not have citizenship along with the Greeks. A Jewish scribe seems to have taken this or a similar genuine decree of Claudius and made sufficient changes for the decree to say the opposite of what it actually said. Of course, the Jews were not the only ones to do this; similar falsifications on behalf of interested parties are found throughout history.

The mixture of early and later forms and the strong flavour of Jewish propaganda in some of the documents suggest that they may have early writings, perhaps genuine Persian administration communications, at their base; however, they have clearly been worked over by Jewish scribes proceeding according to their own agenda. A good example of this is the decree giving permission for the rebuilding of the temple in Ezra 6:2–5. It would not be surprising if Cyrus had issued a specific permit to allow the temple to be rebuilt, but whether this is that decree is questionable. Cyrus would have been extremely busy in his first year of rule after conquering Babylon. How likely is it that he would have issued a decree for the remote province of Judah? If he was giving general directions about the restoration of divine images, he might have looked favourably on a delegation from the Jews. Such a decree in Cyrus' first year is perhaps possible, but he is not likely to have had the time to deal with such trivial matters straight away; one somewhat later on would probably be more likely.

More suspect are the dimensions of the said temple. Why would the Persian king be involved in specifying the particular dimensions of the temple and the mode of building? In any case, something seems to be wrong here since only two dimensions are given, and they look strange. A temple approximately 90 feet wide and 90 feet high appears to be unlikely, especially considering the resources available. Most suspect, however, is the statement that the costs were to be met from the royal treasury (6:4: *min-bêt malkā*'). This is Jewish propaganda pure and simple. The language of the document uses post-Achaemenid grammatical forms, and the name of the great Neo-Babylonian king is given as 'Nebuchad-nezzar', whereas it is more accurately rendered as 'Nebuchadrezzar' (as, for example, in Jeremiah 21:2, 7; Ezekiel 26:7; cf. the form *nbwkdrṣr* in Donner and Röllig 1962–64: text No. 227 obv. 5), from the Babylonian *Nabu-kudurri-uṣur*. These all suggest a document which is either a Jewish invention or which has been edited by Jewish scribes.

The document which is most likely to be authentic is that of Tattenai the satrap of Ebir-nari (Ezra 5:7–17). It was sent by an individual who is now known from cuneiform sources to have been an actual Persian official (Olmstead 1944). Although it is a fairly long letter, it contains only early grammatical forms (5:8: *běyedhōm*; 5:9, 10: *lěhōm*; 5:9: *lěkōm*; 5:10: *šemāhāthōm*; 5:10: *běrā'šěhōm*). Especially important is the picture presented of Sheshbazzar as someone who not only was governor (*peḥāh*) but also began the building of the temple, laying its foundations (5:14–16). This differs from the scenario given in Ezra 1–3 where Sheshbazzar's role is downplayed, nothing is said about his being governor, and the founding of the temple is done by Zerubbabel (see further below on Sheshbazzar). A couple of points might argue for Jewish scribal intervention. It is stated in 5:9 that the 'elders' are in charge rather than the governor as might be expected; however, it is possible that Judah had no governor at this time or that he was not on the scene for one reason or another. The second potential problem is that 5:12 has Nebuchadnezzar instead of the more correct form Nebuchadrezzar, though this is possibly due to the correction of a later scribe.

The alleged reply from Darius is not so solidly based (6:6–12). Reference is made to a 'governor' of the Jews (6:7), though he is listed only alongside 'the elders' and the elders alone occur in the next verse (6:8). The tone of the letter – basically a rebuke in 6:6 – is strange to an official who has only been carrying out his duties. Most suspect is the statement that the expenses of building are to come from imperial funds (6:8–10). Also, the king might well pay for certain sacrifices on behalf of himself and his family (6:9–10), but the carte blanche given here cannot but be viewed with some scepticism (cf. Grabbe 1994: 290–91). Why would the king, under whose benevolent care all the peoples of the empire went about their business, feel the need to issue a curse against 'any king or nation' who might damage the house of God in Jerusalem? This statement is what the Jews would like, not what the king was likely to issue. All in all, the letter looks like a Jewish invention (or possibly a genuine letter which has been heavily edited).

On the letter of Artaxerxes with regard to Ezra (Ezra 7:12–26), see below.

Prophecies of Haggai and Zechariah

Prophecies from Haggai and Zechariah are said to have served to goad the Jewish leadership into resuming work on the temple which had been stopped for a period of time because of the accusations of 'enemies' (Ezra 5:1–2). The content of these prophecies is not given. Two assumptions are possible: either these represent the material in the present books of Haggai and Zechariah 1–8 (or at least a part of this material) or these are prophecies which are not otherwise found in the Bible. It is more likely that the compiler of Ezra 1–6 has drawn on written sources and had no other sources available (Williamson 1983). In other words, we should see the source of these verses as some version of the present books of Haggai and Zechariah 1–8. This opinion is confirmed by the dates within the prophetic books themselves which connect the prophecies with the second year of Darius, precisely the date indicated by Ezra 5:1–2 (Hag. 1:1; 1:15–2:1; 2:10, 20; Zech. 1:1, 7).

If the author of Ezra 5:1–2 has drawn on the books of Haggai and Zechariah, we find some interesting discrepancies between the two. The context of Ezra 5:1–2 is the cessation of work on the temple which had been started but was brought to a halt because of accusations made to the Persian government about the intent of the Jews. As a result of Haggai's and Zechariah's prophecies the work is resumed, without official permission, and Tattenai the satrap comes to investigate. We would expect this to be reflected in the prophecies; however, this is not the case.

In Haggai the problem is not the opposition of 'enemies' or the prohibition of the Persian administration. It is, rather, the people who are more concerned about living in 'luxurious' houses than building the temple (Hag. 1:2–4, 9). They are called on to go to the hills for timber for building (not to the Lebanon for cedar wood, as in Ezra 3:7). The problems people are suffering come not from adversaries or government officials but drought and poor crops (Hag. 1:5–6, 9–11).

Zechariah's message is contained mainly in visions, which makes interpretation more precarious. A major concern is the return of Yhwh himself to Jerusalem (Zech. 1:16; 8:3), after having abandoned it before the exile (Ezek. 10:18; 11:22–23). Another is the removal of the guilt and uncleanness of the exile (Zech. 3; 5). There is also an echo of the lack of prosperity until work on the temple got under way (Zech. 8:9–13). Nothing is suggested about interference from Persian officials or about threats from the surrounding peoples.

An Ezra memoir?

A section of the Ezra story in Ezra 7–10 is in the first person, 7:27–9:15. This has naturally led scholars to propose the existence of an 'Ezra memoir' parallel to the NM. It might seem gratuitous to reject the existence of an Ezra memoir while arguing for a NM. There is some prima facie indication of a genuine personal writing. His embarrassment at asking for an armed escort in 8:21–23 might argue for authenticity, as perhaps would the story of finding Levites to be a part of his emigrating party (8:15–20). Yet I find the attestation of an Ezra memoir problematic and a completely different situation from that of the NM. Rather than argue it in the abstract, the comments on the person of Ezra below form a significant critique of the idea of an Ezra memoir for use as a historical source. See the concluding section of this chapter for further comment.

Narrative passages of Ezra 1–6

The argument that the narrator of Ezra 1–6 had no information apart from a handful of sources (the Cyrus decree, a list of temple vessels, the list of Ezra 2, the supposed Persian documents, and the books of Haggai and Zechariah) and used them in compiling his narrative (Williamson 1983) seems persuasive to me. This means that much of the narrative, both in Hebrew and in Aramaic, is an inference from the preserved documents; consequently, the narrative has no independent authority. A number of implications arise from this.

What is most striking to a modern scholar about Ezra 4–5 is the placement of various letters in the context of the reigns of Cyrus and Darius. They simply do not make sense in the light of what is known about Persian history. The initial return is dated in Ezra 1 to the first year of Cyrus. The indication is that the building of the altar in Ezra 3 is only a few months later, in Cyrus' second year (cf. Ezra 3:8). They meet opposition in Ezra 4 for all the years of Cyrus until the reign of Darius (4:5). The reign of Cambyses is omitted in these chapters, very likely because the compiler did not know of him. (If he was known, his name would almost certainly have been mentioned in 4:5.) An Ahasuerus is mentioned (4:6), who is usually identified with Xerxes, but the letter of accusation is strangely not quoted. Then a letter is written in the time of Artaxerxes; however, those who supposedly write it are different from those mentioned in the letter itself (compare 4:7 with 4:8–10, 17, 23). But then comes the real jaw-dropper: the letter from Artaxerxes is used to stop the building of the temple in the time of Cyrus and to keep it halted until the reign of Darius! Artaxerxes was at least sixty years later. This is like reading that the Charge of the Light Brigade in the Crimean War was devastated by machine gun fire from aeroplanes. The author of the narrative clearly has not the faintest idea of the relationship of the Persian kings to one another, and has placed his documents to produce what in his opinion is the best argument without being aware that it makes nonsense of Persian history.

The documents in Ezra 5–6 fit the context better, though this does not necessarily mean they are authentic. I have argued above that the letter of Tattenai (5:7–17) looks most likely to be authentic, but that the letters in Ezra 6 are suspect for several reasons. There is also no indication for the basis of the statement, 'This house (of God) was finished on the 3rd day of the month Adar, in year 6 of king Darius' rule' (6:15). It could be based on a genuine source, but if so, we have no knowledge of this. None of the assumed sources for the narrative of Ezra 1–6 has such a date in it. It is difficult to believe that there would be the resources available to complete the temple so quickly, even using local wood and stone (despite Ezra 3:7; cf. Hag. 1:8). That the temple was completed some time around 500 BCE seems reasonable, but whether we can trust that it took place in Darius' sixth year (516 BCE) is doubtful.

Sheshbazzar

Possibly the most curious figure in the book of Ezra is Sheshbazzar. He makes a brief appearance in Ezra 1:9–11 as the one who brings the temple vessels back to Jerusalem; he then disappears from the narrative without further comment. We are told nothing about him apart from his designation as a 'prince of Judah' (*hannāśî' lîhûdāh*). What precisely this means is much debated. It was once assumed that Sheshbazzar was to be identified with the Shenazzar who was a son of Jehoiachin (1 Chron. 3:17–18). This would suggest that his title acknowledged him as a member of the Jewish royal family. Further studies make this identification unlikely, however (Berger 1971; Dion 1983), though Sheshbazzar could still possibly be a member of the royal family.

Despite having been forgotten by the central narrative of Ezra 1–6, Sheshbazzar's name still comes up later, this time in a quoted document (5:14–16). This reference is significant. First, the document in which it occurs is the one most likely to be authentic (see above), which would mean that we were likely to have some reliable information about the man. Another reason for the significance of this reference is that it goes contrary to statements in the rest of Ezra 1–6. When he is given the temple vessels in Ezra 1, there is no suggestion that Sheshbazzar was to be governor. This puts a whole new perspective on his importance. He was not just a bodyguard, as it were, to ensure the safe arrival of the vessels; bringing the vessels was only an initial duty which inaugurated his taking up a Persian post. Most interestingly, he also laid the foundations of the temple, according to 5:16. This flatly contradicts Ezra 3:6 which states that Zerubbabel and Joshua set up an altar but the foundations of the temple had not been laid. It is clear that the author of the narrative in Ezra 3 either is ignorant of the Sheshbazzar tradition or he knows it and has suppressed it. It may seem strange that the compiler of the book would have suppressed this information, but it is difficult to believe that he cannot have noticed the information in one of the documents he used. Thus, it seems more likely that he deliberately ignored the information about Sheshbazzar from the document. For him the founders of the temple are Joshua and Zerubbabel. This means that the activities of Sheshbazzar have had to be reduced to conducting some vessels safely to Jerusalem before disappearing into the sunset.

The account in Ezra 5:14–16 is tantalizingly brief. What exactly did Sheshbazzar do to 'lay the foundations' of the temple? How long was he governor? What happened between his governorship and the coming of Joshua and Zerubbabel? Why did he not finish what he had started? And, especially, why did he get 'forgotten' by later writers? What *historian* would ignore dealing with these important questions? The writer is clearly no historian.

Original peoples versus returnees

One of the consistent pictures found in Ezra especially, but also in Nehemiah, is that the people returning from Babylon under Joshua and Zerubbabel were coming back to resettle a land which had remained uninhabited since the Babylonian captivity (Carroll 1992; Barstad 1996). The literary tradition about the Babylonian captivity is ambivalent. 2 Kings suggests a major removal of population at various points, but it admits that the 'poorest of the land' remained in Judah (2 Kings 24:14; 25:12). The expression 'poorest of the land' should be taken with a grain of salt since they were also the only ones supposed to have been left after the deportation in the time of Jehoiachin. Yet according to 2 Kings 25 and Jeremiah, there were plenty of nobles, soldiers, priests, and even the odd prophet around after this – and they were strong enough to withstand a siege of the Babylonians for several years (2 Kings 25:1–3). Both 2 Kings 25:22–26 and Jeremiah 40–43 show not only a large group of Jews, with a governor (king?) in the person of Gedaliah, but also a good deal of general activity. This is hardly the description of an empty land. A group is said to have fled to Egypt (including Jeremiah), but it seems difficult to see this number as being large (though the text may want us to conclude that everyone remaining in Judah left and went to Egypt).

According to the biblical texts, the actual number of deportees is quite small, relatively speaking: 10,000 at the time of the captivity of Jehoiachin (according to 2 Kings 24:14); Jer. 52:28–30 reduces this to 3,000, though that might be Jerusalem alone, with the entire total under Nebuchadnezzar being fewer than 5,000. Thus it is difficult to speak of actual numbers, but the impression in 2 Kings and also at the end of Jeremiah is that only a minority of the population was removed from the land. 2 Chronicles gives a different story. It claims not only that all those who survived the siege were taken to Babylon but also that the land observed its neglected sabbatical years (36:20–21). That is, the land was not being worked; hence, one can only conclude that it was mainly empty.

When the original settlers come, they return to their old habitations (Ezra 2:1//Neh. 7:6: 'each to his own city'). Nothing is said about anyone else living there or about any contest over ownership of the property. The people already in the land are labelled 'foreigners': they claim to have been brought in as settlers imported by Esarhaddon but are also called 'the peoples of the land' (Ezra 4:1–4). The physical location of these 'adversaries of Judah and Benjamin' is not given. One might associate them with Samaria, as the association with Esarhaddon might suggest. Nevertheless, there is nothing to say that they were not (or also not) living in the territory of Judah. It is strange that they are called the 'peoples of the land', a phrase always used in the OT and also in the later rabbinic literature to refer to people reckoned as being 'Israel' (Gunneweg 1983). The term is never used in rabbinic literature for Gentiles (Oppenheimer 1977), so why should those labelled 'peoples of the land' be foreigners here?

An understanding of the message is complicated because of the use of documents which seem to be placed haphazardly in the context. As already noted, the context of the reigns of Cyrus and Darius is inappropriate for a letter alleged to be addressed to Artaxerxes (4:7–16). However, from a literary point of view, Ezra 4:9–10 continues the theme of 4:1–4. The first few verses of the chapter announce the theme of foreignness; these 'foreigners' bribed Persian ministers in 4:5, then 'they' made an accusation in 4:6. Now 4:9–10 continues this theme by claiming that those who wrote in the time of Artaxerxes were those from 'Erech, Babylon, Susa (Elamites), and the rest of those whom the great and noble Asnappar exiled and settled in the city [*sic*] of Samaria and the rest of (the satrapy of) Ebir-nari'. The message is clear: the 'peoples of the land', the 'adversaries', were foreigners brought in by Assyrian kings (though the problem with the name 'Asnappar' is discussed in chapter 2 above).

These 'nations of the land' (*gôyê-hā'āres*) are a problem because they impart 'uncleanliness' (Ezra 6:21). This uncleanness is further elaborated in the Ezra story when the intermarriage between the Jews and 'the peoples of the land' is discussed in Ezra 9–10: 'The people of Israel and the priests and Levites have not separated themselves from the peoples of the lands, whose abominations are those of [like those of?] the Canaanites, Hittites, Perizzites, Jebusites, Ammonites, Moabites, Egyptians, and Amorites' (9:1). Although the 'peoples of the lands' may not quite be identified with the Canaanites and other aboriginal peoples displaced by the Israelites (the translation is uncertain), a strong link is made. Certainly, their 'abominations' – their religious and perhaps other practices – are considered ritually defiling and abhorrent. To 'mix' with them by intermarriage is to corrupt the 'holy seed' of the Israelites (9:2). The theme of their abominable habits is continued in Ezra's prayer (9:6–15). The identity of the 'peoples of the land' in Ezra's time with those at the time of the original Israelite settlement is made much more explicit in 9:11–12. The sin of intermarriage because of the people's abominations is repeated in 9:14. The women of the 'peoples of the land' are said to be 'foreign' in a number of places in Ezra 10 (vv. 2, 10, 11, 14, 17, 18, 44). Similar usage is found in Neh. 9–10 which talk of a similar case involving mixed marriages. The people fast and separate themselves 'from all the sons of the foreigner' (Neh. 9:2). They separate themselves from 'the peoples of the lands' (10:29) and pledge not to marry with 'the peoples of the land' nor to buy from them (10:31–32).

The conclusion seems straightforward: the text simply refuses to admit that there were Jewish inhabitants of the land after the deportations under Nebuchadnezzar. Probably only a minority of the people were taken away, with the tens of thousands still left. These people continued to live in Judah, work the land, raise families, carry on their daily life. Presumably they would have quietly taken over any land abandoned because the owners had been killed in fighting or deported to Babylonia. There is no suggestion that any foreign peoples were brought in to replace those deported. Where are these people – Jews – in the books of Ezra and Nehemiah? They are absent. Instead we find references to the 'peoples of the land' who are identified as foreigners. One can only conclude that many, if not all, these 'peoples of the land' were the Jewish descendants of those who were not deported. In the eyes of the author of Ezra, these peoples were no longer kin; the only 'people of Israel' were those who had gone into captivity.

The Ezra story (Ezra 7–10)

At first glance the story of Ezra seems straightforward enough. He is introduced by his genealogy, tracing his ancestry back to Aaron the priest (Ezra 7:1–5). He is also identified as a scribe and one devoted to study of the law (7:6, 10). He received a document from king Artaxerxes permitting him to return, bring with him various people and gold and silver for the temple, and teach the law (7:12–26). When he arrives, he finds a problem in that certain people have intermarried with 'foreigners'. He sets about resolving this problem, which is how Ezra 7–10 ends, though an additional section on the reading of the law (Neh. 8) should be included here.

As soon as you go beyond the surface level, though, problems immediately rear themselves. The first problem is the letter of Artaxerxes. As noted above, one of the first indications of authenticity of this document should be the language. A document issued under the Achaemenids would be in Imperial Aramaic, the common language of communication in the Persian empire. This letter is indeed in Aramaic, but some of the linguistic forms are those from a later period, known as Middle Aramaic. The older and later forms sit side by side (7:16: 'ĕlāhăhōm; 7:17: ûminḥāthôn, wĕniskêhôn, 'ĕlāhăkōm; 7:18: 'ĕlāhăkōm; 7:21: yiś'ălenkôn; 7:24: ûlĕkōm, 'ălêhōm), which suggests an actual decree that has been heavily edited by Jewish scribes. The content of the letter supports this inference, notably the benevolence of the Persian empire towards the Jews and, especially, the power conferred on Ezra.

The first statement is that anyone of the 'people of Israel, priests, and Levites' who wants to go to Jerusalem has permission to go with Ezra (7:13). The king 'and his seven counsellors' also allow Ezra to regulate (lĕvēqqārā') Judah and Jerusalem by the 'law of your God in your hand' (7:14). Then he is allowed to convey the silver and gold which the king and his counsellors have generously offered to the 'God of Israel whose dwelling is in Jerusalem' (7:15). Even the king and his counsellors tacitly place themselves under the sovereignty of Yhwh. Furthermore, 'all the silver and gold found in all the satrapy of Babylon' is to be given over to the house of their God in Jerusalem; this is in addition to all the gold and silver freely donated by the people and priests (7:16). This money is to be used for purchasing animals, grain, and drink to be offered on the Jerusalem altar (7:17). Whatever money is left over can be used for whatever the priests want, according to God's will (7:18). Indeed, any other needs, such as of temple vessels, are to be paid from the royal treasury, up to 100 talents of silver (7:19–22)!

This generosity is incredible! The king and his counsellors give donations, the people and priests give donations, Ezra is allowed to take all the silver and gold found in the satrapy of Babylon (which includes both Babylonia and the area of Ebir-nari). As if that is not enough, he can take up to another 100 talents of silver from the treasury. God has indeed given Ezra favour in the eyes of the king, if all this should be true. But there is more to come: it was forbidden to tax the priests, Levites, temple singers, and other temple servants (7:24). No wonder that Ezra offers such profuse praise to God at the end of the chapter (7:27–28)! This is all ostensibly done so that sacrifices could be offered on behalf of the king and his sons. But it hardly takes such vast wealth and a relief of taxes to ensure that sacrifices were offered for the king daily on the Jerusalem altar. A simple gift of an animal or two per day would have sufficed. It is one thing to supply gifts to the temple; it is quite another to provide such lavish riches for what was, after all, only a very local cult site.

The authorization does not stop with these measures. Ezra is told that he is 'to appoint officials and judges to be judging all the people in the region of Ebir-nari, both those who know the law and those who do not', according to the wisdom of the law in his hand (7:25–26). He is to teach those who do not know the law. It is often suggested that this refers only to Jews, but there is no basis for this interpretation in the decree. Its most obvious referent is all the people in the satrapy west of the Euphrates, and the mention of the 'law of your God and the law of the king' suggests that not just Jews are being talked about. Any who do not obey are to be punished as appropriate. Ezra has clearly been given some very sweeping powers. The extent of these powers is hinted at in Ezra 8:36 where the orders of the king are handed over to the 'satraps and governors of the province Beyond-the-River'.

Ezra 8 describes the preparation for the journey to Jerusalem and the activities once Ezra arrived there (the journey itself, as so often in the biblical text, is passed over in silence). He collects together a group of those who wish to return, including priests. Finding that there are no Levites among them, he sends to Casiphia and manages to get a handful of Levites and a couple of hundred temple servants to accompany him. Why he needs Levites is not discussed other than their designation as 'ministers for the house of our God' (8:17).

Next Ezra proclaims a fast (8:21–23). Why? Because Ezra 'was ashamed to ask the king' for a bodyguard of soldiers and horsemen to protect them on the journey. This might sound like a simple case of putting his faith in God rather than men. However, the narrative goes on to state that the gold and silver gathered to take to Jerusalem was committed to the care of twelve priests. This gold and silver amounted to 650 talents of silver, 100 talents of gold, and various expensive vessels for the temple. A talent was usually about 3,000 shekels, the preserved shekel weights being about 10 grammes each (a convenient figure, though it might be a bit heavier, even up to 14 grammes; cf. Powell 1992: 6.905–906). A talent was thus approximately 30 kilograms (roughly 65 pounds); 100 talents of gold was about 3 metric tonnes of gold. In this case, the silver amounted to about 19,500 kilograms or 19.5 tonnes. To this were to be added the 100 silver vessels of a talent each, 20 of gold, and two of an exceptionally fine quantity of bronze. Leaving out the two bronze vessels, it all adds up to more than *25 metric tonnes* of silver and gold – truly a king's ransom! According to Herodotus 3.91, the entire satrapy of Ebir-nari produced tribute of only about 350 talents of silver per year.

The amount of treasure that Ezra is said to be carrying takes one's breath away. It is difficult to grasp how much wealth his small band was transporting from Babylon to Judah. Currently, an ounce of silver sells for about $5. But modern prices are not comparable to the value in antiquity. The standard day's wage for a number of centuries in the eastern Mediterranean was a silver quarter-shekel (a drachma in Greek coinage) or about 3 grammes, worth 50 US cents on the current market. Persian economic texts, especially those from Persepolis during the reigns of Darius and Xerxes, give us an insight into values in the sixth century BCE (Dandamaev and Lukonin 1989: 158–77). A minimum wage for the *kurtash* (workers tied to their posts) was about 2 shekels a month (though they were often paid in kind rather than money), though some got more because of seniority, skill, and the like. Free hired labour was usually better paid, up to 8 shekels a month, though 3–4 was closer to the norm. However, the wages in Persia itself were higher than those in other parts of the empire. A ram cost about 3 shekels and 10 litres of wine was a shekel. Without being able to be precise about its value, we can be certain that the worth of Ezra's treasure was phenomenal by ancient standards.

But this raises a serious question: is it likely that the Persian king, having himself donated a large quantity of precious gifts, would have allowed Ezra to risk transporting all this without military protection? Far from Ezra being embarrassed to ask for a guard, the king would have *insisted* on it! The textual statement that the precious metal was assigned to just twelve priests to be 'guarded diligently' (how?) over hundreds of miles looks almost absurd (Ezra 8:24–31). The text here is clearly not interested in reality but in piety: Ezra and his entourage put their faith in God and he protected this unimagined wealth from all enemies during the hazardous journey. This is not a description of a journey but a treatise in theology.

On arrival in Jerusalem the gold and silver and precious vessels are given over faithfully to the resident priests and Levites. Strangely, no high priest is mentioned. Reference is made to 'Uriah the priest' who

141

might be the high priest (since sometimes the term 'the priest' is used of the high priest), but he is only the father of the priest Meremoth and may not even have been alive (8:33). Then appropriate sacrifices are made, presumably to thank God and to celebrate the safe arrival. Finally, Ezra hands over his orders to the royal satraps and governors of the satrapy Ebir-nari. How he was able to do this is not stated. Are we to assume that they all assembled in Jerusalem to receive their orders? This seems to be implied.

After the passage of several months the officials (of Jerusalem? of the province?) approach Ezra to tell him of the problem that some have intermarried with the 'peoples of the land' (Ezra 9:1–2). What does Ezra do? He has been given the power and authority to teach and enforce the law over the entire satrapy, and to appoint judges to fulfil this task. When confronted with an actual situation, however, there is only stupefaction instead of decisive action. Ezra tears his garments and hair and sits on the ground in the square. After sitting in the dust until evening, he then prays (9:3–15). Perhaps mourning and prayer might be what we expect of a pious priest, but we should also expect action. Action does come about in Ezra 10, but who initiates it? Not Ezra! A great crowd of people gather round him, weeping. It is one of these, Shecaniah son of Jehiel, who recommends a course of action to be followed, primarily the swearing of an oath. Finally, Ezra does something decisive: he accepts this advice and acts on it. Then he goes off to fast. In the meantime, 'they' (10:7) send out a decree for all to assemble in Jerusalem (interestingly, it is not said that Ezra was involved in sending the decree; it could have been some of the officers). The rest of the chapter describes the measures taken, in which Ezra seems – finally – to play a full part.

One interesting point in the narrative is the reference to the ones who 'tremble' (*haḥărēdîm*) at the commandment of God (Ezra 9:4; 10:3). It has been suggested that this was Ezra's support group, a pietistic movement who required strict observance of the law and were critical of the current priestly establishment (Blenkinsopp 1990a). Evidence for this group is also found in such passages as Isa. 65:13–16; 66:1–5; Mal. 3:13–21. Although the reliability of the picture in Ezra is very questionable, even a fictional account could still know of and represent a known social phenomenon. In this case, Ezra 10:3 is only one passage which seems to be aware of this group. If such a group existed, much more work needs to be done to ascertain its activities. At the moment, it does not seem to contribute to our evaluation of Ezra's historicity.

A full historical evaluation of the Ezra story can be made only when we consider the 'law in his hand' and the additional piece of the Ezra tradition in Nehemiah 8. The next section looks at these.

Ezra and the law

The question of Ezra and the law is a perennial one (recent treatments include Willi 1995: 91–117; Kratz 1991: 225–60; Blenkinsopp 1988: 152–57). Before evaluating the historical situation, it is important to see the literary picture given to us by the text. As already noted at many other points, the picture of the text is a mixed one.

We can begin with Ezra 7 since this is usually the focus of discussions about the law. This chapter contains two sorts of statements, those in the Aramaic decree ascribed to Artaxerxes and those in the Hebrew narrative. The Aramaic decree has already been discussed above, with attention drawn to some peculiar contents; we shall now focus purely on the document as it relates to law. The Aramaic term *dat* is used for 'law' throughout, whether of 'the God of heaven' (7:12, 14, 21) or of the king (7:26). The 'law of God' is in Ezra's hand and is to be used to regulate (*bqr* pa.) Judah and Jerusalem (7:14). So this law is to become the local law of the province. Much of the letter concerns the temple and its cult, including the vessels and wealth to be given to it, the animals and other foodstuffs to be offered on the altar, and the temple personnel who are to be free of taxes. This indicates a crucial link between the temple and the law. The end of the decree makes an important statement (7:25–26): Ezra is to appoint judges and magistrates to judge the people 'according to the wisdom of your God in your hand', 'wisdom' in this case apparently being another term for 'law'. These judges and magistrates are to judge those who know 'the laws of your God' and teach them to those who do not know them. Finally, anyone who does not obey the 'law of your God and the law of the king' is to be punished severely.

The Hebrew text into which the Artaxerxes letter is set uses the word *tôrāh*. The term 'Torah' means 'teaching' and is thus broader than the English word 'law'. What Ezra possesses is 'the Torah of Moses which Yhwh the God of Israel gave to him' (7:6; cf. 7:10). (Whether it refers simply to a body of teaching or to a specific book will be discussed below.) Ezra had set himself to study the Torah, in order both to carry it out and also to teach the statutes and judgements (*ḥōq ûmišpaṭ*) in Israel (7:10). Ezra is also said to be scribe 'of the words of Yhwh's commandments [*miṣwōt*] and his statutes [*ḥuqqâw*] over Israel' (7:11).

What is the relationship between *dat* in the Aramaic decree and the *torah* of the Hebrew narrative context? As Willi notes, the options are between *dat and torah*, *dat or torah*, *dat equals torah*, and *dat as torah* (1995: 90). All these choices have been taken in some form or other. For example, Rolf Rendtorff (1984) sees two separate entities, the legal, judicial civil law of the Persian empire (*dat*) and Jewish religious law (*torah*). Kratz (1991: 233–41) sees them as more or less equivalent, criticizing Rendtorff's distinctions as having to do with matters of application, not a fundamental difference in concepts (1991: 227–28 n. 330). Willi himself sees the difference in that *torah* is the teaching (especially oral) embracing all aspects of life and also embodied in the written Torah, and its day-to-day, case-by-case application. The Persian government was not interested in making the Torah as such authoritative but it did ratify the application of it in 'commandments, statutes, and judgements' (1995: 101–4, 109). It is the latter to which the term *dat* is applied.

If we first ask the question 'What does Ezra 7 wish us to understand about the terms?', things become simpler. Ezra was a 'ready scribe in the *torah* of Moses which Yhwh the God of Israel gave' (7:6); he was also 'scribe of the *dat* of the God of heaven' (7:12). He 'had set his heart to study the *torah* of Yhwh and to do and teach the statutes and judgements (*ḥōq ûmišpaṭ*) in Israel' (7:10); the king sent him 'to investigate concerning Judah and Jerusalem by the *dat* of your God in your hand' (7:14). Artaxerxes' decree thus authorizes Ezra to teach the law of Moses, which he has in his possession, and to make it the basis of local law in the province of Judah (or, according to 7:25, the basis of the law of the entire Persian territory west of the Euphrates). Thus, in the context of Ezra 7, there seems little doubt that *torah* and *dat* are to be understood as the same thing. The *dat* of Artaxerxes' decree is the same entity as the *torah* which Ezra handles as a scribe and priest. This impression is confirmed when we examine some other considerations.

As has been pointed out (e.g. Kratz 1991: 236) various elements of the Artaxerxes decree can be related to Ezra's activities in Ezra 8–10 and Neh. 8. The law is specifically evoked a couple of times in the episode of mixed marriages. First, in Ezra's prayer the statement is made that they 'had forsaken your commandments which you commanded by the hand of your servants the prophets' (9:10–11). What follows in 9:11–12 is not a quotation from any passage in the present biblical text, though some of the ideas can be found in such passages as Lev. 18:24–30; Deut. 7:1–8; 23:4–7. (The phrase 'your servants the prophets' does not seem to be a reference to the prophetic books but a general term which includes Moses [cf. Deut. 18:15]. The phrase is usually taken to be characteristic of the 'Deuteronomic School'.)

Nehemiah 8 is another key passage and is also part of the Ezra tradition. Here it is not just a case of teaching but of reading from a 'book of the Torah of Moses' (8:1; cf. 8:3, 8). In this case the Torah is a book in which the teaching is contained. So this chapter very much associates the law of God in Ezra's possession with a book which is read and also expounded to the people (8:8). In the context of Ezra-Nehemiah, the law of God in Ezra 7 would also include a book. Ezra was not just coming to Jerusalem with a teaching but was also bringing a book. Anyone who read both Ezra 7 and Nehemiah 8, as they occur in the present Hebrew canon, could not but conclude anything else. The immediate consequence of reading this book is to find that they should be keeping the Feast of Tabernacles, including spending the eight days of the festival in booths, 'which the Israelites had not done from the days of Joshua' (8:17).

A major question is whether the law brought by Ezra is envisaged as a new law. It could not have been regarded as completely new, of course, since it was the law of Moses and by definition had existed for centuries. The question is whether this law had been forgotten and needed to be reintroduced to the Jerusalem community. This might well be a legitimate conclusion from certain passages. For example, the suggestion in Neh. 8 is that the people did not know about the Feast of Tabernacles until they read about it in the book of the law. The whole thrust of Neh. 8 is that the people were hearing something which was new and momentous to them. It needed to be expounded by levitical assistants (8:7–8).

However, this interpretation is contradicted by a number of passages in other parts of Ezra-Nehemiah. In Ezra 1–6 the people who came to Jerusalem in the time of Cyrus already had the law, according to the text. When Joshua and Zerubbabel set up the altar, it was to offer sacrifices 'as written in the Torah of Moses the man of God' (Ezra 3:2). When the temple was completed, the priests and Levites were organized 'according to what is written in the *book* of Moses' (6:18). They celebrate both the Feast of Tabernacles (3:2–6) and the Festivals of the Passover and Unleavened Bread (6:19–22), annual festivals discussed in Leviticus 23 and Deuteronomy 16. It seems strange that according to Neh. 8 the Feast had not been celebrated in such a way since the time of Joshua, yet some decades earlier the Jews of Jerusalem were celebrating it according to the law of Moses. Even the Ezra story speaks of 'all those who know the laws of your God' in the satrapy of Ebir-nari (Ezra 7:25).

A careful reading of Nehemiah 8 also discloses another rather curious situation. The book of the law is read to the people on the 1st day of the 7th month (8:2). One of the things they learn is about the festivals of God, and apply this new knowledge by celebrating the Feast of Tabernacles which falls on days 15–22 of the 7th month (Lev. 23:39–43; Deut. 16:13–15). Yet nothing is said about the Festival of Trumpets which fell on the very day of the first reading, the 1st day of the 7th month (Lev. 23:24–25). Then a little later, on the 24th of that same month, the people assemble, repent about mixing with 'foreigners', and read in 'the book of the Torah of Yhwh' (Neh. 9:1–3). But a reading of the Torah will show that the Day of Atonement was also to have been celebrated on the 10th day of the 7th month (Lev. 16; 23:26–32), and this would have been the ideal time to have repented of the 'sin' of the mixed marriages. Why is such an important observance as the Day of Atonement skipped over without the slightest hint of its existence?

From a literary point of view we can compare the various laws referred to explicitly or presupposed in Ezra-Nehemiah to determine which law the compiler has in mind. Some of the laws are the following:

Intermarriage with other peoples (Neh. 13:1–2 quotes Deut. 23:4–5 [ET 23:3–4]; Neh. 13:25 quotes Deut. 7:3; Ezra 9–10; Neh. 9:1–2, 10:31)
Sabbath (Neh. 10:32; 13:15–22//Gen. 2:2–3; Exod. 20:8–11; Lev. 23:3–8)
Annual festivals:
    Passover/Unleavened Bread (Ezra 6:19–22//Lev. 23:5–8; Deut. 16:1–8)
    Tabernacles (Ezra 3:4; Neh. 8:14–17//Lev. 23:33–36, 39–43)
Sabbatical year (Neh. 10:32//Lev. 25: 1–7; Deut. 15:1–3)
Annual tax of one-third shekel (Neh. 10:33; cf. Exod. 30:11–16)
Wood offering (Neh. 10:35) (no OT parallel)
Priestly dues:
    Tithes (Neh. 10:38; 13:10–13; 12:44//Num. 18:21–32)
    First-fruits (Neh. 10:36//Num. 18:12–13)
    Firstlings (Neh. 10:37//Num. 18:14–18)

Blenkinsopp (1988: 155) suggests that the redactor is thinking mainly of laws in Deuteronomy but supplemented by some of those in the priestly source (P) and the Holiness Code (H). However, this is not the complete story. It is true that a significant number of laws are found in Neh. 10, but as noted in chapter 3 above, the prayer in Neh. 9 also covers some of the main points in the Pentateuch, including Adam, Abraham, the exodus from Egypt, events in the wilderness, and the taking of Canaan. Thus, the information presupposed in Neh. 9–10 in the canonical Ezra-Nehemiah relates to the whole of the Pentateuch and not just the legal sections. When we put this fact together with references to the 'book of the *torah* of Moses' (Neh. 8:1) and the 'book of the *torah* of Yhwh' (Neh. 9:3) and the 'book of Moses' (= *torah* [Neh. 13:1, 3]), there seems to be only one conclusion: the present text of Ezra-Nehemiah wants us to understand that Ezra's law was the complete Pentateuch. We cannot absolutely demonstrate that it had in mind the Pentateuch precisely as we know it today, but it is a fair assumption that something fairly close was in mind.

What was just described is a literary construct. What does this have to do with Jewish law in the Persian period? Most discussions about Ezra and the law, and about what exactly was the law he brought, start from the assumption that this is a genuine historical event. When the problematic nature of the Ezra tradition is recognized, however (see previous section), it becomes clear that one cannot proceed on such an assumption.

Ancient Near Eastern societies, especially among the tribal communities, governed by traditional law (for further discussion and references, see Grabbe 1993a: 23–28). This was not codified or written down in most cases and incorporated a lot of what we today would consider only as societal convention. This applied not only to ancient Israel but even to large Mesopotamian entities. From the famous law codes, such as the *Codex Hammurabi*, it might be assumed that Mesopotamia had a codified legal system comparable to that of the later Roman empire or modern nations. However, a study of Mesopotamian legal decisions known from many records and documents shows that the so-called 'law codes' were never cited as codified law or legal precedent. Judges seem to have judged according to unwritten legal convention and tradition and, of course, personal common sense. The 'law codes' appear to be scribal creations, in some cases for the purpose of enhancing the prestige of the king before the gods (cf. the Prologue to the *Codex Hammurabi*). On the other hand, the contents of the law codes and the documents of actual legal decisions are not completely divorced from each other, either. That is, the law codes seem to a large extent to incorporate the general practice of the society even if there may be an idealized element to them.

Israel of the monarchy fits well this general picture. There was traditional practice and accepted convention. Judges and even the king himself largely followed this in their decisions. The priests also had their traditional law which governed the cult for centuries, probably in unwritten form, with each new generation of priests learning from their elders. At some point, the legal sections of the Pentateuch were written. These look very comparable to the Mesopotamian law codes, meaning that they are scribal creations, that they have a certain utopian aspect to them and often represent an idealized view rather than actual practice, but that they also largely incorporate general convention and custom. The same applies to the 'priestly law' which no doubt summarizes a good deal of cultic practice (see Grabbe 1993a, especially pp. 22–23); on the other hand, the P document was hardly a priestly manual since certain parts of it seem aimed at the lay person (Lev. 1–5), and other parts are unclear (e.g. the distinction between the 'reparation offering' ['āšām] and the 'sin offering' [ḥaṭṭā't]).

There is much in P, the 'Covenant Code' (Exodus 19–23), and Deuteronomy that is idealized and reflects the theological views of the compiler(s). For example, there is no evidence that the jubilee year was ever anything more than an idealized construct; although there is evidence that the sabbatical year was practised in Judaea during the Second Temple period, the instructions with regard to the two celebrations are contradictory (Grabbe 1993a: 94–97). Particular views about God, the cult, and Israelite religion in general are reflected in these codes which may not have been the views of the majority of the priests or the people. Thus, the legal sections of the Pentateuch contain Israelite societal convention and actual legal and cultic practice alongside descriptions of practices which seem only to reflect the theological desires of the compilers and to have been no more than theoretical, at least at the time of writing. This, along with the story of 'Israel' from creation to the eve of entering the promised land, was eventually put together to produce the Pentateuch we know today.

Law under the Persians seems to have been something similar. The traditional teachings of the Persians from an early period are known to some extent in the writings of Zoroaster, even though the dating of his life is still disputed. One of the bases of law and convention among the Persians (as among the other Indo-Iranian peoples) was that of *aša* (Avestan) or *arta* (Old Persian), which included the ideas of 'righteousness, wisdom, justice, order' (cf. the name Artaxerxes 'having a kingdom of *arta* [justice]'). This was opposed to *drauga* ('evil, disorder, folly'). Thus, Darius in his famous inscription preserved at Behistun states (Kent 1953: 117–19 [DB §10:33–35]):

> When Cambyses had gone off to Egypt, after that the people became evil. After that the Lie [*drauga*] waxed great in the country, both in Persia and in Media and in the other provinces.

Another inscription of Darius states (Kent 1953: 135–36 [DPd §3:12–20]):

> Saith Darius the King: May Ahuramazda bear me aid, with the gods of the royal house; and may Ahuramazda protect this country from a (hostile) army, from famine, from the Lie [*draugā*]!

An inscription of Xerxes (sometimes called the '*daiva* inscription') reads as follows (Kent 1953: 150–51 [XPh §46b:35–41, 51–56]):

> And among these countries there was (a place) where previously false gods [*daivā*] were worshipped. . . . Where previously the demons [*daivā*] were worshipped, there I worshipped Ahuramazda and Arta [*artācā*] reverent(ly). . . . The man who has respect for that law [*dātā*] which Ahuramazda has established, and worships Ahuramazda and Arta [*artācā*] reverent(ly), he both becomes happy while living, and becomes blessed when dead.

It was customary for the Persians to respect local law, as long as it did not interfere with the law of the imperial overlord. In antiquity Darius had the reputation of being a 'lawgiver' (Olmstead 1948: 119–34), including the codification of Egyptian law. This was not the creation of new law, though, but the systematization of pre-existing law. It would not be surprising if local Jewish law was allowed to be enforced on the people of the Persian province Yehud, which may be the indication of the expression 'law of your God and the law of the king' (Ezra 7:26; cf. Kratz 1991: 229–36). It would also not even be surprising if the Persian administration encouraged some sort of codification of Jewish law. Whether the Passover Papyrus (Cowley 1923: No. 21) is an example of Persian involvement in Jewish religious law is a moot point since the vital introductory lines are missing (cf. Grabbe 1992a: 54–55).

To summarize this lengthy discursus, the literary picture of Ezra-Nehemiah is a contradictory one. On the one hand, it wants to make clear that the law of Moses was known and practised from the beginning of the return. On the other hand, it also gives the distinct impression that the book of the law read by Ezra was new to the people. The dichotomy can be explained by assuming that the first is the ideology of the author (Moses wrote the Pentateuch long ago) while the second is much closer to reality; that is, the 'book of Moses' was probably something which took shape in the Persian period. By the time that the Hebrew Ezra-Nehemiah was completed it was presupposed that Ezra promulgated some version of the five books of Moses as an authoritative writing for the Jews. Exactly when Ezra-Nehemiah is to be dated is unclear, but it was almost certainly before the time of Ben Sira around 200 BCE. Ben Sira appears to know the Pentateuch and the Prophets in much the form that they later appeared in the Jewish canon (Ben Sira 44–49). He gives no indication that this state of things was new, suggesting that this was already the situation long before his time. This is a whole study in itself, but the Pentateuch and many of the Prophets probably reached much their present form in the Persian period (cf. Davies 1998).

The significance of putting traditional law into a fixed book cannot be overestimated. Before, the community and the priesthood were the guardians and repositories of the traditional and religious law. Change could take place, but it was slow and gradual, and interpretation was a group activity. Once the teaching was codified into a book, anyone who could read could potentially give an interpretation. This had enormous implications which, with the passage of time, came to be realized. These will be further discussed in the final chapter.

Conclusions about the Gestalt of Ezra the Scribe

The more we have looked at the traditions about Ezra in Ezra 7–10 and Nehemiah 8, the more puzzling the figure of Ezra becomes (Grabbe 1994). His priestly origins are emphasized at various points in the story, and one would gain the impression that he held the office of high priest. Indeed, no other person is said to be high priest in the chapters about him. Yet he is not called high priest, and his name does not occur in the lists of high priests elsewhere (Neh. 12:10–11, 22). His concern to bring Levites and temple servants as well as priests with him in Ezra 9 suggest an attempt to restore the cult. Yet there is no hint that the cult lacked ministers, whether priests, Levites, or temple servants. The cult had functioned for decades before Ezra came, and there is no indication when he arrives in Jerusalem that there is anything lacking.

The political powers conferred on Ezra are astounding. One might at least assume that he was appointed governor of Judah, and a number of scholars refer to him as governor without discussion, as if this can be taken for granted (e.g. Margalith 1986). Some of the measures he takes are parallel to those of Nehemiah (e.g. the mixed marriage issue) and might well be taken by the governor of the province. He is nowhere called governor, though this title might have been suppressed by the editor, as it was in the case of Zerubbabel (and Sheshbazzar). However, the commission of Artaxerxes says nothing about being a provincial governor.

If the letter of Artaxerxes gives weight to any political office, it would be that Ezra is over the entire satrapy of Ebir-nari. He has the right to teach and enforce the law in the entire satrapy and to appoint judges to oversee its enforcement. Nothing is said about the satrap over this area, nor was Ezra's jurisdiction and appointment of judges confined to the Jews. One could well assume that Ezra has been appointed the satrap of the entire area west of the Euphrates. This conclusion would be absurd, in the opinion of most commentators, yet it is a legitimate conclusion to draw from the text – certainly as legitimate as assuming he was governor or high priest. The absurdity of the suggestion simply highlights the literary and theological nature of the tradition. Yet with all that religious and imperial authority behind him, he has trouble dealing with a relatively minor problem in Jerusalem. He can only pray and sit in the street; others make the decisions and give the orders; at least, the initial orders from him come as the result of someone else's decision. Ezra's actions are neither those of the high priest nor the governor; they are certainly not those of a satrap.

Most astounding of all is the amount of wealth alleged to have come under Ezra's control. Some of the points made above show contradictions within the tradition. The money given to Ezra contradicts external historical reality. The amount of gold and silver alleged to have been brought by Ezra was sufficient to pay off the national debt of some Third World countries: more than 25 tonnes of precious metal. Despite having all that wealth to use more or less as he pleases, Ezra also has the authority to draw out another hundred talents of silver (three tonnes) plus a large quantity of foodstuffs from the imperial treasury (Ezra 7:22), just on his signature, as it were. The author of Ezra seems to have no concept of the worth of the figures he drops casually into his narrative, or how large a portion of the Persian empire's wealth they represent. More surprising are the number of commentators who have accepted them without question.

The later development of the traditions confirms this impression. As discussed in more detail in chapter 4 above, the Ezra and Nehemiah traditions show a diversity of perspective on Ezra and what he accomplished. 4 Ezra 14 gives activities in relation to the law, but the story here is quite different from the Hebrew Ezra-Nehemiah. In this case Ezra is the conduit for the law and many other books. After drinking from a divine cup, he dictates to five scribes for forty days and forty nights (14:37–48). The end result is the twenty-four exoteric books which are obviously meant to be the Hebrew canon, but in addition there are another seventy esoteric books to be kept secret except for the wise. The emphasis here is not on Ezra as a teacher or expounder of the law but as a preserver of a law which had been lost and as the source of secret books which were available only to the few. It is doubtful that one can call Ezra a lawgiver here in the sense that Moses was, because the law that he dictates is not new but the old law restored.

Other sources do not know of Ezra as a lawgiver, however. The most important witness is Ben Sira who makes Moses the mediator of the commandments and the covenant (44:23–45:5). Nehemiah is the repairer of the walls and houses (49:13), but Ezra is not mentioned. As already noted, Ben Sira either did not know the Ezra tradition or knew it but rejected it. Either way, it demonstrates that the concept of Ezra as lawgiver was by no means a universal view.

Summary and conclusions

Ezra is an enigma. The confidence with which his life and activities are reconstructed by many commentators is simply not borne out, either by a careful study of the tradition itself or by those areas where it can be checked against external data. The tradition itself is self-contradictory. The Ezra story simply does not make sense in its own context. For this reason, the arguments that we have an 'Ezra memoir' in parts of Ezra 7–9 seem unlikely. Either this first-person section is mainly an invention, or Ezra wrote it but deceived us, or it has been heavily worked over by a later editor. There are problems with each of these possibilities, but this is because there are such problems with the Ezra narrative itself. Portions of the story go quite contrary to other parts. Ezra is satrap but not satrap; governor but not governor; high priest but not high priest. He is presented as if he had the power of the governor or even the satrap of the entire region west of the Euphrates, and it could also be surmised that he was the high priest. Yet when it comes time to exercise all this power, he is at a loss. It is as if the person of Ezra 7 is an entirely different person from that in Ezra 9–10. The letter of Artaxerxes in Ezra 7 in some passages could pass as a genuine Persian decree, but in other respects it looks like a piece of Jewish propaganda. This is especially true in the incredibly generous concessions made to Ezra and the Jews by the king, including what seems to be almost a petty cash fund of one hundred talents of silver. When that is combined with the enormous value of the gifts made to the temple (more than 25 tonnes of gold and silver), we know we are not dealing with history but with something else, whether you call it legend, literature, or theology.

It is very possible that there was a historical Ezra. It is striking that a number of the lists have the name Ezra or something close in them. The Artaxerxes letter could well be based on a genuine letter from the king in regard to a Jewish leader, even to Ezra himself, but the letter in its present form is a piece of later Jewish propaganda. Most of the individual episodes within the Ezra story could conceivably have a historical basis, but they could equally have been invented. To decide that one is historical and another not appears to be arbitrary in the light of present knowledge. For example, it is tempting to say that whatever the problems with the Ezra tradition, at least the story that he had something to do with the law is credible. However, this is to favour the later development of the tradition over the earlier. Ezra indeed has an important (if unclear) association with the law in the Hebrew Ezra-Nehemiah, but this is not universal in the traditions. In 4 Ezra he is the restorer of the law, not its creator, because the law went back to Moses. But Ben Sira knows nothing of an Ezra-lawgiver tradition, nor does 2 Maccabees. The Qumran texts emphasize Moses as the lawgiver, even if Ezra is not completely unknown, whereas the New Testament does not mention him at all. Ezra as lawgiver does not seem to be any more established as a historical datum than any other part of the Ezra tradition.

7

NEHEMIAH AND HISTORY

Sources for the book of Nehemiah

As already discussed in chapter 5, it is almost universally accepted that Nehemiah 8 is a portion of the Ezra tradition. Apart from that, much of the content of the book of Nehemiah comes from the so-called 'Nehemiah memorial' or 'memoir' or from a diversity of sources.

The 'Nehemiah memorial' (NM)

A good portion of the Nehemiah narrative is in the first person. It has long been agreed that a writing of Nehemiah of some sort lies at the core of the book. The precise sort of writing has been much debated without any strong consensus (see the survey in Kellermann 1967: 76–84; Williamson 1985: xxiv–xxviii). Some have thought it was a sort of report to the Persian authorities, justifying Nehemiah's actions in Jerusalem (cf. Williamson 1985: xxviii). An explanation which has gained a good deal of support is that it was a 'letter to God', a 'Nehemiah memorial', a personal writing perhaps placed in the temple and meant primarily as a communication with God (Mowinckel 1961; 1964b: 50–104). Tablets written on behalf of the king, detailing his good deeds and pieties, have been found in the foundations of temples of Mesopotamia. Their primary function was to deliver a message to the deity, which means that they were hidden; however, this does not mean that copies might not also be made public. Another explanation is that Nehemiah wrote a variant of the prayer of the accused such as Jer. 18:19–23 and 2 Kings 20:3 (Kellermann 1967: 84–88). Williamson himself explains the origin of the NM in two stages, the first being an Aramaic report for the

Persians and the second a later reworking with the Jewish community in mind (1985: xxvii–xxviii). Each of these theories recognizes some of the characteristics of Nehemiah's writing while also having weaknesses. However, Joseph Blenkinsopp (1987; 1994) has pointed to the closest parallel in the form of a contemporary account of the life and work of another native appointed as a Persian official, the autobiography of the Egyptian Udjahorresnet. Still, Nehemiah's writing is unique in its own way, and we should not expect an exact counterpart. The abbreviation NM (for 'Nehemiah memorial/memoir') will be used henceforth to designate the Nehemiah writing.

Whatever the Nehemiah writing is called and however it is explained, the existence of such a writing by one of the leading participants in the events of the time is a real bonus for the historian. Can we have confidence that such a writing of Nehemiah indeed existed? After all, it has also been proposed that an 'Ezra memoir' existed, but this has been disputed (see chapter 6 above). The striking thing about the NM is the widespread consensus on its existence. Even so sceptical a scholar as Gunneweg accepted that it existed (1987: 176–80). There are several reasons for postulating such a source (cf. Kellermann 1967: 4–8). One is the large amount of material in the first person, an unusual situation in the OT literature. But probably the main argument is the very subjective and personal one that the NM strikes the reader as a real outpouring of an individual at a particular time.

Acceptance of an authentic NM does not mean that all one's problems are over. Two major obstacles still remain to the use of the NM as a historical source. The first is that the NM in its present form has been edited into the book of Nehemiah, with a good deal of other material. The question is, what is the extent of the NM and how much change has been made to the text by the editors? A reasonable consensus can be obtained for much of the NM, even if there is disagreement about where the 'edges' of the document might fall. Usually assigned to the NM are Neh. 1:1–7:5, portions of 12:27–43, 13:4–31. The main area of disagreement lies with Neh. 13, much of which is in the first person. Although most accept that much of this chapter belongs to the NM, a strong argument has been presented that it is by a later writer imitating the distinctive style of the NM (Ackroyd 1970a: 28, 41; Steins 1995: 198–207). If this is right, the chapter does not go back to Nehemiah himself.

A second problem to use of the NM as a historical source is its highly prejudiced nature. Nehemiah is presenting everything from his own perspective, as we might expect, but his perspective is an extremely partisan one (cf. Clines 1990). He seems to make no attempt to see other points of view or recognize that there might be another way of understanding events. Opposition to him came not only from outside the community but from some of the leading figures within the community and even from within the priesthood. Nehemiah gives his side of the story, but that is not the only side. We have to consider how he was perceived by others with whom he worked or otherwise came into contact.

Various lists

A number of lists are included in the books of Ezra and Nehemiah. Also, except for the list of those coming with Ezra (Ezra 8:2–14), all the lists of Ezra-Nehemiah occur in Nehemiah (including the variant of Ezra 2 found in Neh. 7). In fact, apart from the NM and Neh. 8, much of the material in the book of Nehemiah is of lists of various sorts. The different lists often involve names laid out by family, sometimes with the names of ancestors in the form of a genealogy of some sort. It would be naive to take these as straightforward records of actual individuals and actual genealogies. Studies of genealogies in pre-modern societies show that they can have functions other than a simple record of blood descent (cf. Wilson 1977; 1979). They may show social relationships or contain theological messages.

Even where authentic names are included, genealogies tend to evolve on the oral level and become subject to editing when committed to writing. Thus, trying to deal with the lists in the context of history is very difficult. We can only test for plausibility or make intelligent guesses in many cases. A brief survey of these lists quickly shows that they do not fit the situation in many cases and appear to be from a variety of sources, though trying to ascertain these sources at this point is rather difficult. Some of the alleged contexts make no sense at all. A brief review of the comments made in chapters 2–3 above is in order.

The most obvious place to begin is with the list in Ezra 2//Neh. 7. There is almost universal agreement that this list is not a register of those who came with Joshua and Zerubbabel at the beginning of the return from exile (whether under Cyrus or Darius). Some of those on the list have Persian names (e.g. Bagoas), and the names Nehemiah and Azariah (a form of Ezra) suggest a rather later time in the Persian period. The list is laid out partly by extended family and partly by place of settlement. It would be difficult to authenticate the genealogical part for reasons noted above; however, the settlement list looks to be of a different order. The places listed in Ezra 2:21–35//Neh 7:21–38 fall within the boundaries of what is likely to be the small Persian province of Yehud. This is why the list is commonly thought to represent the settled population of Judah perhaps in the late fifth century BCE (e.g. Mowinckel 1964a: 98–109). Beyond this it is difficult to extract much in the way of historical data. There may be other useful information, but this is very uncertain.

The list of those who came with Ezra in 8:2–14 looks artificial. It is part of a first-person narrative, yet it refers to 'those who came up with me from Babylon in the reign of king Artaxerxes' (8:1); surely in context there was no need to specify the current king. This suggests the list was obtained from elsewhere or was made up for the purpose of the narrative. It begins with the grandson and son of Aaron respectively, Phinehas and Ithamar. The name David seems to be king David. Why these should be listed is not clear, nor is any number of returnees given. There are some oddities about the list (e.g. the expression 'sons of Shecaniah' occurs in both 8:3 and 8:5, yet no representative is given in either case and a number occurs only in the second verse; the name Shelomith in 8:10 is a feminine form). If we ignore the two occurrences of Shecaniah, we have eleven names. Nine of these are also found in Ezra 2:3–15; most also occur in Neh 10:15–17 which is a rather different context. It looks as if a standard list has been used (see below).

The list of repairers of the wall is perhaps the most likely to be authentic, though it has long been recognized that it is probably not a part of the NM. Many of those who worked are said to repair the section of the wall near their own homes, which makes a good deal of sense since there would be a considerable degree of motivation in such circumstances. The question of whether the list is complete is debated since a 'second section' is sometimes mentioned without a first (e.g. 3:11, 30) and several even mentioned in a row (3:19–21). The first part of the list (3:1–15) is characterized by the expression 'next to them/him' ('al-yādām/yādô), and the second part (3:16–32) by 'after him' ('aḥărâv). There may be a connection between this differentiation and the topographical line of the wall, with the first half referring to the repair of the old wall and the second half to the new line of the wall established where the old one was abandoned (Williamson 1985: 200; Gunneweg 1987: 71). Interesting is the significant number of priests who participate in the work of building and the fact that Eliashib the high priest heads the list, perhaps suggesting that it was composed by priestly scribes. There is a tendency to give the names of fathers and sometimes even grandfathers, which could suggest that it legitimated the families of those who participated.

The lists in Neh. 10 and 12 have a considerable overlap, despite their different contexts, especially when slight variants of name are allowed for. Neh. 10 is supposed to give the signatories of those who signed a covenant to keep various laws, whereas Neh. 12 lists those 'who came up with Zerubbabel son of Shealtiel and Joshua' (12:1). Despite the fact that almost a century separates these two, the lists of priests in 10:3–8 and 12:1–7, 12–21 have a common core of fifteen names; in addition, each list has half a dozen names which the other does not have. The two lists must have had a common origin in some way, which seems strange given their different contexts. On the other hand, the 'heads of the people' list in 10:15–28 has parallels for two separate sections. Most of the first eighteen names of 10:15–20 have parallels in Ezra 2:3–19// Neh. 7:8–24, whereas most of the names in 10:21–28 have parallels in the list of wall repairers (Neh. 3).

Neh. 11 describes those who settled in Jerusalem, including most of the priests and Levites but also supposedly a tenth of the people. About a third are from Benjamin, which fits the settlement patterns of the new province. No total is given in the text, but the sum of the separate numbers equals about 3,000 which is probably the population one might expect of Jerusalem about this time. The largest group is the priests, which is not surprising given that one would expect the priests to live near the temple. The number of Levites is small, as throughout Ezra-Nehemiah. Some of the places in 11:25–31 were in the area of Edom, not Judah. How to explain this has been debated, with several suggestions, but it is hardly a description of places in the province of Judah at this time. Although the heading (11:3) lists the Netinim, they are not given a number and also appear in 11:21 in what looks like possibly an addition to the list. The 'sons of Solomon's servants' appears in the heading (11:3) but are not listed afterward in the chapter. All this suggests not a straightforward settlement list of Jerusalem in the time of Nehemiah but rather a compilation from other lists. This deduction is strengthened when one notes that 11:4–19 has many points in common with 1 Chron. 9:2–17.

The conclusions are that the various lists in Ezra and Nehemiah can be used only with considerable caution. The list of those who worked on the wall (Neh. 3) could well be from an archive. In Ezra 2//Neh. 7 the list of sites where people settled may be a reflection of settlement patterns in Judah at a particular time, but pinning that time down is difficult to do with any confidence. Knowing that there may be original data in these lists does not tell how to sort them out from the elements created by the compiler.

The Nehemiah story

Nehemiah's commission

A puzzle commences with the first few verses of the book. Nehemiah is told about the sorry state of things in Jerusalem: those 'who have survived the captivity there in the province are in dire trouble and disgrace; Jerusalem's wall is full of breaches, and its gates have been destroyed by fire' (Neh. 1:1–2 NJPS). This is not what we expect to read after having just finished Ezra, where the city and temple had been rebuilt, the temple and cult restored, and the difficulties of mixed marriages resolved. Has something happened in the meantime – some sort of tragedy which has affected both city and people? If so, this is never made explicit.

Or is the explanation to be seen in the development of the traditions? As shown in chapter 6, the various traditions about the restoration of Judah and Jerusalem have been to some extent independent of one another. It may have been that there were several 'origin' or 'founding' stories, each of which had a different individual or set of individuals as the leaders of the restoration. In one story it was Zerubbabel and Joshua, a story more or less intact in Ezra 1–6. Another version of the story may have made Ezra the founder of the new Jerusalem though, if so, this form of the story does not survive in any of the remaining versions. Another form of the story made Nehemiah the rebuilder of the temple and founder of the state. That particular version does not occur in the present book of Nehemiah, but it is not a matter of speculation since it does exist in one of the other versions (2 Macc. 1:18–2:13). The abruptness of Neh. 1 could be due to a literary cause. The story used by the compiler may have had Nehemiah as the one who restored the temple and the city. If so, he could not use it in its original form because the temple had already been founded under Joshua and Zerubbabel according to the earlier part of his account in Ezra 1–6. Thus, the compiler simply changed the founding story into a 'repair of the wall' story, but this led to an abrupt beginning with the state of Jerusalem left hanging and unexplained.

This explanation makes a lot of sense from a literary point of view, but it is harder to accept if a genuine NM makes up much of Neh. 1–2, for the first-person account is definitely to do with a repair of the wall. On the other hand, repair of the wall might have preceded a restoration of the temple, and this part of the story might have been dropped by the compiler. A lot depends on the dating of Nehemiah. If he did not come until the reign of Artaxerxes I at the earliest, it is hard to credit a situation in which the city and temple remained in ruins for about three-quarters of a century before anything was done about it. If we attempt to resolve the problem by literary developments alone, we should probably have to reject the idea of a NM. Yet it seems to me that the arguments for its authenticity (subjective as they are) are convincing. Therefore, the best explanation is that something had happened to Jerusalem in the meantime. This explanation is also the one most easily fitting the present literary context, including the reaction of Nehemiah in Neh. 1. He apparently expected the news to be good, which also presupposes that a community had been settled and functioning there for a long time. On the other hand, it was likely that the compiler did not know what had happened to cause the difficulties described in Neh. 1:3 because he says nothing about it. In other words, the only information he had after the supposed events of Ezra 10 was the NM, in either pure or edited form. Our lack of information was also the compiler's lack of information.

Nehemiah's closeness to the king might be suspect, as is that of Daniel or Esther and Mordecai. But Nehemiah's position is more believable than that in either the Daniel or the Esther stories. The fact that he could be released for years at a time shows that he was not central to the Persian administration. His passage to Jerusalem with letters from the king is also in marked contrast to that of Ezra. Nehemiah simply took a personal bodyguard and went to Jerusalem with some letters of support which he presented to the appropriate Persian officials. He did not bring tonnes of gold and silver; he did not eschew an escort and depend on God; he was not given authority over the established officials in the region of Ebir-nari. The only special authority he had was to obtain timber from the king's park for some of his building work. He was also appointed governor of the province of Judah (Neh. 5:14).

Nehemiah requested of the king to 'rebuild Jerusalem' (Neh. 2:5). How that was understood and whether he may have exceeded his authority are points which could be discussed at length. Nevertheless, the basic commission is clear, and his repair of the walls seems to be a legitimate activity in the task of 'rebuilding Jerusalem'. This task also seems to have been accepted by the Jerusalem authorities without any quibbling. The local people would no doubt be well aware of their vulnerability with the city wall in such a state, and the fact that many of them seem to have worked on the section of the wall nearest to their own homes would have been an additional inducement (Neh. 3). Yet opposition developed – and evidently a strong one, which brings us to the next section.

Opposition to Nehemiah

Nehemiah roused opposition from the start, it seems. He had barely arrived on the scene before a group of local dignitaries were suspicious of what he was up to (Neh. 2:10). There seem to be two reasons for this. The first is that Sanballat and Tobiah, as well as Geshem the Arabian, were local individuals with power who apparently worked together to mutual advantage, and Nehemiah was clearly a competitor. We know from other sources that Sanballat was governor of the province of Samaria, that Geshem was probably an Arab ruler, and that Tobiah was probably a member of an old Jewish upper-class family with an estate in Transjordan (Grabbe 1992a: 132–35). It has also been argued that Judah had been a part of the province of Samaria until Nehemiah came (Alt 1953; McEvenue 1981); if so, Nehemiah had hived off a part of the province of Samaria from its governor, which would be an additional reason for their resentments. However, this thesis is controversial and has been rejected by a number of studies (Smith 1987: 193–201; Williamson 1988); in any case, Sanballat had sufficient grounds to arouse his political concerns even if Nehemiah had come only as a replacement governor.

The second reason for opposition was Nehemiah himself. He evidently had the knack of antagonizing those around him. For example, as soon as he arrived in Jerusalem he made a night inspection of the wall, yet he did this without the knowledge of the local officials (Neh. 2:11–16). Why this secret reconnaissance? He does not explain, and it makes little sense. All he had to do was tell them that he had come with authority to build the wall and then go out in daylight for a proper inspection with those who would be doing much of the supervisory work. The work was apparently undertaken with considerable enthusiasm (cf. Neh. 2:17–18), but from the start of the project they must have felt that he did not trust them.

Nehemiah's own estimation of himself and his importance seems to have been fairly high. Some leaders would have just come and built a wall, but not Nehemiah. He came with both a royal and a divine commission and carried it out through godly assistance – and his own will – despite opposition from vicious and wily foes who are described in practically demonic terms. The description of opposition in Nehemiah 4 almost takes one's breath away. One has the impression that a set of murdering bandits is about to fall upon the poor builders of the wall; when all is said and done, however, no one so much as says 'Boo' to them. We have only Nehemiah's version of the situation, and the text in Neh. 4:6–7 is difficult and probably corrupt. But his claim to be able to read Sanballat's mind is a bit much to swallow, even from Nehemiah. If Sanballat was planning a raid on Jerusalem, he is hardly likely to tell the local Jews about it (as is implied in 4:6). And if he wanted to stop the building of the wall, why would that have endangered 'your sons and daughters, your wives and homes' as suggested in 4:8? He is representing Sanballat and Co. as if they were a gang of thieves and cut-throats, instead of regional dignitaries and Persian officials. One cannot help wondering if the danger from Sanballat was purely a figment of Nehemiah's overheated imagination (see further the analysis of Neh. 4 in chapter 3 above).

The opposition between Sanballat and Nehemiah is quite understandable. It is the perennial political rivalry between officials of a governmental regime, especially one in which local governors of far-flung areas had a good deal of autonomy. This type of rivalry was mild compared to what we read of between satraps in the Persian administration. In many cases, these became almost independent kings with their own armies and absolute power in their own satrapies. Achaemenid history is filled with examples of unruly satraps who gave pain not only to their fellow satraps but to the king himself. Periodically, a satrap would rebel, and the emperor did not always find it easy to deal with his powerful underling. That two Persian officials governing contiguous areas had little love lost between them needs no explanation. From that point of view the conflict between Nehemiah and his fellow governor Sanballat is what we should expect.

What is more surprising – and also likely to have been unnecessary – was the internal opposition to Nehemiah. This antagonism may in some cases have been unavoidable in that some saw him as a rival, but this explanation goes only so far. Entrenched interests there no doubt were (see below), but other bad relations seem to have been cultivated by Nehemiah himself. The example of the secret midnight ride has been mentioned already. But those who found him a pain were not just a few local dignitaries; rather, they included priests, prophets, nobles, and even people who evidently did their best to get along with Nehemiah while still disagreeing with some of his measures. A man who gets everyone's back up is not usually reckoned to be blameless.

The first indication of internal opposition is the statement that although the Tekoaites repaired, 'their nobles' (*'addîrêhem*) refused to help (Neh. 3:5). This is not explained, and there are many possible reasons. It may be that the nobles disagreed with the project. More likely is that Tekoa was some distance from Jerusalem, and they saw no need to get involved in a project which would not benefit their local area. Or perhaps they were quite happy for the 'plebs' from the village to do the work but disdained getting their own hands dirty. There seems little reason to read personal opposition to Nehemiah into this one incident. Yet the enthusiasm with which the priests and the people set to the task of repairing the wall was soon belied by bad feelings which seem to have developed fairly quickly.

Nehemiah 5 is a good example of a situation which was handled badly. In this chapter Nehemiah presents himself as a champion of the poor and oppressed. Some of 'the people [*hā'ām*] and their wives' cried out because they had had to sell property or, in some cases, even their own children into slavery to buy food or pay taxes. Nehemiah criticizes the nobles and leaders for pressing for the repayment of loans. He also cites his own example of buying back some Jews who had been sold into slavery. So far, a worthy cause and a noble example of his own righteous actions. But Nehemiah cannot handle the matter quietly and effectively to resolve the problem, as a good administrator would. Inevitably, he makes a huge public fuss, which is the way of the politician and the demagogue.

He first of all makes a public accusation against those he deems guilty. He says they have nothing to say for themselves, but this is hardly surprising since Nehemiah himself had gathered a crowd against them (Neh. 5:7–8), again the action of a demagogue. He then holds himself up – publicly – as a righteous example. In what is probably another example of public humiliation, he calls the priests and makes them swear to keep the promise to return confiscated property (5:12). Nehemiah completes his account by enumerating the amount consumed daily at the governor's table and then boasting that he had not availed himself of the governor's food allowance to pay for this (5:14–18). Most commentators have viewed his measures with favour, but they usually have not probed beyond the rhetoric to consider the practical implications.

Nehemiah was evidently unaware of the modern adage, 'There is no such thing as a free lunch.' He mentions that, among other things, an ox a day was served at his table. Over the twelve years of his governorship, this represented more than 4,000 cattle – a herd large enough to stock a Texas ranch. Who paid for these, not to mention a flock of sheep six times this size and countless thousands of fowl? Nehemiah claims with elaborate self-righteousness that he did not collect the governor's tax, in contrast to previous governors, but he is coy about saying who paid. One assumes he either collected funds from some other source (a special tax on the nobles, perhaps?) or he had a private income. But previous governors may not have had such advantages. If they were doing their job, why should they not receive appropriate payment? On the other hand, perhaps they did not have such a retinue as Nehemiah who fed 150 locals plus visitors from abroad each day. Did a governor of the small province of Judah need such a large group of administrators, friends, and hangers-on? On the other hand, if such a large group was really needed, it was right that they receive public support. Our modern democracies work on such a principle, which commentators all too quickly forget.

As for the much criticized nobles, we do not have their side of the story. No doubt some had exploited the poor and deserved the censure, but did all? How many of them were not in a financial position to write off large unpaid debts? If those to whom they loaned money could not pay them, could they still pay their own taxes? Had they themselves borrowed money which they expected to pay back when they in turn received payment for money loaned out? The assumption seems to be that the nobles had inexhaustible wealth, and that cancelling debts was of no consequence to them, but why should we assume this?

Finally, what did Nehemiah do for the long-term good of the poor? It was a nice gesture to tell the nobles to cancel their debts. However, when the tax demands came the next year, who was going to loan them money to pay it? Nehemiah's intervention had ensured that no one would lend money in the future because they had no way of getting it back. The essential principle of loaning against collateral had been outlawed, so there was no incentive to make a loan. With no suggestion in the passage that Nehemiah had done anything to help the long-term plight of the poor, the problems described at the beginning of the passage were likely to recur. The difference now was that the poor no longer had anywhere to turn for a needed loan when they had a financial crisis. Thanks very much, Nehemiah!

Nehemiah's penchant of getting involved in all sorts of local matters may explain some of the passages in the NM in which he complains about various individuals being against him. Nehemiah 6 is one long harangue about those who were less than enthusiastic about the governor of Judah. According to his version of events, his main antagonist Sanballat supposedly allied with Geshem the Arabian to 'do evil' (*la'ăśôt rā'āh*) to him (6:2). They sent a message suggesting a meeting. Nehemiah 'knows' that this is a mere ruse to get him away by himself to do some unspecified nastiness to him, so he refuses repeated requests to have a meeting (6:2–4). How does he know it is a trap? Nothing in the text suggests that he does know; in other words, he is only guessing.

Perhaps he was right, and the Sanballat contingent was out to rid themselves of an opponent. On the other hand, would the Persian government allow one governor to murder another? Sanballat and his supporters may have had a genuine desire to reach an agreement, no doubt to mutual advantage, but nevertheless an offer to shake hands and make up. If so, it was not in Nehemiah's nature to deal with them on any terms but his own, and he puts the worst interpretation possible on their invitation.

A further message accuses him of seeking to set himself up as king (6:6–9). Nehemiah rejects this as preposterous, but his own actions belie his suggestion that it was all made up. Whether Nehemiah had any formal designs on a local kingship is impossible to say from the data preserved; nevertheless, he acted like a petty tyrant in Judah. The charge that he was seeking to become king would have rung a bell with many observers. Nehemiah was too astute to try to rebel against the Persian empire, as charged by Sanballat; however, the accusation that there were prophets making such claims (6:7) is quite believable. This would have been a difficult charge to make if no such prophecies were known. Whether rumours that Nehemiah wished to become king reached the Persian emperor's ears is not known; if they did, Nehemiah seems to have weathered whatever enquiry followed. As a politician of some knowledge and ability (he had become royal cupbearer, after all), Nehemiah probably had no plans to proclaim himself the Judaean king. But you do not have to have the title of 'king' to act like one.

Nehemiah had his supporters in prophetic circles, but he also numbered prophets among his internal opponents. First, Shemaiah son of Delaiah calls him into the sanctuary and warns him of a plot against him (6:10–13). Surprisingly, Nehemiah is not grateful but instead assumes that Shemaiah had been hired by his opponents to intimidate him. Why he thought this is not discussed. Shemaiah may have been perfectly sincere in the message he gave Nehemiah. If he was merely one of Sanballat's fifth columnists, as Nehemiah alleges, the reasons for concluding this are not given in the text. As far as we know, Shemaiah was simply acting by the divine spirit within him like any other prophet. The same seems to apply to the prophetess Noadiah, the intriguing female prophet who remains little more than a name to us. She prophesied something which Nehemiah did not like. That she was actually an opponent of Nehemiah is uncertain, though she, Shemaiah, and the other unnamed prophets may have become opponents (even if they were not originally so) because of how Nehemiah treated them. If they were really sincere in the messages passed on to Nehemiah, his attitude to them must have been extremely galling.

The figure who is most interesting in relationship to Nehemiah is Tobiah (cf. Mazar 1957; Grabbe 1992a: 132–35). He is called 'the Ammonite slave' (2:10, 19: *ha'eved hā'ammōnî*) by Nehemiah, which was no doubt intended to be a derogatory epithet. The term *'eved* is ambiguous and can designate anyone from the humblest slave to the high government officials who were 'servants' of the king. Nehemiah's designation is likely to be sarcastic because it fails to recognize Tobiah's Jewishness (Tobiah only lived in the old Ammonite region but was not ethnically an Ammonite) and because Nehemiah calls Jewish servants 'lads' (4:10, 16–17: *na'ar*). Nehemiah sees Tobiah as one of the conspirators against him. Yet Tobiah was a Jew of an influential family and had relations and connections in Jerusalem (6:17–19). At a later date, the high priest even allowed him to set up an office in one of the storerooms in the temple area (13:4–9). Tobiah was clearly a man to be reckoned with in the Jerusalem community.

It is with Tobiah that we begin to see part of the cause of the problem. Nehemiah presents the situation in black-and-white terms. As he saw it, people were either for him or against him, and if you supported Tobiah, you were against him. But others among the Jewish leadership did not see it that way. They did not seem to oppose

Nehemiah as such, and most of them worked on the wall without hesitation, yet they also saw no reason to treat Tobiah as an enemy. So they tried to maintain good relations with both Tobiah and Nehemiah; what is more, they even attempted to reconcile the two by speaking well of Tobiah to Nehemiah (6:18–19). It did not work, of course, because Nehemiah was determined to have nothing to do with Tobiah. What this illustrates, though, is the extent to which the opposition to Nehemiah was his own creation. He simply did not try to get along with the local people. They either did it his way or they were his enemies. No wonder that when he left the province to return to Babylon for a period of time, people were quick to abandon the more extreme of his reforms (Nehemiah 13).

Completion of the wall

As already noted, the story of the completion of the wall gets interrupted by a part of the Ezra tradition on the reading of the law. The completion of the building work is mentioned in Neh. 6:15, though in the context of the opposition to Nehemiah. The rest of the story is not told in one unit but is split between several further passages. As already noted above, Nehemiah was practically paranoid about enemies. Therefore, according to 7:1–5, as soon as the gates were set on their hinges, Nehemiah set up a guard routine. His lack of trust in those about him is once again indicated by his appointing his brother Hanani to be in charge of this procedure. Hanani (also apparently mentioned in Neh. 1:2) is indicated by the context to be a literal brother of Nehemiah. (It is possible that the first part of 7:2 should be translated, 'Hanani my brother, even Hananiah the captain of the citadel'; in other words, only one person and not two is put in charge. The construction of the sentence favours this interpretation, but the matter is disputed.)

Next, Nehemiah decided that Jerusalem's population was too small (7:4–5). He was no doubt right that a reasonable population was needed to ensure that the building work was not damaged by enemies and that Jerusalem functioned as a city. The text states that no houses had yet been built (7:4). This is rather strange in that the previous verse states that each inhabitant was to watch in front of his own house; also, earlier in Neh. 3 the builders had often repaired in front of their own houses. Most commentaries assume that 7:4 is not to be taken literally. In any case, Nehemiah has a plan to register the people, and the rest of Nehemiah 7 is taken up with a list of those who had come in the time of Joshua and Zerubbabel. That is followed by the reading of the law and the issue of mixed marriages. It is not until Nehemiah 11 that the story resumes. Neh. 11:1–2 forms a logical continuation of the account begun in 7:1–5. The question of whether 11:1–2 is a part of the NM has been much discussed (e.g. Williamson 1985: 345–46), with the conclusion that it probably was not. This would make it part of a document which includes the list in the rest of the chapter.

Regardless of whether 11:1–2 is a part of the NM, it illustrates the likely aims of Nehemiah in his measures relating to Jerualem. All of the officials are required to live in Jerusalem. The rest of the people drew lots. The aim was to make a full tenth of the population of the province live in Jerusalem. It was no doubt correct that a minimum population in the city was needed to make it function, but one wonders whether Nehemiah was not thinking beyond this. The effect of building the wall, setting up gates, and increasing the population greatly was to increase the importance and prominence of Jerusalem. It was also possible to control the activities of the city's population. If one-tenth of the inhabitants lived in Jerusalem, this gave a great deal of power to Nehemiah himself. It is more difficult to control people who live in the countryside, especially nobles who have their own estates and perhaps a private retinue of servants. But if all the officials are required to live in Jerusalem, it would be easier for Nehemiah to keep an eye on them. The usefulness of the wall in this control will be further discussed in the next section.

The account breaks off again into a list of those who settled in Jerusalem and does not resume until 12:27–43 when the dedication of the wall is described. Again, this is usually reckoned as a part of the NM, though with various editings and insertions (e.g. Blenkinsopp 1988: 343–48). However, it could have been a separate document; that is, it would not be surprising if someone wrote up a description of the dedication for preservation in public or private archives. If 12:27–43 comes from a separate document, it is still possible that Nehemiah himself wrote it (note the use of the first person in 12:31). The emphasis in this ceremony is naturally on the priests and Levites who make up the bulk of the procession around the city walls. This is the only account in the biblical text of a city wall's being dedicated in this manner. The ceremonies described seem more appropriate to the dedication of the temple; however, it would be thoroughly within Nehemiah's character to give the completion of his building work a divine dimension. From that point of view the report fits well with the NM and Nehemiah's way of going about things.

The nobles, priests, and Levites

Among those who were recipients of the rough edge of Nehemiah's tongue were various of the nobles and priests. This has led Morton Smith to argue that the nobles and priests were Nehemiah's opponents, against whom he enlisted the Levites and the 'new-rich mercantile class' (1987: 96–112). Smith's thesis is stimulating, but it must be kept in mind that it forms part of a larger hypothesis about the 'Yahweh-alone party' and the 'syncretistic party' which, he argues, had a long history from the early period of the monarchy. Although the model presented in the whole of Smith's book has many attractive features, it is really too simplistic; the data suggest a rather more complicated relationship of various groups and movements (cf. Grabbe 1992a: 104–7). Nevertheless, his particular point with regard to Nehemiah deserves consideration. A number of the relevant texts have already been discussed, but at the risk of some repetition the main ones will be summarized here.

There is no doubt that the nobles are criticized at various points, as are the priests. As soon as Nehemiah arrived, he unaccountably keeps the city leadership of priests and nobles in ignorance of his night observation of the damage to the wall (2:11–16). The nobles of Tekoa did not assist in the building of the wall, but this seems to have been an exception, and we do not know that it had anything to do with objection to Nehemiah (3:5). Neh. 5 is a major example of criticism of the nobles and priests. As discussed at greater length above, Nehemiah confronts the 'nobles and officials' with a large crowd of the people and berates them publicly, then puts them under oath. The nobles correspond with Tobiah, who was related to some of them, and they speak well of him to Nehemiah (6:17–19). Finally, when Nehemiah finds examples of Sabbath-breaking, he calls the nobles to account to resolve the problem, perhaps suggesting that they were benefitting from the Sabbath trading (13:15–17).

Yet there are other passages which complicate this picture. Most of the nobles seem to have helped with the wall (4:8, 13–15), which means that the refusal of the Tekoan nobles was probably the exception rather than the rule. The fact that some nobles communicated with Tobiah is hardly surprising since that family was an old established one and had married with the Jerusalem nobility. Nehemiah did see Tobiah as an opponent, but that was his view – why should they have to believe the same? On the other hand, they continued to communicate with Nehemiah as well. This shows no hostility towards him (even if he saw them as disloyal). Thus, we definitely see tensions between Nehemiah and the nobles, caused, it seems, mostly by the abrasive manner of the former, but there is no clear evidence of a breach between Nehemiah and the nobles. At most there is a possibility, but it has not been demonstrated. Also, we need to keep in mind that Nehemiah himself was probably a noble, as suggested by his income and his position.

A similar situation seems to have been the case with the priests. A number of references to the priests are found in chapters whose relationship to Nehemiah is very uncertain, but priests are also important in the NM itself. The priests initially supported building of the wall; they are named throughout Neh. 3, and no opposition is anywhere suggested (even if Neh. 3 is an insertion in the NM). He makes no mention of priests in his tirade in Neh. 5 except to call on them to administer an oath to the nobles. Priests were full participants in the dedication of the wall (12:27–43). Two examples only seem to suggest any breach between Nehemiah and the priests. One is in 13:10–13 which mentions that Levites had left their posts because they were not being allotted their rightful dues. As already noted in chapter 3 above, the mention of only Levites suggests that the priests were receiving support as normal. Therefore, this passage may well hint at the old rivalries within the cultic personnel (cf. Grabbe 1995: 52–53, 57–58, 60–62) but it does not, as Smith asserts, show that Nehemiah had enlisted the Levites as his supporters in opposition to the priests. He uses the Levites as gate-keepers (13:21), but that was one of their functions.

The other example concerns Eliashib the (high?) priest who allowed Tobiah to use a storeroom in the temple area (13:4–9), but the difference between Nehemiah's evaluation of Tobiah and that of others has already been commented on. This one example does not show a special opposition between Nehemiah and the priests, though it seems clear that some priests did not necessarily agree with all aspects of his programme. Again, we see the friction that Nehemiah seems to have created with all groups of any power in Judaean society. What is not demonstrated is that he had the Levites *en bloc* as his supporters, and the priests as his opponents (Smith himself recognizes that the priests were split [1987: 103]).

One of Smith's central supports is the concept of the 'new-rich mercantile class'; however, it is doubtful that we can speak of such a group at the time. Those who gained wealth by trading attempted to assimilate to traditional landed aristocracy (Garnsey and Saller 1987: 44–45). Smith's social divisions look too modern. Granted, we know little about Nehemiah's activities between the building of the wall and the events described in Neh. 13, and much could have taken place which is not recorded in the preserved book, but one would like to see more evidence than Smith has provided. All in all, Smith's thesis seems overly schematic even while recognizing the opposition that Nehemiah created with traditional leadership groups.

The rest of the Nehemiah tradition

Nehemiah 12:44–13:31 has a good deal of miscellaneous material. How much of it belongs to the NM is difficult to say. Most commentators have assigned a good deal of this section to the NM, but it has also been denied that any of it belongs to Nehemiah (Ackroyd 1970a: 28, 41; Steins 1995: 198–207). Nehemiah 12:44–47 is not usually considered a part of the NM by anyone; nevertheless, the present literary context implies that this section represents the activities of Nehemiah. This makes the concluding part of the book an interesting summary of Nehemiah's career. This summary really begins with the dedication of the wall in 12:27–43 which logically would have come earlier but has been postponed until near the end of the book. One presumes that the compiler had a reason for delaying the dedication of the wall until this time. From that perspective, the dedication of the wall and the remaining activities described in the book are a way of making a point about Nehemiah's accomplishments.

Four points are emphasized about Nehemiah's achievements in 12:44–13:31. First are the organizing and maintenance of the temple cult and its personnel, of which several examples are given. Second would be the repair of the wall, whose completion begins the section. Third, the issue of interaction with foreigners is mentioned two or three times. Finally, the enforcement of Jewish law generally is a topic of some importance. The completion and dedication of the wall have already been discussed, but the other points need some expansion.

Matters relating to the organization of temple personnel are mentioned twice in this section. In 12:44–47 the point is made that the various gifts to the priests, Levites, singers, and other personnel were paid in order that the cult might be carried out. Men were appointed (by whom?) over the store areas for the tithes, heave offerings, first-fruits. The implication is that the people gave freely because of their gratitude, but then it is noted that this was in the time of Zerubbabel and Nehemiah. This may suggest that the people were less diligent in other times. The absence of any reference to Ezra in view of his supposed importance for the promulgation and enforcement of the law is interesting. The importance of paying these dues is illustrated in 13:10–14 where Nehemiah returns from an appointment with the king in Babylon to find that the tithes and other dues were not being paid, so that the Levites and singers were working in the fields to make a living.

In the main section on intermarriage with the 'peoples of the land' in Neh. 9–10 (see below) Nehemiah does not take an active role (though he is said to be one of the signatories). Two passages in this section relate to the question. The first at 13:1–3 refers to the Pentateuchal decree against Ammonites and Moabites entering into the congregation of Israel (cf. Deut. 23:4–7) and states that 'the people' removed the 'mixture' from their midst. Nehemiah is not mentioned, and this is not usually considered part of the NM; nevertheless, in this context it goes well with the next section on the subject. At 13:23–31 the Ammonites and Moabites are also an issue, though they are accompanied by Ashdodites in this case. As noted earlier (chapter 3 above), there are a number of unanswered questions about this account, but the basic intent of the compiler is clear: Nehemiah was as diligent in his opposition to mixed marriages as Ezra.

Two other examples relate to the general opposition to foreignness. In 13:4–9 Tobiah insinuates himself into the temple precinct (though it is clear that he has the permission of the high priest). Nehemiah is naturally furious; however, his reaction appears to be as much because of the success of his enemy as of a religious objection to 'foreigners'. As already noted, Tobiah was undoubtedly Jewish and therefore hardly 'foreign'. Similarly, when a son of the high priest Joiada had married Sanballat's daughter, Nehemiah drove him out of Jerusalem (13:28). Thus, zeal against intermarriage and intercourse with outsiders is difficult to distinguish from straightforward animosity towards an opponent.

The examples of enforcing the law all relate to the Sabbath (13:15–22). He first of all upbraids the Jews who carry out agricultural work or transport goods to Jerusalem and sell them on the Sabbath. He next turns on the Tyrian traders, though he takes up the matter with the Judaean nobles rather than the traders themselves. A plan is set up to shut the gates on the Sabbath and guard them against the entry of goods. The traders have little choice but to comply. This is one of the few OT passages in which Sabbath observance is the main issue. This has led some to see Sabbath observance as, therefore, a post-exilic issue, but apart from this passage and Isaiah 56:1–8 the Sabbath is seldom mentioned even in those passages normally designated as post-exilic. Sabbath observance of some sort probably has a long history in Israel, including already the period of the monarchy, but the complete cessation of work and trading may not have been envisaged until a rather later time. In any case, the example looks almost as much a polemic against foreign merchants as an argument for a particular form of Sabbath-keeping.

Nehemiah as reformer

Nehemiah is usually portrayed as a courageous reformer who championed the poor and oppressed and who was zealous in enforcing the law of God in the province. What we have is by and large his own assessment of himself, of course, plus what an admirer passed on to later generations in the present book of Nehemiah. He presents his good deeds on two planes. The first is his solicitude for the people of the province. An example of this is the repair of the city wall. Although this hardly counts as the work of a reformer, it suggests his efforts to help the people of Jerusalem. Where Nehemiah presents himself in particular as a reformer – or at least is seen by moderns as a reformer – is with his economic measures (Neh. 5) and in his religious reforms relating to the intermarriage with 'foreigners' and to keeping the Sabbath (Neh. 13).

The problem with the picture of Nehemiah as a champion of the poor against the rich and powerful is that it is a simplistic and misleading one. Cancelling debts is the work of a reformer and a fairly drastic measure which was unlikely to make him popular with the ones who made the loans, but it was a way of being seen as a champion of the common people. The problem with this particular reform, as already noted above, is that no measures are described which would alleviate permanently the plight of the poor. Cancellation of debts could only be a temporary measure, however welcome it might have been to the debtors in the short term. People on a subsistence income have little surplus, though there is a bit in some years which is sufficient to pay taxes and buy some luxury items. Unfortunately, bad years regularly come in which peasants have to borrow to keep going. Reserves are not usually sufficient to tide them over; hence, the need to borrow. The negative side is that a series of bad years means that the debts cannot be paid off, and the property or other collateral reverts to the creditor. There is no simple solution to the problem; indeed, there may not be any solution if the population is too large for the land which supports it. If there is concentration of land in the possession of the few, land redistribution is possible, but we have no indication that this was an option for Nehemiah. The fact is, judging from the little information available, Nehemiah forced through certain temporary measures but did not go beyond that. His reform in this area seems to have been a limited, one-off measure.

The second area where Nehemiah was a reformer was in the area of religious observance, though it tended to be in those areas affecting the relationship of the Jews with surrounding communities. Nehemiah 13 mentions several of these actions. He took a number of measures relating to observance of the Sabbath. This included putting a stop to Jews working and trading on the day, but especially he forced traders to cease their activities in Jerusalem on the Sabbath. His actions in this case look almost as much an issue of exclusion or control of 'foreigners' as of observance of the Sabbath itself. To what extent the Sabbath was simply being brought forcibly to people's attention and to what extent new modes of observing it were being introduced is difficult to say. Although the Sabbath itself probably has a long history in Israel, complete rest from work and trade may not have been its primary function in the earlier part of its history.

Another area of religious reform relates not only to intermarriage but to restriction of intercourse with all those outside the Judaean community. He expelled Tobiah from the temple area where the high priest had allowed him to set up shop. This may simply have been a way of dealing with an opponent, but it raises a curious issue because Tobiah was Jewish himself. However, many of the Jewish inhabitants of Judah were excluded from the community according to the ideology of Ezra-Nehemiah which refuses to recognize as kin those descendants of the Jews who were not taken captive (see chapter 6 above). This appears to have been Nehemiah's view as well. Anyone not descended from those who returned from captivity was considered 'foreign', however much they were indigenous. Thus, Nehemiah set out to deal with the issue of mixed marriages.

The main passage is in 13:23–28 in which some Jews had allegedly married with 'Ashdodite, Ammonite, and Moabite women'. The actions described are fully compatible with what we know of Nehemiah from elsewhere: he does not just force the violators to separate (as happens in Ezra 10). No, such simple reactions were not Nehemiah's way. He had to curse some and flog others. He even goes so far as to pull out the hair of some of them (unlike Ezra who tears his own hair!). Finally, he expelled the son of the high priest from the community for marrying the daughter of Sanballat. The other references to mixed marriages are not likely to be from the NM but are compatible with the picture of Nehemiah (13:1–4 in which Nehemiah is not mentioned, and Neh. 9–10 in which Nehemiah does occur but only as one of the signatories while the action is taken by the community as a whole; on this passage see the next section).

These various measures instigated by Nehemiah – whether the repair of the wall, the opposition to Sanballat and other 'foreigners', the ban on mixed marriages, or even the regulations about the Sabbath – were not just miscellaneous *ad hoc* decisions. Rather, they seem to have been part of a complete programme. In that sense, Nehemiah was very much a reformer. His goal seems no less than to make Judah into an isolated puritanical theocratic state. This programme is nowhere explicitly laid out in the book, but the whole thrust of the book is towards this goal.

Repairing the wall was an action which could have a number of purposes, physical protection being one of them. Yet there is no indication in the book that Jerusalem needed a wall for physical protection. Most of the people of Judah lived in unwalled villages or in otherwise vulnerable circumstances. The only indication of danger comes when Nehemiah alleges that those working on the wall are going to be attacked, but even if he is right (which is doubtful) it is the repair of the wall itself which invites the attack, not the lack of a wall. If the wall was not needed for defence, what was its function? A wall serves as more than just a means of defending against attack. A city wall can have an important social function. It can serve to enclose people into communities and bond them together; it can be used to hold the outside world at arm's length. A wall can also be a means of controlling those enclosed by it; it can close people off into a ghetto.

In Nehemiah's case the wall would have had a number of uses. It would have made it easier to defend himself and his administration against any possible interference from the outside by military or physical force. If the officials of the city and province were required to live in Jerusalem (cf. 11:1), it would have been much easier for

Nehemiah to keep them under his observation and thus control them. A city whose gates could be shut against outsiders could also serve to minimize contact with unacceptable ethnic and religious groups, and even influences and ideas. In a real sense, Nehemiah was creating his own religious and ideological ghetto. Thus, the city wall – as mundane as it might seem – was far more than just an architectural project; it was essential to Nehemiah's reforms.

All those not a part of the community of returnees are labelled 'foreign' in Ezra-Nehemiah. This, too, was essential to Nehemiah. The bulk of the inhabitants of the region were the descendants of those not deported to Babylon. It was among this group that religious and ideological ideas at variance with those of Nehemiah and his supporters were most likely to be found. They were the group hardest to control, and marriage with them would have eroded the discipline he was able to impose on the *golah* community. Tobiah was a leading representative of the native Jews who had remained in the land and thus of particular danger to Nehemiah's plans. No wonder he was outraged when he found that Tobiah had penetrated not only within the city walls of Jerusalem but even to the temple court, all with the permission of the chief religious leader, the high priest (13:4–9).

Nehemiah has been compared to the city tyrants who were a feature of this period in the Greek world (Smith 1987: 103–12). Greek *turannos*, from which we get the English word 'tyrant', meant something a bit different from the modern connotation which is consistently negative. The Greek word simply meant someone who was an absolute ruler of a city but not part of a hereditary monarchy. To the democrats such rulers would have been anathema, but not everyone in the Greek world was by any means a democrat; it was easy to see from the example of Athens that democracy had its negative traits, too. To the Greeks Nehemiah would have looked like a typical tyrant. The positive side of the description is that he was able to force through his reforms; the negative, that his reforms were considered wrong-headed by many of those within the Jerusalem community.

His actions have led some to compare him with contemporary reformers in the Mediterranean world such as Pericles (Smith 1987: 108) and Solon (Kippenberg 1982: 55–62; Yamauchi 1980). Pericles' main action comparable to Nehemiah's was to forbid intermarriage with aliens (Aelian, *Varia Historia* 6.10). Solon's reforms parallel Nehemiah's mainly in the area of cancelling debts and releasing those enslaved because of debt (*Athenaion Politeia* 5–9). We know about their reforms because both individuals wrote justifications of their actions for posterity. These comparisons are interesting, even if sometimes unprovable; however, the parallels appear to be due not to any organic connection between the reformers but probably because in each case the individual is a politician rather than a hereditary ruler and thus needed to gain a certain amount of popular support (Yamauchi's facile statement [1980: 292] that 'Nehemiah was motivated solely for God's glory' may be fine for Sunday school but hardly belongs in a historical treatment).

A recent study has appealed to a sociological model to explain what Nehemiah was doing (Tollefson and Williamson 1992). Using the 'revitalization' model of A. F. C. Wallace (1956), they find that it fits well the picture given in the book of Nehemiah: 'mazeway' (world view) reformulation (Neh. 1:1–10); communication phase (1:11–2:20); organizational phase (3:1–32); adaptation to the project (3:33–7:4 [ET 4:1–7:4]); cultural transformation phase (7:5–10:39); routinization phase (11:1–13:31). This model fits the final form of Nehemiah fairly well; however, this could be an editorial fit since the actual progress of Nehemiah's activities seems to have been less neat (a possibility which they recognize [1992: 61–66]). Nevertheless, Wallace's model works because he has described the general contents of most reform movements. That is, the reformers see a need for change, then communicate it; if their communication is successful, they have to organize reform, adapt to changing circumstances (or it will not succeed), reach a stage of major change, and finally a period of adjustment to the new (reformed) situation. Where the thesis is weakest lies in the acceptance of the reforms (cultural transformation phase). The authors of the article seem to have more faith in general support for all Nehemiah's reforms (e.g. 1992: 60) than is justified by the text (cf. Grabbe 1998a).

The issue of mixed marriages

Nehemiah 9–10 describes a situation similar to Ezra 9–10 in which the issue of intermarriage with 'foreigners' is addressed. Nehemiah is not a part of the proceedings (except as one of the signatories in 10:2), and these chapters are not clearly a part of the Nehemiah tradition as such; indeed, some make them a continuation of the Ezra tradition of Neh. 8. Yet although the situation is clearly parallel to that in Ezra 9–10, the relationship of the two passages is not immediately obvious. In Neh. 9 the people themselves ('the

Israelites') take the initiative to fast, pray, and separate themselves (9:2–3). They also read the law, with various Levites listed as being on the raised platform before the people (9:4); four of these names agree with those mentioned in Neh. 8 (Jeshua, Bani, Sherebiah, Hodiah). They pray a prayer which is different from Ezra's in Ezra 9 but has some resemblances. Some of these may be coincidental since a prayer in a particular situation is likely to resemble other prayers in a similar situation. Particularly interesting is the reference in both prayers to Jews of Judah as being more or less slaves of the Persians (Ezra 9:9; Neh. 9:36–37).

Nehemiah 10 is particularly interesting. It could be a genuine document preserved in the archives, but how one could prove that one way or the other is hard to say. It begins with a list of signatories. Intriguingly, it begins with the name of Nehemiah who has the official title of Tirshata ('governor'), yet Nehemiah has no part in the preceding narrative. For that reason, it seems unlikely that Neh. 9 is a part of the Nehemiah tradition. Considering Nehemiah's penchant for getting involved in every religious or political issue of significance, his omission here is doubly strange. It suggests that Neh. 9 was compiled by someone who was not necessarily a great admirer of Nehemiah and certainly not by Nehemiah himself.

The signatories and people swear to observe 'the Torah of God given by the hand of Moses' and also 'all the commandments of Yhwh' and his statutes and judgements (10:30). In the present context, it alludes back to the 'book of the Torah of Yhwh' at the beginning of the section (Neh. 9:3) and to the reading by Ezra in Neh. 8. The passage preceding the list of commandments mentioned separating from 'the peoples of the land' (10:29), and the list of commandments sworn to begins with keeping pure from the 'peoples of the land'. Yet the following stipulations cover a wide variety of points of conduct and worship. Although most can be found in the Pentateuch, not all can (e.g. 10:35 on the wood offering). Most of what is said relates to the temple and its upkeep. The fact that this sworn document is presented in the context of ceasing to have intercourse with 'foreigners' – but only partially relating to this context – suggests that it was an independent writing taken over and used in a new literary environment. It would have fitted the issue of marriage with 'foreigners', but a document arising from that situation alone seems unlikely to have been what we find before us in Neh. 10. If we had to find a context for Neh. 10, we would probably see it as being primarily about support for the temple.

The resemblance between Ezra 9–10 and Neh. 9–10 seems more

than coincidental. The situation of intermarriage is the same. The people gather and repent. A prayer occurs in each passage. The situation is resolved by a separation from the 'foreigners'. In both passages a list records those who agreed to abide by the ruling. There are also significant differences. No leader is mentioned in Neh. 10. The list is different in each case, the one in Neh. 10:1–30 being those who signed a contract to abide by the pledge (in a sense signing on behalf of all the people) whereas that in Ezra 10:20–43 is a list of those who had 'sinned' by their marriages. Finally, much of Neh. 10 is taken up with a list of other points of the law which the people pledge to keep.

The differences suggest that these were not seen as just two versions of the same event. Yet it seems strange that the episode of mixed marriages would have recurred so similarly on two separate occasions. For this reason, one cannot help being suspicious that there is a relationship between the two accounts, that one is only a version of the other. Determining which might be the prior account is not easy. Considering the general state of the Ezra tradition (as described in chapters 2 and 6 above), it is tempting to consider Ezra 9–10 as dependent on Neh. 9–10. Finding formal criteria on which to make such a judgement is difficult, however. Perhaps the one point which might argue in favour of this conclusion is that Neh. 10 looks like a community document which may have had a genuine existence and was derived from the archives. In other words, Neh. 10 presents itself as a document with a series of points of agreement and then a list of those who signed on behalf of the entire community. If there was indeed such a document, the entire episode of Neh. 9–10 could have been constructed based wholly on it. In other words, the contents of Neh. 9 were created by the author to give a context for the document which he had before him (and copied out as Neh. 10).

If this was the case, Ezra 9–10 was probably a further development, being a creation on the basis of Neh. 9–10. However, much of this is speculation because it is difficult to demonstrate that Neh. 10 was a genuine document. It could have been, but there seems no way to prove that it was not simply the creation of the literary writer.

Summary and conclusions

Our investigation of Ezra (chapter 7) ran into the sand. The further we went, the further Ezra receded from our grasp. Whatever historical figure lies at the base of the story has been so buried underneath the layers of legend, literature, and theology that it is difficult to ascertain how much relates to history. Things are different with Nehemiah. He emerges as a living figure, even as a larger-than-life character, as one might expect of a strong-willed and obsessively single-minded leader. He invited either love or hate; to his mind there was only one side of the matter and that was his. Compromise or conciliation were anathema to him. Any evaluation of Nehemiah has to recognize his relentless and unyielding nature.

Uniquely among OT writers we seem to have part of a first-person account – Nehemiah's own composition – available to us (this uniqueness is contingent on one's evaluation of the supposed 'Ezra memoir'). True, its precise borders are disputed, and all agree that it has been edited to a lesser or greater extent; at best, only a portion of the NM is extant. Nevertheless, this does not detract from its importance, if the core of the book of Nehemiah was indeed a personal writing by Nehemiah. On the assumption that the NM is genuine, a sort of antique hero has often been constructed. I have also proceeded on the basis that the NM (as far as it can be determined) is genuine, but the personality which emerges is far from a hero according to my analysis. He was quite a peculiar individual. A man of determination and perseverance with a clear vision of what he wanted to accomplish, he was also egotistical, bigoted, narrow-minded, vindictive, and had an unsurpassed ability to alienate most of those with whom he worked.

Nehemiah is presented – indeed, he presents himself – as a champion of the Jews against the 'foreigners', of the poor and oppressed against the wealthy and powerful, of the priesthood and cult against the impious tendencies found among the people. His response to the circumstances of the Judaean and Jerusalem community was a programme of reform which involved some fairly extreme measures. His aim was to cut ties with the outside community as much as possible and to turn the returnee community into a dictatorial theocratic state which enforced endogamous marriage and the strict observance of the Jewish religion as he interpreted it. He fits well the mould of the Greek city tyrant of which there were many contemporary examples, especially in Asia Minor.

Nehemiah's personality was such that he could force his way by mental will and physical threat. With the authority of the Persian king behind him, it was not difficult for him to have his way as long as he was on the scene to monitor the activities of the people. As soon as he left the area, however, things began to develop to a more open and cosmopolitan society – or, as he might have put it, to fall into sin and transgression. It was not just the masses, the common people, who deviated from his reforms. The decision to try to accommodate those whom Nehemiah viewed as enemies was made at high levels in the community, by the nobles and the leading priests. Some of these seemed to oppose Nehemiah, but others evidently tried to work with both him and such 'enemies' as Tobiah who headed an ancient and influential family in the Transjordanian region.

Nehemiah was a failure, at least in the short term (cf. Grabbe 1998a). Granted, he built the city wall and was able to accomplish his goals during the twelve years or so that he was in Jerusalem, but even a temporary absence was sufficient for some of his measures to be abandoned or reversed. Our ignorance of what was happening in Judah in the next two centuries makes it difficult to be precise about details of how Judaism developed. Yet when we finally find a partial lifting of the veil two centuries later, we find a Judaism which was certainly not in Nehemiah's image. From the Zenon papyri and the 'Tobiad romance' we know that the family of Tobiah not only continued to prosper but even increased its influence in the region (Grabbe 1992a: 192–98). If the Tobiad romance in Josephus is to be believed, Tobiah's descendants became the major tax farmers for the region, with direct access to the Ptolemaic court and practically civil rulers of the Palestinian area. Nehemiah would have had apoplexy.

Nehemiah's attempt to isolate the Jewish community was no more successful. Long before the so-called Hellenistic reform of the mid-second century BCE, the Jews had come under Hellenistic influence, and many found it a very congenial culture (see Grabbe 1992a: ch. 3). Contrary to what Nehemiah probably feared, few Jews appear to have abandoned their religion, but they found little incompatibility between their Judaism and Hellenistic culture. Some, a minority but with the greatest numbers among the priests and aristocrats, obtained a Greek education and became acquainted with Greek literature and learning. There is no evidence that the isolation of Jerusalem instigated by Nehemiah was maintained; trade and social and intellectual intercourse seem to have been carried out with the surrounding peoples. Most important of all, many of those labelled 'foreigners' in Ezra-Nehemiah seem to have been accepted as Jews by the Jerusalem community. Although the so-called Samaritans continued to hold to their own separate identity (cf. Grabbe 1993b), the inhabitants of Judah seem all to be identified as Jews, whether they were descendants of the returnee community or of those left in the land by Nebuchadnezzar.

The Jews show a great concern for all aspects of the Torah. The Sabbath was meticulously observed as were the annual festivals and many of the purity laws, for all we can tell. The influx of pilgrims from those living in the Diaspora, especially the Greek-speaking Diaspora, was no doubt an important catalyst for the development of Jewish culture. But Nehemiah's concern to create an inward-looking community trapped in its own self-imposed ghetto came to little. From that point of view, Nehemiah failed. His reforms seem not to have outlasted his own period of governorship. The openness to the surrounding cultures and peoples continued to characterize much of Judaism until the fall of Jerusalem in 70 CE.

Yet in the long run Nehemiah did win. The Judaism which survived through the centuries was not the liberal Judaism which freely partook of the surrounding culture. It was the conservative Judaism – the Judaism of the *stetl* and the ghetto – which kept the religion alive. Even today the real crisis is perceived by many to be in such liberal societies as America where Jews are assimilating at an alarming rate. The debate begun in Ezra-Nehemiah goes on, and Nehemiah remains the champion of those who argue for an exclusivistic religion.

8

SUMMARY AND
CONCLUSIONS

My study of Ezra and Nehemiah has had two main aims: (1) to ask
what the books say, and (2) to investigate how their message – their
picture of the actions of the Jewish people and their leaders in the
first part of the Persian period – relates to history as reconstructed
by a critical historian. In some ways, this has been done many
times before, but in other ways it is a fairly radical departure from
previous studies. Most studies have not tried to achieve both aims.
It is traditional for commentaries to discuss the relationship of
Ezra and Nehemiah to history, but they often do this by first
trying to reconstruct the literary and textual history of the book.
Thus, the question of what the books actually say in their present
form is often by-passed. Those who concentrate on the final form
of the books, on the other hand, are usually not interested in the historical question (or they read history directly from the texts according to a naive fundamentalist perspective, which is much the same
thing).

The consequences of a close reading

The first part of this study was devoted to asking what the books say
through a close reading of the text. For the most part, opinions of
others and questions of source criticism and growth of the tradition
were put aside in chapters 2–4 (though they were occasionally introduced in anticipation of later discussion). The purpose of the close
reading was not just to investigate the structure of the text and its
theological message, both of which were important. The various
structures and devices used by the compiler to convey his message
were certainly looked at, but also noticed were the aspects of
the text which showed lack of complete accord: contradictions, in-
coherences, attempts to impose a particular message on the material,

ideological assumptions. These were as much features of the text as the gross structure which was the chief means of conveying the overall message.

Two aspects of the text thus disclosed themselves. First, we were able to recognize the skill with which the narrative was put together to convey its meaning. We were able to see how the compiler took diverse elements and sources and welded them into a unified whole with a coherent message. He created a progressive narrative of Yhwh's dealings with his people over a considerable period to reconstitute a nation which had been destroyed and a people who had been cruelly exiled from their native country. The story describes how the people became re-established in their homeland, with the temple at its heart, under the guidance of Yhwh who inspired even the Persian kings to accomplish his aims, and how the threats to the welfare of the community were countered and averted. It was a story of the triumph of the will – human and divine.

But there is a second aspect to the text. Below the surface of this artistic edifice was discovered considerable evidence that the traditional material used had not been beaten into a smooth, homogenous pabulum. Quite the contrary, the diversity of material and point of view still extant in the text showed that the compiler had put the story together from a variety of sources and traditions with their own distinctive messages and outlooks. Consequently, a full account of Ezra-Nehemiah seemed not just to allow for a source and tradition analysis, but indeed to *demand* it. The skilled work of the compiler had left copious details which showed the text singing not with a single melody but a whole polyphony of songlines, some of which created some very interesting dissonances and even cacophony. By looking at both the concords and the discords within the texts, we hoped to come to a clearer understanding of the books as a whole. The consistent grand themes flowing through both books did not drown out the many little voices which said something else. These discordant notes were vital for the second part of the study which asked about questions of history. The close literary study was thus a necessary precursor to asking how the books relate to history.

The message of Ezra-Nehemiah is straightforward, even simple. It consists of a narrative with a story, interlarded with which are a number of theological ideas that the narrator considers important. The narrative tells of a people who had been exiled from their native land because of certain sins, including the non-observance of the sabbatical year. When the seventy years of their punishment were finished, Yhwh intervened to inspire the Persian conqueror of Babylon himself to issue a decree letting the Jews return and build their temple. A large group returned, bringing the stolen temple vessels, and settled in the land. Then they began to build the temple. Various enemies (associated significantly with the old Northern Kingdom) attempted to thwart their efforts and succeeded temporarily, but when the people resumed the work under the instigation of prophets, they succeeded under the patronage of the Persian king.

Then the Persian king decreed that a priest and scribe by the name of Ezra was to bring the 'law in his hand' and use it as the basis of judging in the province and even the satrapy. He brought another entourage and a huge sum of gold and silver, plus some (more) temple vessels. When it was reported to him that the people had sinned by contracting marriages with the surrounding peoples, he fasted and prayed and eventually required them to abandon the wives and families acquired in this way. Then Nehemiah came, also with the favour of the Persian king, to rebuild the city wall and settle the city with a suitable population. He also stopped abuse of the poor who had lost property, homes, and even children over loans they could not repay because of the poor crops. During his governorship Ezra read the law publicly, and the people embraced it and took it to heart. A(nother) problem of intermarriage was resolved with a pledge from the people, the wall was finally dedicated, and in the concluding part of the story Nehemiah had to address several social and religious problems, some of which warned of the need for continuing vigilance since some of the old problems were still a potential threat.

Several significant themes arise out of the narrative or are mentioned incidentally in the text. The main one is God's providence and care for his people; even the king of the greatest empire on earth is putty in his hands, a mere instrument shaped and wielded by the deity himself to benefit his people. But being the people of Yhwh entails certain responsibilities; Yhwh must be obeyed at all times. A second theme is a part of this obedience: to keep pure by eschewing marriage to and even contact with 'foreigners' and the 'peoples of the land'. It is these 'foreigners'/'peoples of the land' who hamper the building of the temple (Ezra 4–6) and also the repair of the wall (Neh. 3–4). They are the cause of all sorts of evil (not often spelled out) and must be kept separate from the pure community – the 'holy seed'.

Another theme is the importance of 'the book'. The Hebrew word *sēfer* can mean not only 'book' but also 'document' and 'writing'. Ezra-Nehemiah is filled with 'books' of lists of people: the settlement list (Ezra 2//Neh. 7//Neh. 12:1–25); those who came up with Ezra (Ezra 8:1–14); those who pledged to separate from their 'foreign' wives (Ezra 10:18–43); those who repaired the wall (Neh. 3); those who pledged to obey the Torah (Neh. 10:1–28); those who lived in Jerusalem (Neh. 11). Various documents are used in Ezra 4–6 both to hinder and to aid the rebuilding. A 'book' issued by Cyrus authorizes Ezra's mission (Ezra 7:12–26). However, the book at the heart of the narrative is that read by Ezra (Neh. 8) or by the people (Neh. 9:1–5).

A further theme manifests itself especially in Ezra but also in certain sections of Nehemiah. This is the emphasis on the actions of the people, as opposed to those of the leaders ('the great men'). This theme does not always fit well some of its contexts and seems imposed upon a narrative which once apparently centred on leaders such as Joshua and Zerubbabel, Ezra, and Nehemiah. But the value of communal action is a particular emphasis of portions of the books. All these themes serve as an important theological vehicle to get across particular messages to the readers. They advance the main goals of the book or supplement the central thrust with additional subsidiary messages.

These themes, along with the structure and other elements of the books, serve to unite Ezra-Nehemiah into a literary, narrative, and theological whole (chapter 5 above). For centuries the books were read and interpreted as a literary unit and a holistic theological entity describing the post-exilic period. This final-form reading has also characterized some recent scholarly treatments. A structuralist model (Eskenazi 1988) has received a good deal of deserved attention, but there are other models which could serve equally well to argue that the two books should be read as a single item (e.g. the chronological scheme in the two books, the narrative line, the intertextual elements, even sociological models). This has led even to the view that the unitarian reading should take precedence over all others.

Yet the close reading of chapters 2–4 above shows many details and less obvious elements of the narrative which go against the holistic view. Not all of these are best taken account of and given their due weight by reading the books as a coherent whole. The close reading demonstrated that the unity of the two books is an editorial unity. A dominant voice has been imposed on the materials, but other voices are still heard beneath the surface. It is proper that these voices should be allowed to speak as well. The nature of the traditions demonstrates that it is perfectly legitimate to read the text diachronically as well as synchronically; indeed, one could say that one must do both to do justice to all that one finds there. Just because an editor once imposed his vision on the traditions received, why must we be bound by this particular view? Why cannot we look behind the carefully crafted façade to examine the original materials that he has welded together and see them from our own perspective? The critical historian also has a right – nay, a duty – to ask whether, using the same materials, a different story cannot be told, perhaps a better story or one likely to be truer to the historical reality. It has been this last – the story as reconstructed by a critical historian – which has been the goal of the last part of this book.

Three independent 'founder legends'

Several recent studies have argued for reading Ezra and Nehemiah as separate books. My own study found that the traditions in the book of Ezra and the traditions in Nehemiah were once separate and continued to exist as independent accounts after they were brought together in the Hebrew Ezra-Nehemiah. There were three complexes of tradition, each surrounding particular individuals: the Joshua-Zerubbabel tradition, the Ezra tradition, and the Nehemiah tradition. In certain important ways 1 Esdras especially seems to represent the earlier Ezra tradition but also the Joshua-Zerubbabel story (even if the present book is a redacted form of that earlier account with some particular developments).

My view about originally separate traditions is supported by a survey of the traditions in other sources. The Joshua-Zerubbabel complex does not occur by itself anywhere, though it may be paired with Ezra alone (1 Esdras) or with Nehemiah alone (Ben Sira 49:12–13). The Ezra tradition by itself is found in portions of 4 Ezra, and a separate Nehemiah tradition occurs in 2 Maccabees 1:18–2:13. In this last Nehemiah is the rebuilder of the temple and the restorer of the cult, not Joshua-Zerubbabel. A close study of Ezra 7–10 suggests that the present story has been adapted to the context to take account of the activities of Joshua-Zerubbabel; however, there are signs that originally Ezra himself was seen as the rebuilder of the temple and the one who got the cult going again after the exile.

Some modern commentators seem to go out of their way to avoid the most obvious outcome about the Hebrew Ezra-Nehemiah arising from these variant traditions. When 1 Esdras completely omits any of the Nehemiah tradition, tortuous explanations are devised to establish that 1 Esdras was still excerpted from Ezra-Nehemiah, or when Ben Sira is silent about Ezra, he still must have taken his information from Ezra-Nehemiah. Similarly, even though Josephus used 1 Esdras and has a Nehemiah story with significant differences from the Hebrew Nehemiah, nevertheless, it is still assumed that he must have known Ezra-Nehemiah and even used it for his Nehemiah story. Not one but three clear examples are explained away in this way. For some reason there is a strong reluctance to follow these data to their logical conclusion: that none of these three knew the Hebrew Ezra-Nehemiah or, at the very least, that they were not very taken with it.

The reasonable inference is that there once existed three independent *cult and city founder legends*, each of which made a different individual or set of individuals the one who returned and restored the cult and/or the city after an extended period of exile. Describing these as 'founder legends' is to describe a state reached in the development of the tradition, not necessarily their shape when they originated. The original NM apparently presupposed some sort of earlier return, and Nehemiah's main task was the repair of the wall. Nevertheless, the tradition developed to become a founder legend in which he also restored the cult and temple (2 Macc. 1:18–2:13). It seems likely that the three separate founder stories have been brought together in the Hebrew Ezra-Nehemiah and have been edited in such a way as to remove some of the more obvious contradictions created by this union of independent traditions. But they also continued to exist and develop on their own as well.

From a literary point of view, each of these traditions (or combinations) has its own integrity with a definite structure. Each can be analysed in its own right and the particular message discovered. The message of one form of the tradition may not be the same as that of another, and only an appreciation of the integrity of the individual versions will be able to draw out that special aim and significance of each in its own right. An approach which simply conflates them is likely to miss a good deal. In other words, the holistic reading has its weaknesses as well as its strengths. From a historical point of view, a diachronic reading is definitely a must, though one should begin with an appreciation of what the final form of the text actually says.

The existence of different traditions and different versions of the same basic tradition should tell us something significant when we start to ask historical questions. It may be that one tradition was the primary source and another a secondary account, in which case the secondary one is less trustworthy. An edited text may have lost something in the process. A text which strikes one as sober and reliable may turn out to be much less so if it happens to have been created by redacting a text which originally contained implausible elements and untrustworthy data.

Especially revealing was a close reading of the text without attempting to harmonize with or impose a specific structure. A unity at the 'macro-level' may look decidedly artificial when all the details are taken into account. The close reading of Ezra and Nehemiah and their traditions in chapters 2–4 found many conflicts between the statements in the texts. The unity pointed out above has been achieved by glossing over these many discrepancies; indeed, the compiler was probably unaware of them in many instances because of his own ignorance of the history of the times.

The Nehemiah account

This close reading was particularly instructive with regard to the story of Nehemiah. The widespread agreement that a NM is a major source of the book was borne out in this study (in so far as it was touched on). Having a first-person account as the basis for the narrative is perhaps unparalleled in the biblical text (unless one also accepts an 'Ezra memoir'). It provides a unique insight into a powerful and important personality. We get a glimpse of his own mind and thoughts. This inside knowledge is balanced, on the other hand, by the heavily biased nature of the NM. If Nehemiah ever had doubts about himself, there is not a hint of it here. From all we can tell, he is incapable of seeing the situation from any perspective but his own. We get his point of view and no other; tolerance and openmindedness seem to be anathema to him.

As cupbearer of the Persian king Nehemiah was in a prime position to ask a favour which the king willingly granted. This was to repair the wall and otherwise restore the sorry state of the city of Jerusalem. We are not told how the city got into that state and can only speculate, but it seems likely that some disaster had been visited on the city not all that long before Nehemiah's visit. (The alternative, that the city was in much the state it had been left in after the destruction of Nebuchadnezzar, might well be the perspective of a founder legend, but is not likely to have been the content of the original NM.)

Nehemiah was quite successful with his wall building, but in the process he quickly acquired enemies, some of them potential friends. The enmity between him and Sanballat was probably inevitable. They were evidently equals in the Persian administration and therefore rivals for status and power. Nehemiah claims that Sanballat was prepared to launch a murderous attack on those building the wall, but there is no evidence of this, and some parts of the account seem unlikely. We have to accept that this may have all been in Nehemiah's imagination; Sanballat would have been taking a terrible risk to contemplate such an action, though he may have taken some pleasure in spreading rumours that he was about to send in raiders. On the other hand, the invitations to meet, which Nehemiah interpreted as ruses to do him in, could have been genuine efforts to come to some sort of *modus vivendi*. Sanballat might have realized that he had to accept Nehemiah's presence and a move at conciliation could be to mutual advantage. Having only Nehemiah's version of events means that evaluating the truth behind his accusations is difficult.

Nehemiah's suspicions towards Sanballat are understandable, but not the way he treated potential allies. As soon as he arrived in Jerusalem, he took an unannounced ride to inspect the walls, suggesting that he did not trust the local leadership. Despite this snub, the list of builders in Neh. 3 shows considerable support for the project. But his uncompromising attitudes were resented by many who could have been his supporters. There were those who had ties with Tobiah and saw no need to break them but also tried to work with Nehemiah. He interpreted it as disloyalty and treason, but no doubt they saw it as common sense and tried to win him over to their way of thinking (Neh. 6:17–19). Some hope! Also, when he was out of the province, people reverted to their more relaxed way of doing things, abandoning Nehemiah's stringent attitude towards the surrounding peoples, many of whom were Jews, after all (e.g. Tobiah). The (high-)priest Eliashib allowed Tobiah to set up a base in one of the temple storerooms (Neh. 13:4–9). The reason for this is not given, but the priests would have had the right to make such decisions, and to the best of our knowledge no law was broken. Nehemiah was able to overturn the permit partly by force of personality but also by his position as provincial governor.

One area where Nehemiah's activities are most applauded (because they fit modern sensibilities so well) are those described in Neh. 5. His championing of the poor and oppressed is often cited as a positive example of true religion for moderns. The analysis made is usually fairly superficial, however, not going beyond the surface account. The commendable desire to cancel debts and release the lands and even the persons of the debtors masks several negative considerations. First, it fails to recognize that those who lend money have a right to be repaid and are not necessarily in a position to turn the loan into a gift. Nehemiah's actions may well have bankrupted some of the creditors (contrary to the definitions of some, 'creditor' does not automatically mean 'greedy, grasping, unjustly wealthy' or any of the other negative assumptions so often made). What he certainly achieved was to make sure that no one would loan to the poor in future, which would have meant disaster in the long term because many agrarian workers could not survive without access to credit in times of hardship. Nehemiah's measures made no future provision for the debtors. He cancelled current debts, but this would not mean that those affected would not become indebted again (assuming anyone was willing to lend them money). From the point of view of common-sense economics, Nehemiah may have been creating more problems than he was solving. Certainly, he could have gone about it in a different way.

Some leaders might have resolved the problem by private talks with the debtors and an attempt to reconcile all sides in the equation. Not Nehemiah. He had to create a scene and publicly humiliate some of the creditors. If there had been no other way, this might have been justified, but we have no indication that he tried any other means. Moreover, it was done in such a way as to aggrandize Nehemiah himself. He holds himself up as a shining example, but in fact he himself was a creditor as well. The difference is that he could afford to cancel the debts; others may not have been as wealthy as he was. Nehemiah also boasts that he did not make use of the governor's allowance for food, unlike previous governors (Neh. 5:14–15). Again, this is all very well if you are rich enough not to need it. After all, government has to be paid for. The income to run the governor's household had to come from somewhere, and it must not be forgotten that among the previous governors whom he castigates were Sheshbazzar and Zerubbabel. Nehemiah was evidently independently wealthy, perhaps acquired through his position as cupbearer to the king, but other governors may not have been so fortunate. And one has to ask why he required to feed 150 people per day at his table (Neh. 5:17–18), a rather large entourage for a provincial governor.

Nehemiah seems to have been a failure, at least in the medium term (Grabbe 1998a). As long as he was around to strong-arm the people into following his ways he succeeded. He had considerable power granted to him by the king, but the strength of his personality was probably enough to keep many in line. But the indications are that this was only a temporary acquiescence which disappeared fairly soon after he was off the scene. We have little knowledge of what happened in the later part of the Persian period; however, what we know of the Ptolemaic and Seleucid period does not show the narrow exclusion of contact with the surrounding peoples. Indeed, the 'peoples of the land' rejected by Ezra-Nehemiah as foreign seem to have been accepted as a part of the community in later times. Hellenistic culture influenced the Jews as much as any other people, culminating in the making of Jerusalem into a Hellenistic city in the time of Antiochus IV. However, in the long term the views espoused by Nehemiah were more successful in promoting survival during the long centuries of statelessness and persecution than some of the more liberal views.

The Ezra story

The Ezra narrative is a difficult one. At first blush it looks like a straightforward story of a man, a priest and scribe, who was given a commission by the Persian king to bring the law to the Jews in the western part of his empire. Ezra came to Jerusalem, tackled a problem of intermarriage with the native peoples, and then read the law to the people, just as he was authorized. It seems simple enough. As one begins to look more closely at the narrative, though, the story immediately begins to blur and even disintegrate. The apparent similarities with the Nehemiah story turn out to be superficial, and the contrasts come more and more to dominate one's view. Ezra's commission looks unambiguous. A short statement by the Persian king would have sufficed (in the case of Nehemiah we have no document at all). Yet for some reason, a long decree is needed (Ezra 7:12–26), with all sorts of benefactions enumerated. The decree seems to have been tailor-made for use by a Jewish propagandist, and an investigation of the language shows some linguistic features uncharacteristic of Achaemenid administrative practice and from a later period.

At first it looks as if Ezra was being appointed governor of Judah since he was given the task of 'regulating Judah and Jerusalem by the law of your God in your hand' (7:14). Not only was he permitted to administer on the basis of the Jewish law in Jerusalem, he was also given permission to make it the official law of the entire province to the west of the Euphrates. He was to set up judges and magistrates to judge 'all the people of Ebir-nari, all those who know the law of your God, and to teach it to all who do not know it' (Ezra 7:25). All who did not serve this law and the law of the king were to be punished severely (7:26). Nothing was said about this being confined to Jews. For all practical purposes, Ezra had been made satrap of the entire satrapy of Beyond-the-River-Euphrates. He also had the phenomenal favour of the king and his counsellors in receiving large financial gifts (7:15). Along with the offerings of the people this came to the enormous sum of 25 or more tonnes of silver and gold (8:26–28). Yet this was not all; in case this king's ransom turned out to be insufficient, he could draw on another 3 tonnes of silver from the royal treasury – no questions asked – as if it were his private petty cash fund (7:22). By contrast, Nehemiah, who was the king's own cupbearer, received none of this largess. Also, Nehemiah was supplied with an armed escort (Neh. 2:9), yet Ezra – bringing this huge sum of money – was ashamed to ask the king for a guard against robbers (Ezra 7:22). It seems very strange that the king thought that Nehemiah needed a body-guard, but he happily permitted Ezra's unarmed band – with many elderly people and a valuable cargo of gold and silver – to travel hundreds of miles without any protection at all.

In a portion of the order remarkably parallel to Cyrus' decree (Ezra 1:1–4), Ezra was permitted to take whoever of the people, priests, and Levites wanted to accompany him (7:13). However, when Ezra assembled his band of returnees, he found no Levites and went to considerable effort to coerce some into joining him (8:15–20). Why? There is no indication that Jerusalem lacked Levites and temple servants; a substantial number had supposedly gone up with Joshua and Zerubbabel (Ezra 2//Neh. 7). Even if we allow these lists to represent the situation later than Zerubbabel, the narrative about the rebuilding of the temple presupposes Levites, singers, and other temple servants (3:8–12; 6:20); in fact, Joshua and Zerubbabel organized them for the cultic service (3:8–9). Thus, Ezra 8 leaves one with the impression that Ezra is trying to do what Joshua and Zerubbabel had already done. Is this because the Ezra story originally had Ezra restoring the temple and cult? I have already suggested so above.

Portions of Ezra 7–9 are in the first person, which has led many to postulate an 'Ezra memoir' as the basis of this section. In theory, there is no reason why there should not be a first-person Ezra account just as there seems to be a Nehemiah one. But whereas further investigation confirms the first impressions about the NM, a careful look at the Ezra story finds much that is incongruous and unlikely. Either Ezra is leading us up the garden path, or the account is someone's invention, or some later scribe has taken great pains to 'improve' Ezra's account by considerable changes. Some of the content is simply impossible. If you read it in a modern book, you would immediately label it fiction or even fantasy.

The narrative makes a strong connection between Ezra and the Jewish law, and later Jewish tradition places particular emphasis on this, as have many modern scholars. But if he was so important for the law, why was he ignored in a number of traditions? It is difficult to believe that Ezra was so strongly associated with the law historically and yet was completely forgotten or ignored in some circles from an early period. Our earliest witness after Ezra-Nehemiah was Ben Sira, but in all his comments on and admiration for the law, he totally ignores Ezra. This confirms the situation already described about the Ezra story: its connection with actual history is extremely dubious.

And yet the emphasis on Ezra and the law found in so many modern treatments is a correct one, although too often wrongly focused on the question of which law Ezra brought. In the light of the problems with the Ezra tradition just noted, to try to identify his law could well be a vain endeavour. On the other hand, even if the narrative is fictional, it can still tell us about the state of and attitudes towards the Torah at the time the compiler worked. The picture in Ezra-Nehemiah is of a community possessing a written, authoritative law – a new situation replacing an older one in which traditional law was a possession of the priesthood and the whole community. Therefore, a more fruitful approach is the following: the real focus should be on the significance of the change in concept of law when it moves from oral priestly instruction and community ethos to written codified book.

The significance of putting traditional law into a fixed written text cannot be overestimated. Previously, the community and the priesthood were the guardians and repositories of the traditional and religious law. Change could take place, but it was slow and gradual, and interpretation was a group activity. Once the teaching was encompassed in a book, anyone who could read could potentially give an interpretation. How quickly this potential was realized has been exaggerated. The codified Torah was still in the hands of the priests, and its interpretation continued to be their job (as Neh. 8:7–8 and 9:3–4 indicate). As long as the temple stood, the priests were still the main guardians of the law. Nevertheless, the way was open for others to appropriate the Scriptures for themselves. Dissident priestly groups were likely to have been the first to take this route, of which a good example seems to be Qumran. Whether the Pharisees were primarily a lay movement, as so often asserted, remains to be determined (we know that some of them were priests), but many of their rules or *halakot* (if perhaps not all) seem to arise from or to be connected with specific laws in the Pentateuch.

We should be cautious about assuming a rapid development of this approach to the Torah. There is little evidence that Jewish religious writings now became primarily interpretative literature, as so often claimed. The prime example is 1 and 2 Chronicles which are usually seen as a midrash on Samuel and Kings (though even this has recently been doubted by Auld [1994]). Yet an examination of much early Jewish literature shows the continued production of original religious writings; the fact that many of these did not ultimately make it into the canon is irrelevant. There may even have been some attempts to produce rivals to the Pentateuch or at least portions of it, depending on how one accounts for the *Book of Jubilees* and the *Temple Scroll* (11QT).

And yet we also find a good deal of biblical interpretation as well. We find examples of 'rewritten' Bible in such books as the *Liber Antiquitatum Biblicarum* (Pseudo-Philo) and the various books on Adam and Eve. Among the *Fragmentary Writers in Greek* (Holladay 1983, 1989, 1995) are examples of biblical reworking and development such as Ezekiel the Dramatist (Exodus) and Eupolemus (Kings). But probably the best examples are found among the Qumran scrolls with *pesharim* (commentaries), collections, paraphrases, rewritings, and para-biblical texts. One cannot help feeling that the codification of the Pentateuch and other writings which came to form the Bible stimulated and eventually led to the creation of a whole industry of religious writings which presupposed 'Scripture'. Biblical interpretation and commentary became very important, even if later and less pervasively than conventionally thought.

'The end of the matter'

We know what the books of Ezra-Nehemiah want us to believe. We know what the story is that they want to tell, and that story has validity in its own right, as theology and literature. It is perfectly legitimate to read the books from a theological point of view, following the dominant theme and message. The metaphor of exile/return/success-against-great-odds has been a powerful symbol for Judaism through the ages, helping the Jews to sustain their identity and hope through many dark, oppressive centuries. The Hebrew Ezra-Nehemiah has been a vital support in keeping this central symbol alive. Nevertheless, we do not have to make that story our own. We can ignore it or even disagree with it.

A close reading of Ezra-Nehemiah shows not only unity in the gross structure (which supports the theological reading) but also many signs of diversity in detail. It is right and proper to take account of this fact as well. The nature of the text itself thus shows the complete legitimacy of reading the text diachronically as well as synchronically. There are hints in the text of other stories, stories downplayed or suppressed in the editing of the tradition. Why should we be bound to tell only the story imposed by the editor? For the full set of stories in the text, we must read both synchronically and diachronically. We can also ask whether a particular story – whether a dominant one or one suppressed by the editors – is history. Ezra-Nehemiah is rooted in history, but it is not a work of history; if we ask historical questions, we must forget the theological agenda. The last question is the one I have chosen to address in the final part of the book.

The first of the 'other stories' to be told is that of the indigenous Jews whom Ezra-Nehemiah consistently labels as 'foreigners'. For most of them, we can only guess at how they must have viewed the attempt by the *golah* community (or at least some of it) to demote them as second-class citizens. Especially oppressive in their eyes would have been the aim to displace them from land they had farmed for many decades. The one family we do know something about is that of Tobiah; in a sense his story has already been partially told because we at least know what happened to his descendants. Their success during the Seleucid period may be a clue to their fortunes during the Persian period. Another we would like to see told is that of the wives and children who were expelled when their marriages were ruled unlawful by certain community leaders. We get only a hint of their reaction, but it is a poignant glimpse into the personal suffering they experienced. A further story is that of those in the Samaritan region. We have some small knowledge of Sanballat from brief information in the Elephantine and Wadi

Daliyeh papyri, and also of his sons. These are just some examples of the many stories enclosed in the two books.

The compiler of Ezra-Nehemiah has told one story. Other voices in the text suggest others. I have taken the words of Ezra and Nehemiah and created a different story, one drawing on the tools of critical scholarship but also using data from sources other than Ezra-Nehemiah. This story reconstructed from a critical perspective is yet another story, one found neither on the surface of the text nor in the cracks. This reconstructed story – my story – is not as good as that in Ezra-Nehemiah because I refused to fill in the gaps or provide an invented scenario where I do not know what happened. I ask questions, but I do not answer them if there is no answer. Who was Ezra and what did he do? I wish I knew, but I do not and am not confident that the story in Ezra is anything more than an invention. So I do not tell Ezra's story; I only point out the problems with the story in the book. With Nehemiah it is different. I tell his story as I see it, but it is a different one from the book. I have not simply made up this story; it has been deduced from the stories in the book, but it is in some respects a quite different one. I have also suggested that there are other stories still to be told, though we do not have enough information yet to tell them.

Some may wish to confine themselves to the canonical version and accept it as authoritative theologically or perhaps even just literarily. That is the privilege of any reader. But the state of the tradition also allows one to ask about other voices and stories which the dominant narrative line overshadows and suppresses. When it comes to the question of history, the historian will say that it is not just legitimate but even essential to look for these other voices. It is by listening to the entire chorus of the text that we begin to tap its riches.

BIBLIOGRAPHY

Ackroyd, Peter R. (1958) 'Two Old Testament Historical Problems of the Early Persian Period', *JNES* 17: 13–27.

—— (1968) *Exile and Restoration*, Old Testament Library, Philadelphia: Westminster; London: SCM.

—— (1970a) *The Age of the Chronicler*, Supplement to *Colloquium – The Australian and New Zealand Theological Review*.

—— (1970b) *Israel under Babylon and Persia*, New Clarendon Bible, OT 4; London: Oxford University Press.

Alt, Albrecht (1953) 'Die Rolle Samarias bei der Entstehung des Judentums', *Kleine Schriften zur Geschichte des Volkes Israel*, Munich: Beck: 2.316–37 (reprinted from *Festschrift Otto Procksch zum 60. Geburtstag* [Leipzig: Deichert und Hinrichs, 1934] 5–28).

Auld, A. Graeme (1994) *Kings without Privilege: David and Moses in the Story of the Bible's Kings*, Edinburgh: T. & T. Clark.

Barstad, Hans M. (1996) *The Myth of the Empty Land: A Study in the History and Archaeology of Judah During the 'Exilic' Period*, Symbolae Osloenses 28, Oslo/Cambridge, MA: Scandinavian University Press.

Batten, Loring W. (1913) *A Critical and Exegetical Commentary on Ezra and Nehemiah*, ICC, Edinburgh: T. & T. Clark.

Berger, P.-R. (1971) 'Zu den Namen ששבצר und שנאצר (Esr $1_{8.11}$ $5_{14.16}$ bzw. I Chr 3_{18})', *ZAW* 83: 98–100.

Berquist, Jon L. (1995) *Judaism in Persia's Shadow: A Social and Historical Approach*, Minneapolis: Fortress.

Bickerman, Elias J. (1976) 'The Edict of Cyrus in Ezra 1', *Studies in Jewish and Christian History*, AGAJU 9; Leiden: Brill: 1.72–108 (= partial revision of *JBL* 65 [1946]: 244–75).

Blenkinsopp, Joseph (1987) 'The Mission of Udjahorresnet and Those of Ezra and Nehemiah', *JBL* 106: 409–21.

—— (1988) *Ezra-Nehemiah*, Old Testament Library, London: SCM.

—— (1990a) 'A Jewish Sect of the Persian Period', *CBQ* 52: 5–20.

—— (1990b) 'The Sage, the Scribe, and Scribalism in the Chronicler's Work', in J. G. Gammie and L. G. Perdue (eds), *The Sage in Israel and the Ancient Near East*, Winona Lake, IN: Eisenbrauns: 307–15.

—— (1994) 'The Nehemiah Autobiographical Memoir', in S. E. Balentine and J. Barton (eds), *Language, Theology, and The Bible: Essays in Honour of James Barr*, Oxford: Clarendon: 199–212.

Boyce, Mary (1975) *A History of Zoroastrianism*, vol. 1, HdO I.8.1, Leiden: Brill.

Brueggemann, Walter (1996) review of L. L. Grabbe, *Priests, Prophets, Diviners, Sages*, in *JBL* 115: 728–30.

Carroll, Robert P. (1992) 'The Myth of the Empty Land', in David Jobling and T. Pippin (eds), *Ideological Criticism of Biblical Texts*, Semeia 59, Atlanta: Scholars: 79–93.

Clines, David J. A. (1984) *Ezra, Nehemiah, Esther*, CBC, London: Marshall, Morgan & Scott; Grand Rapids: Eerdmans.

—— (1990) 'The Nehemiah Memoir: The Perils of Autobiography', *What Does Eve Do to Help? and Other Readerly Questions to the Old Testament*, JSOTSup 94; Sheffield: Sheffield Academic Press: 124–64.

Cowley, A. (1923) *Aramaic Papyri of the Fifth Century B.C.*, reprinted Osnabruck: Otto Zeller, 1967.

Dandamaev, Muhammad A., and Vladimir G. Lukonin (1989) *The Culture and Social Institutions of Ancient Iran*, Cambridge: Cambridge University Press.

Davies, Philip R. (1998) *Scribes and Schools: The Canonization of the Hebrew Scriptures*, Louisville, KY: Westminster John Knox.

Dion, P. E. (1983) 'ששבצר and סמנורי', *ZAW* 95: 111–12.

Donner, Herbert (1986) *Geschichte des Volkes Israel und seiner Nachbarn in Grundzügen, Teil 2: Von der Königszeit bis zu Alexander dem Großen, mit einem Ausblick auf die Geschichte des Judentums bis Bar Kochba*, Grundrisse zum Alten Testament, Das Alte Testament Deutsch Ergänzungsreihe 4/2, Göttingen: Vandenhoeck & Ruprecht.

Donner, Herbert, and W. Röllig (1962–64) *Kanaanäische und aramäische Inschriften*, 3 vols, Wiesbaden: Harrassowitz.

Driver, G. R. (1957) *Aramaic Documents of the Fifth Century B.C.*, revised edn, Oxford: Clarendon.

Eskenazi, Tamara Cohn (1986) 'The Chronicler and the Composition of 1 Esdras', *CBQ* 48: 39–61.

—— (1988) *In an Age of Prose: A Literary Approach to Ezra-Nehemiah*, SBLMS 36; Atlanta: Scholars.

Fitzmyer, Joseph A. (1979) *A Wandering Aramean: Collected Aramaic Essays*, SBLMS 25, Atlanta: Scholars.

Frei, Peter, and Klaus Koch (1996) *Reichsidee und Reichsorganisation im Perserreich*, 2nd edn, Freiburg (Schweiz): Universitätsverlag; Göttingen: Vandenhoeck & Ruprecht.

Galling, K. (1964) *Studien zur Geschichte Israels im persischen Zeitalter*, Tübingen: Mohr (Siebeck).

Garnsey, P., and R. Saller (1987) *The Roman Empire: Economy, Society, and Culture*, London: Duckworth.

Grabbe, Lester L. (1987) 'Josephus and the Reconstruction of the Judaean Restoration', *JBL* 106: 231–46.

—— (1988) 'Synagogues in Pre-70 Palestine: A Re-assessment', *JTS* 39: 401–10.

—— (1991) 'Reconstructing History from the Book of Ezra', in P. R. Davies (ed.), *Second Temple Studies: The Persian Period*, JSOTSup 117; Sheffield: JSOT: 98–107.

—— (1992a) *Judaism from Cyrus to Hadrian*: vol. I: *Persian and Greek Periods*; vol. II: *Roman Period*, Minneapolis: Fortress (British edition in one-volume paperback, London: SCM, 1994).

—— (1992b) 'The Authenticity of the Persian 'Documents' in Ezra', read to the Aramaic Section of the Society of Biblical Literature annual meeting, San Francisco, November 1992, publication forthcoming.

—— (1993a) *Leviticus*, Society for Old Testament Study, Old Testament Guides; Sheffield: JSOT.

—— (1993b) 'Betwixt and Between: The Samaritans in the Hasmonean Period', in E. H. Lovering, Jr (ed.), *Society of Biblical Literature 1993 Seminar Papers*, SBL Seminar Papers Series 32; Atlanta: Scholars: 334–47.

—— (1994) 'What Was Ezra's Mission?' in T. C. Eskenazi and K. H. Richards (eds), *Second Temple Studies: 2. Temple Community in the Persian Period*, JSOTSup 175; Sheffield: JSOT: 286–99.

—— (1995) *Priests, Prophets, Diviners, Sages: A Socio-historical Study of Religious Specialists in Ancient Israel*, Valley Forge, PA: Trinity Press International.

—— (1997) (ed.) *Can a History of Israel Be Written?* European Seminar in Historical Methodology 1 = JSOTSup 245; Sheffield: Sheffield Academic Press.

—— (1998a) 'Triumph of the Pious or Failure of the Xenophobes? The Ezra/Nehemiah Reforms and their *Nachgeschichte*', in Siân Jones and Sarah Pearce (eds), *Studies in Jewish Local Patriotism and Self-Identification in the Graeco-Roman Period*, Journal for the Study of the Pseudepigrapha Supplement 25; Sheffield: Sheffield Academic Press: 48–63.

—— (1998b) (ed.) *The Exile as History and Ideology*, European Seminar in Historical Methodology 2 = JSOTSup 278; Sheffield: Sheffield Academic Press.

—— (in preparation) *Yehud: The Persian Province of Judah*.

Grayson, A. K. (1975) *Assyrian and Babylonian Chronicles*, Texts from Cuneiform Sources 5, Locust Valley, NY: J. J. Augustin.

Gunneweg, A. H. J. (1981) 'Zur Interpretation der Bücher Esra-Nehemiah: Zugleich ein Beitrag zur Methode der Exegese', *Congress Volume, Vienna 1980*, VTSup 32, Leiden: Brill: 146–61.
—— (1982) 'Die aramäische und die hebräische Erzählung über die nachexilische Restauration – ein Vergleich', *ZAW* 94: 299–302.
—— (1983) 'עָם הָאָרֶץ – A Semantic Revolution', *ZAW* 95: 437–40.
—— (1985) *Esra*, KAT 19.1; Gütersloh: Mohn.
—— (1987) *Nehemiah*, KAT 19.2; Gütersloh: Mohn.
Hanhart, Robert (1974) *Esdrae liber I*, Septuaginta 8/1; Göttingen: Vandenhoeck & Ruprecht.
Holladay, Carl R. (1983) *Fragments from Hellenistic Jewish Authors, Vol. I: Historians*, Society of Biblical Literature Texts and Translations 20, Pseudepigrapha Series 10; Atlanta: Scholars.
—— (1989) *Fragments from Hellenistic Jewish Authors, Vol. II: Poets: The Epic Poets Theodotus and Philo and Ezekiel the Tragedian*, Society of Biblical Literature Texts and Translations 30, Pseudepigrapha Series 12; Atlanta: Scholars.
—— (1995) *Fragments from Hellenistic Jewish Authors, Vol. III: Aristobulus*, Society of Biblical Literature Texts and Translations 39, Pseudepigrapha Series 13; Atlanta: Scholars.
Japhet, Sarah (1968) 'Supposed Common Authorship of Chronicles and Ezra-Nehemiah Investigated Anew', *VT* 18 (1968): 330–71.
—— (1982) 'Sheshbazzar and Zerubbabel – Against the Background of the Historical and Religious Tendencies of Ezra-Nehemiah', *ZAW* 94: 66–98.
—— (1983) 'Sheshbazzar and Zerubbabel – Against the Background of the Historical and Religious Tendencies of Ezra-Nehemiah', *ZAW* 95: 218–30.
Kellermann, Ulrich (1967) *Nehemia: Quellen, Überlieferung, und Geschichte*, BZAW 102, Berlin: Töpelmann.
Kent, Roland G. (1953) *Old Persian*, 2nd edn, AOS 33, New Haven, CT: American Oriental Society.
Kippenberg, H. G. (1982) *Religion und Klassenbildung im antiken Judäa*, 2nd edn, SUNT 14, Göttingen: Vandenhoeck & Ruprecht.
Kraemer, David (1993) 'On the Relationship of the Books of Ezra and Nehemiah', *JSOT* 59: 73–92.
Kratz, Reinhard Gregor (1991) *Translatio imperii: Untersuchungen zu den aramäischen Danielerzählungen und ihrem theologiegeschichtlichen Umfeld*, WMANT 63, Neukirchen: Neukirchener Verlag.
Kuhrt, Amélie (1983) 'The Cyrus Cylinder and Achaemenid Imperial Policy', *JSOT* 25: 83–97.
Margalith, O. (1986) 'The Political Role of Ezra as Persian Governor', *ZAW* 98: 110–12.
Mazar, Benjamin (1957) 'The Tobiads', *IEJ* 7: 137–45, 229–38 (revision of articles in *Tarbiz* 12 [1941]: 109–23, and *EI* 4 [1956]: 249–51).

McEvenue, S. E. (1981) 'The Political Structure in Judah from Cyrus to Nehemiah', *CBQ* 43: 353–64.

Mowinckel, S. (1961) '"Ich" und "Er" in der Ezrageschichte', in A. Kuschke (ed.), *Verbannung und Heimkehr: Beiträge zur Geschichte und Theologie Israels im 6. und 5. Jahrhundert v. Chr., Wilhelm Rudolph zum 70. Geburtstag*, Tübingen: Mohr (Siebeck): 211–33.

—— (1964a) *Studien zu dem Buche Ezra-Nehemiah I*, Skrifter utgitt av Det Norske Videnskaps-Akademi i Oslo II. Hist.-Filos. Klasse. Ny Serie. No. 3; Oslo: Universitetsforlaget.

—— (1964b) *Studien zu dem Buche Ezra-Nehemiah II*, Skrifter utgitt av Det Norske Videnskaps-Akademi i Oslo II. Hist.-Filos. Klasse. Ny Serie. No. 5; Oslo: Universitetsforlaget.

—— (1965) *Studien zu dem Buche Ezra-Nehemiah III*, Skrifter utgitt av Det Norske Videnskaps-Akademi i Oslo II. Hist.-Filos. Klasse. Ny Serie. No. 7; Oslo: Universitetsforlaget.

Myers, J. M. (1974) *I and II Esdras*, AB 42, Garden City, NY: Doubleday.

Olmstead, A. T. (1944) 'Tattenai, Governor of "Across the River"', *JNES* 3: 46.

—— (1948) *History of the Persian Empire*, Chicago: University of Chicago.

Oppenheimer, Aharon (1977) *The 'Am ha-Aretz: A Study in the Social History of the Jewish People in the Hellenistic-Roman Period*, ALGHJ 8, Leiden: Brill.

Pohlmann, K.-F. (1970) *Studien zum dritten Esra: Ein Beitrag zur Frage nach dem ursprünglichen Schluss des chronistischen Geschichtswerkes*, FRLANT 104, Göttingen: Vandenhoeck & Ruprecht.

—— (1980) *Jüdische Schriften aus hellenistisch-römischer Zeit, Band I: Historische und legendarische Erzählungen, Lieferung 5: 3. Esra-Buch*, Gütersloh: Mohn.

Porten, B., and A. Yardeni (1986) *Textbook of Aramaic Documents from Ancient Egypt: 1 Letters*, Hebrew University, Department of the History of the Jewish People, Texts and Studies for Students; Jerusalem: Hebrew University.

Powell, Marvin A. (1992) 'Weights and Measures', in D. N. Freedman (ed.), *The Anchor Bible Dictionary*, New York: Doubleday: 6.897–908.

Rendtorff, Rolf (1984) 'Esra und das 'Gesetz'', *ZAW* 96: 165–84.

Rudolph, Wilhelm (1949) *Ezra und Nehemia*, HAT 20, Tübingen: Mohr (Siebeck).

Saley, R. J. (1978) 'The Date of Nehemiah Reconsidered', in G. A. Tuttle (ed.), *Biblical and Near Eastern Studies*, Essays in Honor of W. S. LaSor, Grand Rapids: Eerdmans: 151–65.

Smith, Morton (1987) *Palestinian Parties and Politics That Shaped the Old Testament*, London: SCM; corrected reprint of New York: Columbia, 1971.

Steins, Georg (1995) *Die Chronik als kanonisches Abschlussphänomen: Studien zur Entstehung und Theologie von 1/2 Chronik*, Bonner Biblische Beiträge 93; Weinheim: Beltz Athenäum.

Stolper, M. W. (1987) 'Bēlšunu the Satrap', in F. Rochberg-Halton (ed.), *Language, Literature, and History: Philological and Historical Studies Presented to Erica Reiner*, AOS 67, New Haven, CT: American Oriental Society: 389–402.

Tcherikover, V. A., A. Fuks, and M. Stern (1957–64) *Corpus Papyrorum Judaicarum* (3 vols), Cambridge, MA: Harvard; Jerusalem: Magnes.

Tollefson, Kenneth D., and H. G. M. Williamson (1992) 'Nehemiah as Cultural Revitalization: An Anthropological Perspective', *JSOT* 56: 41–68.

Torrey, Charles Cutter (1896) *The Composition and Historical Value of Ezra-Nehemiah*, BZAW 2; Giessen: Ricker.

—— (1910) *Ezra Studies*, reprinted with a Prolegomenon by W. F. Stinespring; New York: Ktav, 1970.

VanderKam, James C. (1992) 'Ezra-Nehemiah or Ezra and Nehemiah?' in E. Ulrich, *et al.* (eds), *Priests, Prophets and Scribes: Essays on the Formation and Heritage of Second Temple Judaism in Honour of Joseph Blenkinsopp*, JSOTSup 149; Sheffield: Sheffield Academic Press: 55–75.

Vaux, Roland de (1971) 'The Decrees of Cyrus and Darius on the Rebuilding of the Temple', *Bible and the Ancient Near East*, London: Darton, Longman & Todd: 63–96 (= translation from *RB* 46 [1937]: 29–57).

Wallace, A. F. C. (1956) 'Revitalization Movements', *American Anthropologist* 58: 264–81.

Willi, Thomas (1995) *Juda–Jehud–Israel: Studien zum Selbstverständnis des Judentums in persischer Zeit*, Forschungen zum Alten Testament 12, Tübingen: Mohr.

Williamson, H. G. M. (1977) *Israel in the Books of Chronicles*, Cambridge: Cambridge University Press.

—— (1983) 'The Composition of Ezra i–vi', *JTS* 34: 1–30.

—— (1985) *Ezra, Nehemiah*, WBC 16; Waco, TX: Word Books.

—— (1987) *Ezra and Nehemiah*, Society for Old Testament Study, Old Testament Guides; Sheffield: JSOT.

—— (1988) 'The Governors of Judah under the Persians', *Tyndale Bulletin* 39: 59–82.

Wilson, Robert R. (1977) *Genealogy and History in the Biblical World*, Yale Near Eastern Researches 7, New Haven, CT: Yale.

—— (1979) 'Between "Azel" and "Azel": Interpreting the Biblical Genealogies', *Biblical Archeologist* (Winter 1979): 11–22.

—— (1984) *Sociological Approaches to the Old Testament*, Philadelphia: Fortress.

Yamauchi, Edwin M. (1980) 'Two Reformers Compared: Solon of Athens and Nehemiah of Jerusalem', in Gary Rendsburg, *et al.* (eds), *The Bible World: Essays in Honor of Cyrus H. Gordon*, New York: Ktav: 269–92.

INDEX OF MODERN AUTHORS

INDEX OF CITATIONS

N.B. In chapter 2, references to verses of a particular chapter of Ezra being discussed are not indexed; however, any citations from Ezra outside that chapter are indexed. E.g., under the heading 'Ezra 5', any citations from that chapter are not indexed; however, under Ezra 6, any citations from Ezra 5 will be indexed. The same applies to Nehemiah in chapter 3 and 1 Esdras in chapter 4.

Hebrew Bible

N.B. The Hebrew order of the books is followed here.

Deuterocanonical Books/ Apocrypha